W9-CFK-209

"Excellent book. ... My clients can benefit from reading it and I intend to recommend it to them."

> Dr. Jeanne Farley, psychologist
> *New York City*

"Thank you from my heart. *The Thin Book* has helped me and many others along the road to recovery. Many times I've shared the positive, energetic pages of this book at OA meetings and many times I've seen the understanding of your positive force light up faces."

> Kathi B.
> *Buzzards Bay, Massachusetts*

"A fabulous book filled with ... inspiration."

> Joyce Thompkins
> *Minot, North Dakota*

"A thoughtful daily message in *The Thin Book* just successfully diverted a trip to a cracker machine. Thank you for this aid for living."

> Cynthia S. Ramb
> *Springfield, Virginia*

"Excellent and filled to overflowing with creative, sound, and practical ways to handle the pain of overweight. I recommend it often to patients, colleagues, and friends alike."

> Barbara C. Raven, Registered Dietitian
> *New York City*

THE THIN BOOK

JEANE EDDY WESTIN

Hazelden
Center City, Minnesota 55012-0176

ISBN: 1-56838-065-8

Cover design: Nancy MacLean

Editor's note
Hazelden offers a variety of information on chemical
dependency and related areas. Our publications do not
necessarily represent Hazelden's programs, nor do they
officially speak for any Twelve Step organization.

To Helen and Joanne, who gave
me positive help with my weight
problem, and who allowed me, in
turn, to help with theirs.

Foreword

Few health problems in our society compare with overweight. On any day of the year, millions of Americans are dieting or thinking about dieting, and still more millions probably should be.

The overweight are young and old, affluent and broke, urban and rural, educated and ignorant — they represent every ethnic and racial group and live on every street in America. *Clearly obesity is an equal-opportunity problem.*

Although overweight is a health worry of national proportions, it is also unique. Not only do the fat afflicted face a lonely self-cure, which sometimes calls for weeks or even months of food-deprivation, but they also must face a continuous barrage of ego-deflating propaganda from thin America which says: "You are *not* sexually attractive, not employable, and you lack the moral fibre (will power) to push yourself away from the table."

Never mind that science really doesn't know what chemical, hereditary, environmental and psychological factors combine to cause obesity — television, magazines and well-meaning friends advise: stop eating so much.

But is the answer that simple? Not really. It might have been once, but today overweight is wrapped up with such *negative* images that many dieters don't like themselves well enough to work day-after-day for a thinner, healthier body.

Most dieters today need reassurance, a release from guilt, and identification with others in the same boat. That is one reason why therapeutic groups such as Weight Watchers, Diet Workshops, TOPS and Overeaters Anonymous are proliferating. In these groups, the overweight receive emotional props which help them follow a weight-losing diet. However, even weekly meetings don't offer enough support. That is why these organizations encourage daily contact with other members — they recognize that everyday inspiration is an integral part of successful weight loss and weight maintenance.

I hope *The Thin Book* will provide the day-to-day inspiration you require to "stick to it," when every cell in your body cries out for more food. Each day's reading is designed to help you build your deflated self-esteem with *positive thinking, positive feeling* and finally, *positive doing.*

You will see that these daily readings are not clinical, but straight talk to you from one who feels what you feel, someone who's lived in the world 100 pounds overweight, someone who's been there and back.

There are many good diets around, but it's doubtful whether any one diet is good for every body. Anyone who wants to take off excess pounds should see a qualified doctor for the diet and medical supervision he or she needs to lose weight safely. But beyond medical care, most doctors admit they haven't the time to give their dieting patients the *daily* help most of them need. Here's where *The Thin Book* comes in. It doesn't matter what else dieters do — belong to a group, go to the doctor, exercise in a spa — they can use this book every day to enhance their total weight-losing program.

When it comes right down to it, taking off weight and establishing the living and thinking patterns which will help you to keep off extra pounds is a pretty lonely business. I hope you will use this book daily, as a supportive friend, to help make dieting less lonely for you than it ever was before.

October, 1977
Sacramento, California

You know what day this is. It's diet resolution day. Whether you're 10 pounds or 200 pounds overweight, New Year's day is D-day in the ranks of overeaters.

Your "civilian" friends may vow to be more punctual, not yell at the kids so much, or take a self-improvement course in liquid embroidery.

But not you.

What will you promise yourself and anyone else who might be listening? *"This is the year I'm going to get thin, never to be fat again."*

What a bright future those words envision. How much hope they contain. But how often, in the past, have they lost their meaning all too soon.

Well, get ready for the surprise of your life. This time your New Year's promise is not just so many brave words flung defiantly at the calendar. This year, you have 365 new chances to get on a weight-losing diet that really works. What miracle diet is this? Simply the one you are on today.

Because every day is today. That high-calorie food you ate yesterday (and feel guilty about) and the one you might eat tomorrow (and fear) don't count. What *does* count is what you eat this day — and how you feel about it.

January 1st is your 24 hours. It's the day you get off the dieter's see-saw, the one that's had you going up and down the scale for so long. No more saying "yes" to one bite after another. Today is the day you say "yes" to yourself, a confident yes to life without excess food.

Remember, the trick is not to worry about how many pounds you must lose or how long it will take you to lose them. You'll live through those days, weeks and months anyway. The question is: *How* will you live them — overwhelmed by diet disaster, or successfully facing your weight-losing program one day at a time?

Go ahead. Say it out loud. *"This is the year I'm going to get thin, never to be fat again."*

And that's a promise.

Before you reach for that extra bite today, ask yourself:
Have I said "yes" to a fresh, new life without excess food I don't need? Have I exchanged endless promises for one day after another of diet success?

January 2   You Can "Kick" a Tough Habit With Help

Country soul singer Johnny Cash has wrestled with a lot of bad habits in his lifetime. "First it was whiskey and then smoking," says the big man behind the guitar. "Later came pep pills, tranquilizers and fattening foods."

You can guess which problem had Cash strumming the blues. That's right — food.

"Eating is the toughest habit I've ever had to kick," confirms the singer after a two-month diet and a twenty-pound weight loss.

Cash's diet success wasn't entirely due to substituting protein and vegetables for Tennessee treats. "My wife, June, helped me stay on my diet," he admits.

Johnny Cash didn't have to diet alone. And neither do you. Most people who have successfully dieted off excess pounds have had the help and support of an understanding friend — be it wife, husband, fellow dieter or, that rarest of all persons, the good listener.

Who is the most sympathetic friend or relative you know? It should be someone who loves you in moments of failure as well as success. Contact that person. Ask if he or she would help you kick a tough habit. Explain that you are taking off weight one day at a time, and may need some help occasionally.

Reassure your friend that this won't be a full-time job. It might mean simply lending an ear in times of stress — times when you're tempted to side-step a problem by eating unneeded food. Find a good listener who approves of your efforts and encourages you to become the thin person you want to be.

Of course, there's one person whose understanding you need above all others. *Your own.* You will find it helpful to face yourself squarely one day at a time, admit you have an eating problem, and watch your confidence quotient go up as your weight goes down.

Sometimes pride prevents us from asking for help. Don't let pride stop you. Take all the help you can get — and kick the toughest habit of them all.

Before you reach for that extra bite today, ask yourself:
Do I realize that food cravings will come and go, but I can overcome them with help from others and myself? Have I decided not to "feed my habit" any longer?

January 3   You Need a Constructive "Workout"

The word exercise is loathsome to many overweights. The reason is obvious. As one young woman put it: "When I run, *everything* moves." But there's one exercise that isn't embarassing, tiring or costly — and that's a daily exercise in positive thinking. Let's call it your constructive workout for the day.

Combating negativism is a dieter's first line of defense. So try to begin this day and every day by thinking of all the things *right* about you. In the beginning, it's a good idea to actually list them on paper so you can *see* them. Later you may only want to make a mental list. But do make a list; review it often; and as you grow thinner keep adding new, positive attributes to it. Don't let one negative image creep in.

Why is it so important to flex your positive muscles? It's simple logic. In order to diet victoriously you must first feel good enough about you to go to work for yourself. Continued diet success is rare when it's done for another person because eventually the person for whom we sacrifice food will anger us. The first get-even thing we do is to overeat, and there goes another diet.

It may sound selfish but victors in the fight against fat are generally people who want to lose weight for themselves.

Doing your daily constructive exercises can work miracles. Nothing brings out your best, better than a winner's self-image.

It activates positive forces and sets them to work for your mind and body. It illuminates your thinking, revealing good about you that you may never have seen before.

Being human, maybe you've fallen short of your diet ideal in the past and stumbled. That doesn't mean you have to live with a flabby, negative image of yourself forever — not if you work out daily in a positive mental way.

Before you reach for that extra bite today, ask yourself:
Have I found something new and praiseworthy about myself to add to my positive image list? Does my weight loss depend entirely on how someone else reacts to me, or am I losing weight for myself?

There are times in every dieter's day when five little words can spell disaster. Ever catch yourself in one of these three rationalizations?

1. One little bite won't hurt. It's the most common and deadly dieter's excuse of all, because it sounds so true. What harm can one little bite do? Just this. One bite doesn't add a lot of calories, but it does break down your ability to control the next bite and the next. The results can sabotage your day. Like this for instance: "I never meant to eat the whole cake," moaned a diet club member at weigh-in. "I just put it on the kitchen table and slivered it to death."

Psychologists who specialize in modifying eating behavior know that each time you take a bite, you weaken yourself for the next time. Each time you don't eat when you want to, you are stronger the next time you're tempted.

2. I'll make it up tomorrow. The food you overeat today is not magically cancelled out by what you don't eat tomorrow. It is impossible to predict 24 hours in advance what your mood will be and whether, by some superhuman effort, you"ll be able to eat even less than your diet plan calls for.

3. To hell with diets anyway. Most overeaters use this defiant excuse after they've already taken that first bite. They rationalize: "I've blown it, so I might as well go all the way."

But think a minute. There's a great deal of difference between a fifty-calorie bite and a 500-calorie helping. And don't kid yourself that you don't care. Later, you may care very much. Then your guilt could drive you back to the refrigerator for a real binge!

Those "five little words" are hidden deceivers. They tell us what we want to hear for the moment — not the facts. They are unrealistic alibis for defeatism.

As excuse-makers, most overweights are champions. But, we can get rid of false rationalizations by learning to recognize them for what they are.

Remember, after you get rid of "one little bite won't hurt," "I'll make it up tomorrow," and "To hell with diets anyway," there *are* five little words you can live by. They're what this book is all about — *one day at a time.*

Before you reach for that extra bite today, ask yourself:
Have I abandoned all my excuses for eating food I don't need? Am I getting stronger each time I'm able to pass up excess food?

"Oh, I've failed again," is the cry of every dieter at one time or another. A little slip can set off a chain of unnecessary guilt. It needn't. Perhaps you're just treading a harder road than most today, and demanding self-perfection at the same time. Take it easy. You can give yourself a chance to succeed on the most difficult day by setting simpler goals.

Try making a few easy-to-accept rules in advance. In this way, what you eat later will not be subject to whim — or hunger. If you suspect today's problems will make it tough to stick to your dietary program, set up a contingency plan early in the day. Say to yourself, "If I cannot eat weight-losing meals today, I will drop back to maintenance meals — but no further."

The point is: by careful contingency planning, you will not have to drop back *all the way to overeating.* Like a computer, you have built-in success and programed-out failure.

But what if you do slip off your plan, despite your best intentions? The most important thing for you to remember is not to punish yourself for a slip by yet more overeating. For years, we overweights have been told, and have told ourselves, that it is bad to overeat, because we're less attractive and more likely to lose our health. These things may be true, but their effect is to make us feel guilty, and feeling guilty tends to increase our overeating — setting up that vicious circle every overweight knows so well.

If you have a slip, forgive yourself immediately. Set yourself free from any need for future self-punishment. In that way you can start tomorrow with a clean slate, without any hold-over guilt. Sure you have problems. Problems are part of being a sensitive human in a complex world. But there is no known illness, economic disaster or personal trouble that has yet been cured by massive doses of chocolate.

Setting simple goals and backing them up with careful contingency planning is a good way for you to face the challenges of living day by day — without slipping off your diet. Try it.

Before you reach for that extra bite today, ask yourself:
Have I stopped demanding impossible heights of perfection from myself? Do I have a diet contingency plan, so that I will not have to fall back all the way?

More than four million new scales are sold every year. Considering the ones already sitting in bathrooms or under beds, that means a lot of Americans follow the little needle from pound to pound. The great debate isn't whether or not it's a good idea to keep track of your weight, but how often you should do it.

Doctors generally insist on weighing patients at the beginning of each visit. Most doctors' offices are equipped with giant white scales that can be absolutely overwhelming in their accurany — especially if you haven't lost weight since your last office call. No matter how hard you try to explain to the thin nurse that you're wearing heavier clothes, just finished drinking a pitcher of diet soda and have been constipated for a week — she grimly notes the pounds on your chart exactly as they show up on the scale.

Even home scales, while weighing lighter as a rule, are just as menacing to some dieters. But they can become a dieter's best friend, if used regularly.

How often should you weigh yourself?

Most diet clubs have rules about weighing. Weight Watchers prefer their members not to hop on the scale between weekly class weigh-ins. On the other hand, some behavior therapy groups insist on daily weighing with corresponding weight charts, although they discourage compulsive weighing at all times of the day or night.

Perhaps the most unique plan belongs to Overeaters Anonymous. They suggest weighing only once a month to prevent members from becoming too easily discouraged at a slow weight loss, or overly excited by a quick one. Diets, says OA, have been broken for either of these two reasons.

Most dieters find a comfortable weighing plan somewhere in between, based on their doctor's wishes, the rules of their diet group, or their own preferences.

The trick is not to give too much power to your scale. Some people allow a drop in pounds to trigger increased eating. If you're honest with yourself, you'll use the scales to determine only how much weight you're losing, not how much more food you can eat today.

Before you reach for that extra bite today, ask yourself: Have I exchanged scale-hopping for a sensible weighing schedule? Have I stopped rewarding weight loss with additional food?

The trouble with most diet programs, especially the ones in best-selling books, is that they assume people are already motivated. Sometimes, just getting psyched up to begin another diet is the biggest problem of all. Long time dieters, like distance runners, don't have too much trouble starting, if they can just get to the starting block.

Many times that all-important motivation comes in a *moment of recognition,* a moment when you realize you cannot postpone beginning any longer. You wake up one morning saying, "I've had it, living this way. I'm going on a diet." You decide with great determination not to postpone starting until after the next snack, tomorrow, or even until next Monday. You are compelled by a strong, irresistible urge to start RIGHT NOW.

If you are having trouble with motivation, how can you get to your own moment of recognition? Try these two steps:

1. Admission — It seems unnecessary to tell an overweight that the first step in self-motivation must be an admission that you're fat. And yet, if it weren't necessary, why would members of Overeaters Anonymous always preface their talks with, "Hi, my name is Mary, and I'm a compulsive overeater"? The reason for the admission is simple. We overweight people are notorious self-deceivers. How often have we characterized our extra poundage as baby fat, big bones, gland problems — or a host of other euphemisms? Most of us call ourselves anything but fat. The admission that we are fat is the first step toward self-honesty, without which there is no motivation.

2. Acceptance — Now that we've admitted we're fat, the next step is easy. Right? Wrong. Saying it and accepting it are two different things and, of the two, acceptance is harder. If you are one of those individuals who say, "Yes, I'm fat," and continue overeating and gaining weight, then you are not accepting yourself as you really are. The act of acceptance implies action. It is not passive, but active. When you have accepted the reality of your overweight, you will be ready for your own moment of recognition, a moment which will take you to the starting block of your race for a healthier body, a happier outlook and an inner peace. On your mark. Get ready. Get set. Go!

Before you reach for that extra bite today, ask yourself:
Have I stopped using euphemisms for my problem and admitted that I am fat? Am I accepting the reality of my problem and taking action?

January 8   How's Your IQ (Impatience Quotient)?

Most overweight people have a low Impatience Quotient. We are impatient with the *dailyness* of a balanced, disciplined way of eating. Most of all, we are impatient with our progress. Although it may have taken years to gain our excess weight, we would like to have it disappear like magic, overnight.

There's nothing wrong with a little impatience. It helps give us our drive, and pushes us into getting jobs done. But too much impatience, as the poet said, "is too near neighbor to despair." Psychologists add that despair is a useless emotion because it serves no purpose.

Maybe you have impatiently pushed yourself to the point of despair. "I've been on this diet a whole week and only lost three pounds. I quit!"

You can see that impatience is especially hurtful to people trying to maintain reasonable eating programs. It is all too easy to slip from impatience into despair, and then trade despair for a numbing food binge.

Remember the best way to develop the patience you need is to learn to deal realistically with the rhythms of living. You can seldom write a timetable for your life and expect everything and everybody to fall into line. Far better to live a day at a time, to deal with the everydayness of eating healthfully and moderately — without sabotaging your best resolve with extra food.

If you do, you'll find your Impatience Quotient going up, and your weight coming down.

Before you reach for that extra bite today, ask yourself:
Am I trying to raise my IQ by dealing with the true rhythms of my life? Have I decided to practice patience so that I can rid myself of that useless emotion, despair?

Eastern philosophers say that concentration is the master art, because all other arts depend on it. Imagine Van Gogh painting his sun-drenched French fields, or Shakespeare writing his sonnets without a well-developed ability to concentrate. How did they develop their powers of concentration? Through practice, of course, just like they developed their art.

Concentration, simply stated, is paying full attention to what is happening at the moment. When you concentrate, you are able to experience more fully, everything from childbirth to losing weight. Yes, losing weight requires concentration, too.

During a diet group meeting an unsuccessful member exclaimed: "I can never concentrate on what I am doing. I cut out dresses, send for writing courses, even sign-up for real estate school, but I always drop out and go back to eating full-time."

It is difficult to concentrate on losing weight, to fully experience life, when excess eating gets in the way. *Food is the great distracter.* Try practicing the art of concentrating on your eating plan for today. Try concentrating on the positive aspects of the next twenty-four hours. Don't let your mind become preoccupied or diverted, or you will not have the deep experience concentration will bring you.

Do you have one thing you want to fully experience today? Perhaps you have a mountain to climb, a job you've left half done or some other interest on which you have not been able to focus your full attention. Maybe you just want to concentrate on improving your self-image.

Whatever you choose, try to practice concentrating on one thing at a time, and finishing what you start. Real growth is possible from what may seem like an ordinary experience.

Van Gogh and Shakespeare weren't born masters of their art. They developed their talent and inner consciousness through the power of concentration. So can you.

Before you reach for that extra bite today, ask yourself:
Have I practiced concentrating on living without excess food? Am I willing to finish what I begin?

If Nobody's Perfect, Then Why Do You Have To Be?

At one time or another you've excused a friend's mistake with the comforting words, "Don't worry. Nobody's perfect," and you really meant it. It's too harsh to shower blame on someone who is already down. The question is: can you say it to yourself and really mean it? Apparently not. Most of us suffer from anxiety and guilt over imagined mistakes and exaggerated standards.

One self-help group for ex-mental patients, called Recovery, Inc., considers the fear of making mistakes the prime target of their group therapy. Members are continually reminded that making mistakes is only "average behavior" after all.

No one needs this philosophy more than dieters. We have gone off our diets many times, picked ourselves up and begun again. Self-recrimination is a waste of time and not very fair.

The late psychiatrist Rudolph Dreikurs went even further than Recovery, Inc. He said there are no mistakes; they are just an expression of our perfectionist way of living.

People with food problems sometimes tend to be perfectionists in other areas of their lives. In a way, we're saying, "Don't look at our bodies, look at what we do so well." But perfectionism is an intolerable burden. It requires us to be unkind, impatient and intolerant with ourselves.

What's the answer? Simply this. Try having the *courage to be imperfect.* Don't demand perfection from yourself and your life will become more manageable, will have more balance. This is the atmosphere which will promote steady inner growth. It is a way of being gentle with yourself. And you deserve the gentle touch. You are coping with the cunning problem of overweight. You are seeking daily answers to the question marks in your life. The next time you don't come up to the standards you've set, tell yourself softly, "Don't worry. Nobody's perfect." And really mean it.

Before you reach for that extra bite today, ask yourself:
Have I stopped blaming myself for mistakes that are really only average behavior? Will I pick myself up gently when I fall?

When you were a child in school and turned in an especially good paper, the teacher often gave you a gold star. Sometimes, after a series of gold stars, you could look forward to an extra treat — usually sweet — for being such a "good boy/girl."

Do you know, that some of us (who've been adults longer than we care to remember) are still giving ourselves gold stars? Take this experience of a diet group member: "I went to a family dinner — you know, one of those affairs where every cook tries to outcook the next — and I stuck right to my eating plan," she reported. "Everyone admired my will power as I turned down one fattening dessert after another.

"I felt really good about myself, until I got home. Before I knew it I had eaten just about everything in my refrigerator — much more food than I had turned down at the dinner. Why did I do that?"

The answer is really quite simple. This dieter, like so many of us, is a member of the "good boy/girl" league. We reward ourselves with gold stars for turning in a good dieting performance and when we accumulate enough stars we turn them in for an overeating binge.

This syndrome is so ingrained in some dieters that they can experience it over and over again without understanding the subtle game they're playing. Indeed, some are so confused by their behavior that they begin to doubt their intelligence, if not their sanity.

The antidote to the gold star syndrome is to know this truth: dieting to lose weight, or to maintain a desired weight, is its own reward. Your gold star comes in the form of lost pounds, new happiness, and a mind unclouded by overeating. There is more lasting satisfaction in living your life without being dependent on excess food than in all the fool's gold food rewards you could give yourself.

Before you reach for that extra bite today, ask yourself:
Have I discovered, finally, that my diet is its own reward?
Am I willing to resign from the "good boy/girl" league?

Ever watch sports champions in a tense competition? They actually give themselves little pep talks as they play. The next time you're viewing an athletic match, take note of how the big stars behave when the pressure is on. It might go something like this: a tennis pro is about to serve a crucial point. "Come on, get it in there," the player says, "you can do it. I know you can do it."

Winning the weight game for overeaters is every bit as important as winning the world's championship for athletes. Why not use some of their techniques? One dieter reported to her group: "When I found my hand reaching for an unneeded dessert, I talked to myself out loud. 'You don't want that. You really want something better for your body and mind!' "

Answer the self-indulgent baby of overeating with the authority of an adult in charge of your own body. You can gradually change your need for oral satisfaction by changing your reaction to it. Instead of giving in, time after time, day after day, be firm in your refusal and get on with the many new, positive aspects of a life where eating is under control.

Sure it's a struggle to change. But you will get to the day when your feeling of exhilaration will be boundless. Finding the real you emerging from under your excess weight will be a complete and satisfying reward.

Nobody said losing weight and learning to live in a complicated world without a food crutch was going to be easy. To get over the rough spots, try talking to yourself like the champions do. You may even get an answer.

Before you reach for that extra bite today, ask yourself:
Have I given myself a pep talk lately? Am I getting on with the positive side of life where my rewards will be more permanent than temporary food indulgence?

Nothing is more deadly than negative thinking. It saps energy, causes facial wrinkles, makes us unpleasant companions,and plays havoc with the development of sensible eating habits.

"There is a silent, subconscious internal conversation taking place within our minds," say psychologist Dr. Jerry Schmidt. "This conversation actually determines how we feel about what is taking place in the external world." Often, says the doctor, this inner conversation is so negative it can immobilize us.

Of course, no one can be entirely positive, but daily effort can bring negativity under control.

How can you get rid of internal negativism? Each time you feel yourself thinking negatively, try to pinpoint what you told yourself to cause the feeling. For example, you may be telling yourself: "I can't stand this diet," when you have stood it very well for a long period of time. As you can see, negative thoughts are usually not very rational. Counter them immediately with reasonable, positive thoughts, such as, "Of course, I can live very well with this diet."

Perhaps you've been making yourself miserable by telling yourself you should always be happy. Counter this with, "I can't think of anyone who is happy all the time, and I am no different."

The important thing for dieters is to not let that negative thought take root. For instance, if you really begin to believe you can't stand your new way of eating, you can soon convince yourself that you shouldn't be dieting in the first place. If you really begin to believe that everybody else is happy all the time, while you alone are miserable, you are leaving the way open for compensatory eating — "Nobody cares about me, so why shouldn't I eat all I want."

Ridding yourself of destructive negative thinking can't happen overnight. It takes time like anything else worthwhile, but with persistence, you can learn one day at a time. Have a positive day!

Before you reach for that extra bite today, ask yourself:
Have I fallen into the trap of negative thinking? Am I trying to counter negative thoughts with positive ones?

How many times have you heard an overweight say, "I'm tired all the time?" How many times have you said it yourself? Sometimes it seems that we overeaters don't have the energy we want, even after our eating is under control. Part of this lack of energy may be just the old habit of sedentary living.

You're going to start having more get-up-and-go when you begin avoiding calorie-rich foods. But there are other things you can do to help lick the problem of excess fatigue.

Try a change of scenery at least once every day, even if only for five minutes. Walk in your back yard, or to the end of the block. Try to involve your whole body, moving your arms and legs, your head and eyes. Breathe deeply, taking several breaths through your nostrils and exhale the same way. This will help push oxygen deep into your lungs, increasing the oxygen in your blood supply. You'll feel peppier right away.

Another energy-sapper is indecision. Worry over unmet problems can leave you drained. Practice being decisive. Do things. Energy thrives on activity. The more you do, the more your self-confidence will grow, which is a great energy booster.

Find an activity more real than any pleasure you imagined receiving from overeating. Build it into your daily schedule. When you perceive you have more energy than you once had, emerge from your shell. Don't just sit around waiting to be asked to do something. Make overtures.

Remember the story of the elderly man sitting in the rocking chair? "My get-up-and-go," he said, "got up and went."

Maybe yours did too, burdened with excess weight and too much guilt. But you can build a new reservoir of energy by committing yourself to a daily program where overeating is not the most important thing in your life. You are.

Before you reach for that extra bite today, ask yourself:
Have I looked for a new source of energy? Am I building new activities into my daily life?

There are times, even during the best of weight-losing programs, when pressure builds. In a way, pressure, like a spring, is just wound-up energy. If you don't jump off at the right time, you can hit the ceiling.

There are many ways to deal with the feelings of pressure. Most of us used to overeat to quiet these feelings, but that is no longer the way we want to handle them. We have to find an escape valve less destructive than food.

You can always read a book, lose yourself in a movie or work on your hobby. Nothing wrong with any of these tension relievers. But sometimes we need more. If we find ourselves reaching a boiling point, then we better take action before we overeat.

Try talking it out. Don't bottle it up. Talk is cheaper than a blow-up and often relieves strain. Surprisingly, many times others can even help with a problem that has you climbing the walls.

Try getting out of yourself. Do something for someone else. Do not discount the value of a purpose or a cause. At least they take your mind away from yourself.

Don't sulk at home with old hurts for fair weather friends. Get out with others, relax and have fun. Relaxation absorbs pressure like a sponge. It might even be a good idea to hang this sign somewhere in your mind. *Having fun is essential to emotional health.*

You may have other tension-relieving techniques that help you cope with everyday pressure. Go right ahead and use them. The idea is not to fall back into the old habit of meeting every problem with extra food which isn't a solution to anything.

Before you reach for that extra bite today, ask yourself:
Have I tried using tension-relievers, other than food, for the stresses of my day? Am I convinced that overeating is a destructive way for me to handle pressure?

Are you eagerly anticipating today? If you can get some real enthusiasm into your life, it will be far more exciting.

One of the best ways to become vibrant and alive is to get rid of fat thinking. Of course, you know the main component of fat thinking is the false feeling that excess food (especially those things we call "goodies") are necessary to living. Like an alcoholic who can't imagine having fun at a party without liquor, we can't imagine living through a day without sweets to soothe the way.

Another component of fat thinking is how we relate to people. Often, we play the jolly fat man or woman, or sometimes settle for any kind of relationship we can get, and become foils for other people's emotional problems.

As you lose your extra poundage, you will find that people's attitudes toward you certainly change. It takes a period of time for your own mental image to catch up to your new physical image, but soon you'll find it unnecessary to play either jolly clown or fawning foil.

With fat thinking gone, real enthusiasm can enter your daily life. You can honestly greet each day with exuberance and confidence. Look in the mirror and say, "You're going to have a fantastic day!"

Many of us overweights have had the capacity to be enthusiastic, exciting people all along, but we have allowed our problems to desensitize us to the positive things in our world. No more. As one young member of Weight Watchers put it: "I never thought being alive could be so much fun." Try living enthusiastically. It's certainly better than fat thinking.

Before you reach for that extra bite today, ask yourself:
Have I tried looking at the world with exuberance? Why don't I trade fat thinking for enthusiasm?

January 17   Overcoming Your Fears of Rejection

Are you thinking: Oh sure, it's easy to tell me to get out and be with people? But it's a lot harder to do it. After all, we overweights have been snubbed and left out of things for years.

Sometimes overeaters hide behind their weight, and don't even attempt to conquer fears of rejection. But if you give it a try, a happier, more relaxed life will open up to you. Instead of moving away from people, *try moving toward people*.

Perhaps your fear of rejection has caused you to unconsciously adopt behavior and attitudes which actually demand rejection. To cover up fear, you may display an attitude of aloofness toward people. They, in turn, have termed you as a snob.

Some people constantly ruin relationships because they have a secret fear of getting too close to people. Sarcasm and an "I don't care" attitude help keep others at arm's length.

So how can you get over your fear of rejection and have the kind of life you've always wanted to live?

Start by recognizing attitudes you have that invite the rejection of other people, people you would really like to know better. Think before you speak, because old habits of responding are hard to break. Finally, recognize that you are not alone in your problem. Nearly everyone, at times, has felt rejection, even people whose bodies are thin.

One of the saddest things about being overweight in a thin world is that many of us gradually withdraw because of rejection — real or imagined. The new attitudes you are learning will help you reenter that world where you will find the majority of people really are accepting, given half a chance.

Before you reach for that extra bite today, ask yourself:
Have I started moving toward people? Am I giving up old "I don't care" attitudes?

There's a lot to that old saw about "getting up on the wrong side of the bed." Sometimes people think they're going to have a bad day — and that's just exactly what happens.

Tell yourself this morning that you are going to have a great day. Try to bring all your enthusiasm to bear and it will lift you higher and help you overcome any of the day's minor difficulties.

Say to yourself:"I'm greater than I think!" Everyone has low moments, so the least you should do is start off each day with a good opinion of yourself.

Think about the possibility of prosperity which will come to you today. Not prosperity in terms of money, but in terms of being able to enjoy the food you eat, without overeating.

Give yourself some motivation for this day. Make a mental list of all the good reasons you are trying to make a reasonable eating plan a part of your daily life.

And what about other people? Why not try to give one person some extra love today? Remember love is a two-way street, so any you give out comes back to you again. And you can sure use all you can get.

Look in the mirror and see yourself as you really are — not just the way you look, but the positive, powerful personality within you.

It doesn't really matter what side of the bed you got up on — but it matters a great deal what you do with the rest of your day. By cultivating a more positive approach to daily living, you'll be better able to lose weight and open a window to your inner self.

Before you reach for that extra bite today, ask yourself:
Have I given enough thought to the positive way I should start my day? Am I enjoying the emotional prosperity that freedom from overeating brings?

Some people might ask: What on earth has spreading happiness got to do with losing weight? Just this. It's the best way to make yourself happy, and happy people aren't as likely to go on an eating binge.

Most of us, dealing as we do with the worrisome need for excess food, sometimes just get bogged down with the problems of dieting and living. What's the best way to get off this merry-go-round? Spread a little happiness. It's contagious and you'll find you're apt to catch it.

Do something kind and unexpected today. When you're shopping, tell the clerk who waits on you that he really knows his merchandise. He'll get a real thrill from your approval.

Give yourself away today. Give someone your time, your friendship and your ideas. Look for opportunities to say or do the thing that will make another person feel good about himself/herself. You could make someone's whole day by simply saying, "I know you always try your very best."

Sometimes you can give happiness and never say a word. A silent hug, a smile, a friendly pat on the back may be all that's needed to spread happiness — happiness that will turn around and come back to you.

The point is that while you are searching for little ways to give yourself away, you can't possibly take the time to overeat or even bemoan the fact that you have an eating problem.

Think about it. Maybe there is something to all this "giving" business. All of the world's religions and most of the world's philosophers advocate selflessness. There must be a good reason for such uniformity. Why don't you try it? What have you got to lose?

Before you reach for that extra bite today, ask yourself:
Have I stopped thinking of happiness as "getting," and started thinking of it as "giving"? Am I willing to give away a little part of myself?

Stress is the number one enemy of every overeater trying to control food intake and build a more healthful life. Too much stress can manifest itself in nervousness, sleeplessness, irritability, inability to concentrate and even loss of muscle coordination — and, it almost goes without saying, that stress is sure hard on weight-losing diets.

In the past, most or all of these stress symptoms have led us into overeating and the guilt and unhappiness that follow. How can a dieter stress-proof his life? Here are a few suggestions.

Driving — It won't speed up heavy traffic to reach for a high-calorie snack in the grocery bag on the car seat next to you. Instead try to check seething rage and accept the traffic situation as momentary — unpleasant though it may be. While you're waiting, turn on the radio and sing. (Next to your shower, your car makes your voice sound great.)

In public — The secret to de-stressing public appearances, according to Dr. Melvin Heller, is to dress for comfort to keep calm. Strangely enough, many people (not just overweights) are ill at ease on the job or at social gatherings because they are dressed uncomfortably. They dress for others, or for fashion, but not according to the way they *feel* in their clothes.

At home — relieving stress in the home is probably most important because that's where overweights do most of their overeating. The important idea is to arrange your home to give the message: "Relax."

You can find other ways to stress-proof your life if you look for them. Just being aware that you can do something about it will help.

Come to think of it, there aren't many things in your life you can't do something about. You're a pretty powerful person.

Before you reach for that extra bite today, ask yourself:
Have I tried to stress-proof my life as much as I can? Do I look for ways to do something positive about the stresses of life?

A lecturer on living in the present once said of his former life: "I had one foot in yesterday, one foot in tomorrow, but today was kicking hell out of me." His meaning was graphically plain, especially for dieters. If we worry about what we overate yesterday, and are afraid of what might happen tomorrow, today will give us a very bad time indeed.

Regret over past overeating is like crying over spilled milk and usually involves harsh self-criticism. "What a bad thing I did," is usually rapidly translated into the more destructive, "What a bad person I am."

Fearful mind trips into the future usually go something like this: "I know I'll probably go off my diet tomorrow," which through a unique mental process known only to overeaters rapidly becomes, "As long as I'm going to overeat later, I might as well start now."

When mental trips to the past and future start, try to stop them as soon as you realize what is happening. Bring your mind back to the now. *Today is the only day you can do anything about.* As you begin to keep your mind in the present, you will learn to develop resources to deal with real day-by-day situations.

The same lecturer had another aphorism worth remembering: "Yesterday is a canceled check, tomorrow is a promissory note, but today is ready cash." The point is that today is the only day you can really spend. The growth you seek can never be found in the past or the future but by living in the NOW.

Before you reach for that extra bite today, ask yourself:
Am I spending the "hard cash" of the present? Do I believe this day is the only day I can really live?

If you were to ask a group of people, as one Zen master did, what was the most important word in the English language, you would probably get a variety of answers, as he did. Peace, love, money, truth, courage — all were wrong. "Let," he said, "is the most important word." Let go. Let it be. Let it happen.

The word "let" is really not a passive word, but instead implies a trusting acceptance of life. It means allowing love to come into your life instead of manipulating others to your will. It means allowing natural beauty to touch you instead of manufacturing what you think ought to be.

Let life happen to you. Try to get in touch with your inner love and beauty. Think, as you practice new and sane ways of eating, that what is going on inside you is as important as what is going on outside you.

Many people carry around in their heads an image of the kind of individual they want to be. When our behavior, especially our eating behavior, doesn't measure up to our ideal, we grow despondent.

The process of inner growth is less the process of stuffing self-improvement into our brains, than it is uncovering petal by petal the rose already there.

You are all the things you think you are. It's your thinking that must change more than your being.

Be quick to give yourself credit and reluctant to blame. You've already had enough of that. Personal growth, like the fly of the old saying, is attracted more to honey than to vinegar.

Today as you prepare to live without more food than your body will need, remember the most important word in the English language. *Let.*

Before you reach for that extra bite today, ask yourself:
Have I allowed life to happen to me? Do I believe that I am the best I think I am?

Do you agree that you have the power to change your life for the better by changing your attitudes? If not, think how many times your thoughts have had a powerful influence on your behavior in the past. For instance, once you must have liked someone a great deal, but now you can't understand what you ever saw in him or her. Nothing has really changed, except your attitude about that person. Now do you agree that thoughts can give you the power to change?

The same idea is true when it comes to liking yourself. If you don't like yourself very well — because of your weight problem or because you don't approve some behavior — the power of your thoughts can give you a negative outlook on all of your life.

It pays overeaters to develop a good opinion of themselves, and the pay-off is in lost pounds.

You will also become more understanding of others and of yourself. And, most delightful of all, you will become more popular with other people, not to mention enjoying your own company more.

You'll be surprised to learn that the more you honestly like yourself, the less vulnerable you will be to the criticism of others. If you are truly happy with yourself, the opinions of other people will do little to alter your self-image.

Today is the day to make changes in your attitude about yourself. You have the power. Nothing can stop you but a negative attitude.

For overeaters, there's another and more tangible reward for liking ourselves. We become more willing to give ourselves the chance to gain a slender, healthy body. If you create a happy, likeable, slender image in your mind's eye, it's a law of nature that you will later see that image in your mirror.

You be the judge. Sentence yourself to a negative mental image and an unhappy life, or sentence yourself to liking yourself more every day you live.

Before you reach for that extra bite today, ask yourself:
Have I changed my negative self-image to a positive self-image? Am I willing to serve a life sentence for liking myself?

Most of us approach a weight-losing diet with little enthusiasm. Who can blame us? Chances are we're no strangers to the long white diet sheets our doctors hand out with such consistency. Perhaps we've tried and failed, tried again and failed again. But today, following a program of growth-centered living, we can realize that failure is never final. It is just another opportunity to grow. A philosopher once said, "Failing is not falling down, but staying there."

Have you ever thought that a positive way to approach weight-losing would be to make friends with your diet? There's nothing we need more than a controlled way of eating, especially when we have spent an evening gorging ourselves on calorie-rich food only to awaken to a morning hungover with guilt. There's nothing we need more, when we dress in new clothing we bought just two weeks before only to find that the buttons and seams are already straining.

You need this friendship more than you know. Like the chicken and the egg, a friend and success go together . Can you imagine how difficult it would be to live with an enemy every day? If you make an enemy of your eating plan, sooner or later, you will find an excuse to get rid of it. But if you make your diet your friend, it will not be too long before the two of you will learn to live together comfortably.

As with any new relationship, it won't happen overnight. It will take time and trust. But if you will try to stop making an adversary experience of weight-losing, the guilty overeating hangover and the too-tight clothes will soon be just a memory.

Before you reach for that extra bite today, ask yourself:
Have I made friends with my diet? Do I know that if I make an enemy of my eating plan, I will find an excuse to get rid of it?

Do you know people who never admit they're wrong? Whatever happens it is always someone else's fault. Such people are experts at passing the buck. The two go hand in hand you know, because if you cannot admit you're wrong, you have to blame others.

All of us, at one time or another, have too much false pride to admit we are wrong. We are afraid of being ridiculed, so we bluff it out. The problem such behavior causes dieters is that we take out our secret shame on ourselves by yet more overeating. For that reason, the Anonymous programs suggest their members promptly admit it when they are wrong.

It takes a high degree of self-esteem and self-appreciation to admit you have acted wrongly. How do you teach yourself to make such honest and courageous admissions?

First, be realistic about yourself and your position in relation to others. Try listing the people who love you — family and friends, for example. This will show you that you should hold yourself in higher esteem.

Second, analyze the reasons why you are unwilling to admit you are wrong. Look for the key factor that keeps you from making this admission. Is it fear? Examine it. Ask yourself if it is real or only a shadow fear that you've invented.

Third, if false pride is the reason you cannot admit you're wrong, take a look at the real accomplishments of your life and learn to dismiss the occasional lapses.

The great Eighteenth Century English poet Alexander Pope said: *"A man should never be ashamed to own he has been in the wrong, which is but saying, in other words, that he is wiser today than he was yesterday."*

Pope's advice is as fresh and true today as it was 200 years ago. Being wrong is no disgrace or disaster. But, for dieters, not admitting it, can be.

Before you reach for that extra bite today, ask yourself:
Am I overeating because I've neglected to admit I'm wrong? Have I added up the real accomplishments of my life so that I can learn to forgive myself?

A Weight Watcher was heard to comment after stepping away from her weekly weigh-in: "It's no wonder I haven't lost any weight. I've been trying to sell my home, take care of three teenagers, keep up my golf lessons and start a stenography course."

That's not an empty excuse. It would be a wonder if she could stick to any eating plan, trying to do so many things at once. If there's one thing every dieter needs to do, it's to eliminate the feelings of confusion, nervousness, hurry and anxiety that doing too much bring to the surface.

If there is one time in your life when you should set priorities, it is now, when you are trying to cope with your food problem.

There's a special reaction dieters have who are always in a hurry. Sometimes we tell ourselves we are just too busy to prepare the proper foods and reach for "fast foods." It's not long before we're not even pretending to follow a moderate eating plan.

Set your priorities and try to *place eating to live, instead of living to eat, at the head of your list.* Concentrate all your awareness, all your responsiveness on this one thing. You will find this concentration strangely relaxing. You will be free of the feeling of hurry and able to think your very best.

You will need all your wits about you today. It is an important day in your year, a day to set priorities.

Before you reach for that extra bite today, ask yourself:
Am I trying to do too much? Have I placed eating to live, instead of living to eat, at the head of my priority list?

Do you recognize this problem? You've been eating nutritiously and losing weight for some time now. You are beginning to feel very good about your inner changes and your new body. At this point, your best friends and even your family begin a strange litany. "But your face looks so drawn." "Are you sure you haven't lost too much?" "I liked you better the way you were."

Psychologists recognize that sometimes the people closest to overweights react strangely once you start to pare down your familiar shape. They unconsciously set out to sabotage even the most successful diet.

Apparently, they don't like to see radical changes in those close to them. It confuses and disturbs them, so they say irrational things like, "You're looking older and more wrinkled."

Don't listen to them. Don't let your motivation be watered down. You probably aren't losing too much weight. Ten to one, you're only halfway there, and in the end you're going to look and feel younger, healthier and happier.

If you are one of those dieters (rarer than an extinct passenger pigeon) who does lose too much weight, your doctor will let you know. Take your doctor's medical advice, not that of your friends.

Don't worry too much about the adjustments others have to make because *you* are changing. The important thing is how your new way of eating and thinking is affecting your life for the better. As you travel toward your goal you are finding this to be a most creative, enjoyable experience. If you are firm with them, it will not take your friends long to discover you are going where you want to go.

Before you reach for that extra bite today, ask yourself:
Have I listened to well-meaning but negative voices? Do I refuse to allow others to sabotage my new lifestyle?

Many years ago, the late songwriter Johnny Mercer wrote a hit song called *Accentuate the Positive* which could easily become the anthem of overweights everywhere. In it, Mercer suggested lyrically that people should "latch on to the affirmative and eliminate the negative."

It's no wonder that many of us, regardless of Mercer's good advice, are prone to accentuate the negative instead. Overweights in the American society are bombarded with visual messages which tend to reinforce a negative self-image. Television tells us, in so many words and pictures, that we are not physically attractive if we are not the thin ideal. Somehow, some of us have decided that physical attractiveness and self-worth are one and the same. They are not.

Sure we want to have healthy bodies, uncluttered with excess fat so that we will look better and feel better, but the shape of our bodies has little to do with our value as human beings.

Our negative thinking suggests that, if we are overweight, we deserve unhappiness. The slightest cutting remark poisons our day and affirms our own bad opinion of ourselves.

Why not eliminate negative thinking like the song says and accentuate positive thinking? Remember, if you have a healthy self-image, the thoughtless remarks of others will not threaten you. *You have a right to happiness.* Your weight problem hasn't made you a second-class citizen unless you wish to become one.

Day by day you can develop self-reliance and emotional independence. You can leave yourself open to wonderful inner experiences — to affection, approval, acceptance and understanding.

Before you reach for that extra bite today, ask yourself:
Have I "latched on to the affirmative" in my life? Do I believe that my worth as a human being has nothing to do with the shape of my body?

Some people with extra pounds can find a sound diet, go on it, and lose weight with no more help than they get from their doctor, mate or best friend.

Others find the stuggle to suppress their desire for excess food a constant battle of loss and gain. They travel from wild success back to the pits of failure in a lonely circle that usually finds them back at their own starting point.

For these dieters, the benefits of group support may make a significant difference. They may be able to accomplish their dream of permanent weight control with a group of others in the same boat.

One diet group member explains the meaning of group strength: "I can place my hands under this side," he said, grasping the edge of large table, "and I can't lift it alone. But, if others get around the table and lift, too, then I can do with their help what I was never able to do alone."

What does group participation mean to overweights? First, you discover that other people have eating problems, sometimes far worse than yours. This identification is essential to an increased feeling of well-being. At least you are no longer alone.

Second, you learn to accept help. There are people all about you in various stages of recovery, who are willing to freely give you the same help that has been given them.

Finally, as you begin to have more success with your own eating problems, you will be able to help other newcomers do what you have done.

Everyone wants to be strong and self-reliant, but if you're drowning in a sea of food, swim for the group lifeboat.

Before you reach for that extra bite today, ask yourself:
Am I tired of fighting my food problem alone? Have I considered joining a group to gain the extra strength I need to control my weight?

Too often the ups and downs of reforming destructive eating patterns get you into the habit of negative thinking about your future. Perhaps doubts and fears of failure lurk in the corners of your mind, ready to leap out and destroy your confidence.

When you expect to fail or you have reservations about your ability to succeed, you can hardly expect success.

The important thing for every dieter to practice is an *attitude of expectancy*. Expect the best. Expect that your future is bright, and that you will overcome the problem that has you, literally, by the throat.

Of course it doesn't sound easy. Undesirable thoughts of self-pity and just plain pessimism can keep our expectations very low. "Why should life be any easier today than it was yesterday?" we ask, doubtfully.

One way is to expect it to be so. Inspirational columnist Doug Hooper says, "In the long run, nobody can stop your succeeding except yourself." Every thought, he goes on, becomes an action according to the strength and desire contained in that thought.

Think about that. If you have a strong desire to put into action, the action, itself, can become as strong as the thought.

If you expect the best of yourself today, you may surprise yourself with the strength of your ability to act on your desires. If you expect that you will give your best to a better way of eating today, there is absolutely no one who can stop you. Don't be so surprised. You've always been that strong. You just didn't know it.

Before you reach for that extra bite today, ask yourself:
Have I learned that I can expect the best of myself today and get it? Have I made my desires strong so that my actions will match my expectation?

If there's one thing on which the saints and great teachers of the ages agree, it's the point that human beings should seek self-knowledge. Trying to live in a complex world without this essential information would be like climbing the Matterhorn with a paper bag over your head — you wouldn't know where you were, couldn't see where you were going and would be placing yourself in dangerous situations every step of the way.

Take off the paper bag of your negative self — the one that has kept you in the dark for so long. Now you can get to know yourself the way you really are — not the fearful you, stumbling in perpetual night, but the confident, positive you, climbing in the sunshine.

First, you should throw away the assumption that nothing can be done about your weight problem. "Nothing can be done about it," is the false belief you have been nurturing in the blackness of self-deception. You have an innate ability to change your life, to become that slim person which is your mind's ideal.

Next, you should inventory the positive and powerful things you do every day. This *positive inventory* will help you alter your feeling that somehow you are a victim of fate. Taking your mental inventory is much like cleaning house. You throw away the garbage, but keep what is serviceable.

Get rid of mind garbage — the negative "I can'ts," that have been running your life until today. Shine up your positive self. Put your mind back into full service. Get to know this positive self. It's the self you'll enjoy living with the most.

Make it a habit to take a positive inventory every morning. Take a long look at this new self you're getting to know. If you are being introduced for the first time, you may like this person more than you ever knew you could, enough to be friends for a lifetime.

Before you reach for that extra bite today, ask yourself:
Have I been stumbling in the darkness of self-deception? Am I willing to rid myself of mind-garbage and shine up my positive self each morning?

For on-again, off-again dieters, the fear of failure can prevent them from giving themselves another chance to succeed.

Some have resorted to desperate acts to insure success — from having jaws wired together to going on Ghandi-like fasts. Why? Because they desperately fear failure if left on their own.

Suppose you eat a small piece of candy not on your eating plan. Does that mean you have to overeat on everything else in sight? Psychologists call this the overeaters "all or nothing" syndrome. "Some dieters," says behaviorist Dr. Joseph Morrow at California State University, "allow one wayward bite to wipe out weeks of successful dieting."

If you're slimming down a day at a time, and never take a wayward bite, that's fabulous. But if you do err, you know that each day is a new chance you can give yourself. It doesn't matter what you ate yesterday. Today you are committing yourself anew to following your weight-losing eating plan.

Commitment each morning to living without excess food will free you from the fear of failure, and allow you to concentrate on the positive things in your day.

And there are so many positive things. The composure that comes when you're working for the image you've always wanted. The confusion that leaves your daily life when you follow a disciplined way of eating.

Today your mind will not be clouded by the effects of too much high-calorie food. You will see self-confidence replace fear. One by one the problems that bother you will become manageable. You will not be depressed about your weight because you can honestly say, *"I'm doing something about it."*

Today is your day to be happy. Enjoy all your gifts — especially the bright new chance you give yourself day after day after day.

Before you reach for that extra bite today, ask yourself:
Do I no longer fear failure? Am I committed to giving myself another chance if I ever need one?

Many dieters have found, and some independent psychological research confirms, that there are three behaviors to watch if you're serious about losing weight and maintaining it:

1. Never get too bored.
2. Never get too tired.
3. Never get too hungry.

These three problems faced positively could help you lose weight.

Bored — Two psychology researchers tested fat students while they performed exceedingly boring or very interesting tasks. They discovered that the students ate far less when they were really interested in what they were doing.

Overweights know that they have eaten to escape the unpleasant emotional state of boredom. Learning to alternate necessary, but boring, jobs with ones you find more intriguing could give you the crucial edge in appetite control.

Tired — Getting too tired for a dieter often means that this becomes an excuse to eat whatever is handy, rather than to prepare foods on our diet menu. Excessive fatigue is also a signal for many of us to have a quick-energy pick-me-up — which to us can only mean extra food.

Try to alternate periods of heavy energy use with some form of relaxation. Put your feet up for a few minutes, loosen your clothing, close your eyes and breathe deeply. They'll be minutes well spent. Don't try to fool yourself that you don't have the time. It will take a lot longer to quit work for a bout of overeating just because you got too tired.

Hungry — This "never" speaks for itself. If you allow yourself to get so busy that you go way past your regular mealtime, you can get so hungry the meal you have won't fill you up, and you may find yourself reaching for extra calories.

Nobody likes to be told, "you can't do that!" But smart dieters, who know their limitations, remind themselves of the three "nevers" every day.

Before you reach for that extra bite today, ask yourself:
Do I know when to stop? Am I allowing myself to get too bored, tired or hungry?

Are you one of those people who try to do too much in too little time? Many overeaters seem to fall into the trap of overscheduling their day and then becoming so anxious they fall back into negative eating and thinking habits.

Here's how you can avoid this pitfall.

1. Try to work out a plan for your day each morning. Don't try to accomplish too much. Take on one or two major jobs and a few minor ones. Studies prove that planning ahead is time well spent. You'll be able to accomplish your work faster.

2. Take breaks when stress and tension accumulate. If you're doing a physical job, switch for a few minutes to some mental task and vice versa.

3. Strive to do the best you can, but avoid becoming a perfectionist. Perfection, because it is rarely attainable, is a waste of time.

4. Learn to say no if you can't spare the time for another activity. You can be firm, yet tactful.

5. Don't procrastinate, but don't try to do too much too quickly. Take one little thing you've been postponing and do it right now. Perhaps you owe someone an apology. If you make it, you will have done the most unpleasant chore of the day and have it over with.

6. Don't go too far and become a workaholic. Place working in perspective with the rest of your life.

Above all, if you want to manage your time instead of having it manage you, learn to cultivate the attitude of "Do It Now."

The English author John Ruskin has an even more succinct reminder. On his desk was a small marble block with one word carved on its face. That word was "TODAY."

Before you reach for that extra bite today, ask yourself:
Have I made a plan so that I don't fall victim to the urgency of constant sudden decisions? Have I placed my new eating plan at the top of my list of things to do today?

Recovered alcoholics know that if they think too much about the real or imagined pleasures of the bottle, it is virtually certain they will return to drinking.

The same is true for overeaters — perhaps even truer. Unlike the alcoholic who can live very well without alcohol, the overeater must eat to live. But, like the alcoholic, who believes "thinking is drinking" the overeater must learn to control mental food fantasies.

A member of Overeaters Anonymous told her group at a weekly meeting:"When I started my food plan, I began making a mental list of all the foods that I missed. After a week of this daydreaming , I went off my diet, ate my way through the list, and gained another twenty-five pounds."

Our food fantasies, if we dwell on them, can insure that sooner or later we will succumb to these negative temptations. But fantasizing can be fun, so let's learn to do the positive kind.

Try closing your eyes and imagining yourself having your clothes altered to a smaller size. Listen to the voices of your friends exclaiming how well you look.

Imagine walking down a street toward a mirror without shrinking from the sight. The image you see is slender and vibrant, and you walk with purpose and pleasure.

You're at a party and someone behind you is laughing. You continue your conversation, calm and self-assured, because you know that laughter is not aimed at the slim you.

Focus your mind on the new life you want to live, a life where the need for excess food is no longer a preoccupation. You'll discover this fantasy is better than any one you ever had before.

Before you reach for that extra bite today, ask yourself:
Am I controlling my mental food fantasies? Do I believe that my new life will be better than any real or imagined pleasure I ever derived from overeating?

Now that you're getting to know yourself better, it won't be difficult to improve your relationships with other people if you work at it a bit. Sometimes we overweights have had a hard time with friendships. We have either expected too much or too little from others. Here are ten ways which will help you strike a happy balance. Why not try them today.

1. Speak cheerfully to people.
2. Smile at people.
3. Call people by their names.
4. Be friendly.
5. Be cordial. Act like the friendship of others gives you real pleasure.
6. Be genuinely interested in others.
7. Be generous with praise.
8. Be considerate of the feelings of others. (Criticize with caution, if at all.)
9. Be thoughtful of the opinions of other people. (If you're always right, something is wrong.)
10. Be alert to give service when you are needed.

None of these suggestions will cost you either a great deal of money or time, but they are one of the wisest investments you can make in your new way of living. You will find it is difficult, if not impossible, to sit at home alone, stuffing unneeded calories into your mouth if your thoughts and efforts are often directed toward others.

That doesn't mean you should neglect yourself. You should find the same balance with other people that you are searching for in your eating behavior.

How can you do this? Think of the friendliest man or woman you know, and try to imitate them today. There is a real joy in being a truly friendly person. Some of that joy will inevitably rub off on you. And couldn't you use a little joy in your day?

Before you reach for that extra bite today, ask yourself:
Am I getting to know others better? Am I trying to strike a better balance in my friendships, neither expecting too much nor too little?

Not What You Are Giving Up, But What You Are Getting

One of the most harmful attitudes dieters can have is to approach a new way of eating to lose weight with their minds focused on what they are "giving up." If you review your past unsuccessful attempts at weight-losing, you will probably find that your thoughts turned often to the foods you had eliminated from your diet.

Overweights with a long history of diet struggle can change the odds in their favor by a simple twist of thinking: *Don't focus on what you are giving up, but on what you are getting.*

"I stopped thinking, 'I can't have that,'" said one successful dieter, "and started thinking, 'I don't choose to eat that food any longer.'"

The change in performance after this change in attitude is often quite startling. One TOPS teen member said, "Always before, I lost nothing because I felt sorry for myself every time my stomach growled.

"But now I've lost 80 pounds by deciding to be happy when I am hungry, because I know my body is busy using up all that fat."

When you decide to give yourself a new eating plan for better, more healthful living, what are you giving up? Lonely nights. Guilty days. Clothes that don't fit. Job promotions that go to others. Self-hatred.

What are you getting? A chance to live closer to yourself and to other people. Confidence. A new, thin image. Inner peace. The ability to concentrate.

Getting excess food out of the way of real living is the greatest gift you can give yourself.

Today, don't allow your thoughts to focus on those so-called "goodies" you've chosen to eliminate, the ones that have caused you so much grief. Focus instead on the new life you're giving yourself.

It will take concentration. But you can do it.

Before you reach for that extra bite today, ask yourself:
Have I concentrated too much on the foods I'm giving up and not enough on the new life I am getting? Have I learned to concentrate on what I really want in life?

Doctors and psychologists are becoming increasingly aware of the sabotaging spouse. These are husbands and wives who deliberately or unconsciously tempt us to overeat or disparage our need to lose weight in the first place. Why? Jealousy and insecurity are the prime motivators for these spouses, who sometimes go so far as to set chocolate "fat traps" all over the house.

Of course, every loving spouse sometimes offers too much of, or the wrong kind of, food. There's no cause to see a diabolical plot behind every bonbon. But if your mate consistently brings home food gifts, and insists that you should eat them, then you may have a sabotaging spouse on your hands.

Just becoming aware of it helps a lot. And reasoning with your partner helps, too. Sit down and discuss the situation. Perhaps he or she doesn't really understand how serious you are. (One doctor prescribes more drastic action. "Put the 'goodie' under a turned-on faucet while your mate watches. That will show how serious you are.")

Chances are, you won't have to go so far. Most mates will respond to a sincere talk about the problem. If not, you will have to convince your spouse over a period of time that fear of change is groundless. The changes you are making in your life are positive ones which will make you a happier, healthier individual, and a better partner.

Patience and time will help. Eating over it certainly won't. Remember — there are no chocolate solutions to life's problems, especially not this one.

Before you reach for that extra bite today, ask yourself:
Am I overeating to please someone else? Do I realize that overeating will not cure another's insecurities?

Some overweight people, who have little success with diet after diet, excuse themselves saying, "Well, I might become too thin and bony." There is a condition called *anorexia nervosa*, which translates loosely as a severe aversion to food. If you're nervous over *anorexia nervosa*, you needn't be. This rare psychological disorder, which causes people to literally starve themselves to death, affects a miniscule number of overweight people. Most sufferers only imagine they're fat.

Have you been postponing starting down the road to a slimmer you, because you fear you might get too thin? One dieter at a group therapy session, put this excuse in perspective: "I always defended my weight by saying, 'I'd rather be too fat than too thin,' just as if there were no in-between."

Look for the in-between, the middle ground, the balance of life. (Your life may have careened from one extreme to another — from fasting to feasting — from elation to depression.) Most overeaters who discover the middle ground of sensible eating find their total life becoming more manageable. By controlling their appetite for food, they are able to better control the other appetites of life as well — especially the destructive, emotional ones.

If you find you are giving yourself (and others) the tired, old excuse, "But I might get too thin and bony," don't you believe it. Others won't.

Trade false fears for a balanced way of life, one that will eventually give you the image you desire. You can do it. Yes, it is possible to become and remain healthfully slender for the rest of your life. But first, you will have to learn to walk without using such "thin" excuses for a crutch.

Before you reach for that extra bite today, ask yourself:
Am I using an excuse to justify my weight? Do I realize that between too fat and too thin there is a wonderful in-between?

Are you sure you're ready? Sometimes we overweight people go on a diet because we think it will please others, or because somebody told us we should do something about our weight. Unfortunately, this is hardly the motivation it takes to become thin.

When our motivation isn't high, we invariably slip and fall off even the most sensible eating plan. What do we say? "It didn't work." "It made me too uncomfortable." Typically, we have relied on *it* to make us slender, rather than on building a new growth-centered lifestyle.

Is your desire to lose weight and change your life stronger than your desire for food? That is the question, and only you can answer it. If you have had enough — yes, suffered enough — you are ready.

Which is the real you? The overweight, overburdened person who stares back from the mirror, or the slender image you think you can be. You must decide which image you want to "identify" with — the one in the mirror or the one in your mind. You must want to be thin. You must believe you can be.

Of course, it's not that simple. No one wants to insult your intelligence. But it is the place to start. Unless you *really* want it, the motivation to diet for weight-losing is never there.

This motivation, this deep desire to be thin, isn't just something you need for a few minutes at the beginning of a diet. It is a lifelong feeling kept alive by the memory of the food-centered life you gladly left behind. Remember your mind's desire, the thin you, is not mere daydreaming. It is the way you really see yourself. It is your blueprint for change.

Before you reach for that extra bite today, ask yourself:
Am I convinced my desire to lose weight is stronger than my desire for food? Am I willing to start using the blueprint in my mind to build a new growth-centered life?

Remember Scarlett O'Hara in *Gone With The Wind?* Her philosophy of life was, "I won't worry about that today, I'll worry about that tomorrow." Of course, in a way, she's right. Tomorrow *is* another day. But what's wrong with right now?

Too often for dieters, tomorrow never comes. There are too many tomorrows. The old story about the too-fat person who says, "I'm starting my diet next Monday," is a national joke. Delaying tactics work if you're angry. But counting to ten before you start a life without excess food is bad advice for an overeater to give himself.

Do it now. If you have a strong urge to do something about yor life today, not taking immediate action usually means a lot of time and distraction gets between the desire and its fullfillment. When that happens, desire dies.

If you truly want to live a life that isn't dominated by what you are going to eat next, get started now. If you are sick and tired of your dependency on certain foods, do something about it today.

Don't look at the obstacles, look at the possibilities. And what are they? You will be able to take off your excess weight and lighten your emotional load as well. You will gain a new self-respect, a healthier body you'll like to look at and a new alertness that will no longer be dulled by the physical assault of too many calories.

These are the happy promises you can give yourself today. You know where delay gets you — another twenty-four hours of confusion and pain.

Don't let your mind play old tricks on you. Refuse to respond to delaying tactics that would keep you from your mind's idea of real living. Tomorrow may have been fine for Scarlett, but for you, now is better.

Before you reach for that extra bite today, ask yourself:
Am I tired of my food dependency? Have I decided today is the best day to begin my new life?

So often we become embroiled in the "everydayness" of living our lives. We go to work, care for our families, perform our obligation faithfully. And yet, as fulfilling as these necessary activities are, something is missing in our lives. Perhaps it's only a vague sense of uneasiness. Usually we can't even put a name to it.

What's the answer? You may need a vacation far more often than you think. Since it's not always possible to actually pack your suitcase and leave town, it's a good idea to learn to take a "vacation in your mind."

Poets since Roman times have written of the refuge of a quiet mind, where you can withdraw and renew yourself. Quiet isn't easy to find in the hectic lives most of us lead in the modern world, but it is possible to set aside a quiet corner of your mind (Dr. Maxwell Maltz calls it a "decompression chamber") where you can be at peace, and meditate.

Try taking a short vacation to the quiet place in your mind, whenever you have a free moment. Don't wait until crisis strikes, but build up your reserves of serenity in advance so they will be immediately available to you when you need your own help.

Take a few minutes to vacation in this tranquil corner several times a day. Use the magic of imagination to conjure a peaceful scene where you have no decisions and no worries. Get away from it all.

When you return you will be better able to cope with your day, whatever it brings, without undue anxiety.

Anxiety for dieters is a double bind. It not only keeps your performance level low, but it makes following your ideal plan of living and eating much more difficult.

How many of us have held down anxiety with a heavy layer of extra food?

Go ahead. Find your own quiet place and take a little vacation.

Before you reach for that extra bite today, ask yourself:
Have I learned to treat the anxiety of "everydayness" with a rejuvenating mental vacation? Am I willing to visit the quiet place I've set aside in my mind as often as I can?

Today is Abraham Lincoln's birthday. As far as anyone knows the sixteenth president never had a weight problem, but as every school child knows, preserving the union, was an enormous weight to bear. Even before his presidency he exclaimed: "A house divided against itself cannot stand." He could have been talking to those of us who, more than a century later, are engaged in a lifetime struggle against our need for excess food. We cannot be divided in the house of our mind or we will not be able to stand up to life.

To succeed in what may be the most important endeavor of your days, you will need to be wholly committed to learning to think, eat and live a new way. Halfway commitment won't do.

What do you really believe about yourself? Perhaps you think you are a victim of fate, because something always seems to happen which causes you to fall short of your diet goal. Maybe you feel unworthy to succeed, and that you deserve to fail.

If you think these things, chances are good that you will make your prophecies come true. But if you think, "I can't do that," and the answer comes right back, "The hell you can't," then you will most likely be successful.

You *can* really believe the best about yourself and your chances for a new lifestyle, one that doesn't include periodic food binges, if you will allow yourself to believe.

Have you ever had a super-critical parent or teacher tell you that you were bound to fail, get mad, and make the opposite come true just to show them? Try some of this reverse psychology on yourself. If you find your mind divided against itself, with the negative half pulling the positive half apart, get mad at your negative self. Become indignant with the half of you that predicts your failure, indignant enough to succeed at your new way of living.

If you do, you'll just about make Abe Lincoln's day your own.

Before you reach for that extra bite today, ask yourself:
Is my mind divided against itself? Am I tired of allowing the negative half of my mind to rule the positive half?

Many of us are professional dieters. We've been on about every diet ever invented, and some that we invented ourselves. As a result, we tend to think we know all about nutrition. In some ways we do. Of course, it's not possible to be as aware of food and of eating as we are, without becoming aware of the basic components of good nutrition. For instance, most of us know instantly that we gain more weight eating chocolates than rutabagas. Nonetheless, we may not be as nutrition-wise as we think we are.

Few of us eat a truly balanced diet, containing proper proportions of fats, carbohydrates and proteins together with vitamins and minerals. Some overweights are almost protein-starved because of their tendency to concentrate on carbohydrates.

If you have any doubts about the nutritional balance of the eating plan you are following to lose weight or to maintain your normal weight, consult a doctor and, to be on the safe side, a professional nutritionist. (Some physicians admittedly are not expert in nutritional matters.)

The main reason for our caution, which may include reading some recommended books on healthy eating, is to *find food facts*. Only then will we be able to drop some of our cherished, but erroneous, ideas about food. For example, one dieter was convinced he had to have two tablespoons of honey before breakfast. He couldn't remember where he first heard his misinformation, but he had religiously followed it for years, adding unnecessary calories to his daily intake. He hadn't bothered to count these extra calories. "After all," he reasoned, "honey was *good* for me."

Other diet club members have reported (indeed, insisted) on a ludicrous list of what they considered "necessary" foods for good nutrition — everything from bologna to English muffins.

Find out what your body needs for good health. Take time to investigate the nutritional balance of your eating plan. Once you have this out of the way, you can get beyond what you are eating to what is eating you.

Before you reach for that extra bite today, ask yourself:
Have I learned enough about good nutrition to feel safe with my eating plan? Am I ready to look at what's eating me?

Today, Valentine's Day, is the day you can remind yourself that love does not have to come in chocolate packages to be sweet.

Instead of giving or accepting sugar treats, why not give the people you love the gift of yourself?

Tell someone that you really care about them. Tell them that your life is brighter and happier because they are part of it.

Share some of your strength and hope with another dieter, perhaps one who is traveling a harder road than you. Tell them you need them as much as they need you.

Be a sounding board for someone you love. You cannot prevent the pain in another's life, but you can support them with your love and understanding. *You can listen.*

Give yourself a Valentine's Day gift of love. Just for this day, don't judge yourself harshly and punish yourself with overeating.

It's too bad this day comes only once a year. Giving the gift of love helps us block the destructiveness of negative resentment and fear. A day set aside to show love helps us to practice tolerance and good-will toward others and ourselves. Each such day lays the foundation for positive feeling and positive action in our own lives, not to mention the beautiful effect it has on others.

Come to think of it, there is no real reason that you have to limit loving days to twenty-four hours in February. You could decide that you wanted to make every day Valentine's Day. It wouldn't really be difficult. All you'd have to do is put your heart into it.

Before you reach for that extra bite today, ask yourself:
Have I given someone I love a gift of myself? Am I willing to put my heart into being a more loving person each day?

Is there anything so bad about being too fat, ask some overweight people? It's not illegal like drugs are. It's not like being drunk. "I can't get a ticket for fat driving," one dieter said defiantly.

All of this reasoning is true on the surface. To paraphrase the old joke, overweight is not illegal or immoral. But there are parallels between the alcohol/drug user and the food user. Group therapy members have reported they stole money to buy extra food, that their weight helped ruin their marriages and that overeating actually acted as a narcotic, causing them to sleep away much of their day.

The argument about which is the worst vice seems silly. If overeating has become an out-of-control compulsion, it doesn't seem to matter much that it could be worse. It's bad enough.

The problem is: what are you going to do about it? If your eating behavior makes you unhappy, then that is an abnormal way for you to live. Striving toward happiness is the normal way to live.

How can you do that if food has you down? You will simply have to close the doors of your mind to rationalizations, however true, and concentrate on the problem you have. Human beings are naturally goal-oriented. Try setting up a goal for today. How do you want to think and feel by this evening? Work toward your goal.

Remember, rationalizations are merely negative thoughts in pleasant disguises. Learn to see them for what they really are, so that you'll be able to concentrate on the happiness that is normal for you.

Before you reach for that extra bite today, ask yourself:
Am I kidding myself that I could have a worse vice, while the problem I have has me down? Is my goal for today to rid myself of empty rationalizations?

Most weight-loss programs suggest some form of self-monitoring. Many behavioral plans ask the dieter to write down everything eaten during a day, where it is eaten and the dieter's state of emotions at the time. Overeaters Anonymous wants its members to write down their daily menu each morning and check it over with a more experienced member on the telephone.

Why is awareness such a prime factor in successful dieting? Because it tends to break up the habit of eating indiscriminately. Awareness adds another dimension to your response to food — thinking.

Many times members of diet-therapy groups claim they ate without being aware of what they were doing. "I had already finished the whole box of candy," one moaned, "and I didn't even remember picking it up. I just sort-of 'came to' with it in my hand."

It's true that some dieters are not really conscious of their overeating habits. Through repetition, these habits become so much a part of everyday living that a dieter must deliberately place something between the thought of eating and the act.

To break up old eating patterns and make yourself more aware of what you are doing, try some awareness-jogging tricks. Place reminders of your new eating program on the doors to refrigerators and kitchen cabinets. Don't eat while you are doing something else — eating while watching television, for example, becomes automatic, one bite following another.

Increasing your awareness by breaking up old eating habits is an indispensible element of successful dieting. It may seem a bit childish to write down daily menus, or paste diet program slogans all over the kitchen, but that may be where you have to start — at the beginning.

Before you reach for that extra bite today, ask yourself:
Am I truly aware of my eating habits? Am I willing to interrupt the pattern any way I can?

Doctors who work with the overweight say that motivation only insures that a person will start a diet; but even the strongest motivation won't predict success. What character trait *will* predict success? Doctors say, persistence.

No one is trying to fool you by telling you persistence is a snap. Anytime you interrupt a habit, reduce a compulsive activity, there will be distress because you've stopped doing something you've always done. It's during this time of distress, when the going gets rough, that persistence makes all the difference.

How do you build the ability to persist into your life? Enduring the discomfort you may feel, instead of reaching for something to eat, some morsel to soothe the pain away. Sometimes, if you have an emotional pain, you may just have to let it hurt.

The first few days of any new eating regimen are usually the time when you need to persevere and call on all the persistence you can muster, but don't let up as the pounds come off. Sometimes dieters think they are safe because they are nearing their goal weight. This may be the very time they have to work their old ally persistence all the harder.

People who have been more than a few pounds overweight often find they can *never* stop persisting in their new positive way of eating. Keeping the ability to persevere at a high level is their insurance against slipping back into old, destructive eating patterns.

Haven't you always admired the persistent person, the one who never gives up, the one who doggedly endures and gets on with the job? You can be such a person by acting like one. People become who they are, by acting like who they want to be. Think about that.

Before you reach for that extra bite today, ask yourself:
Am I willing to persist in seeking a new way of living? Will I be able to stand some emotional pain without soothing it with excess food?

One of the techniques of modern psychology is called *positive reinforcement.* This term simply means that the therapist points out the good results of what the patient has accomplished.

You can be your own psychologist. Point out to yourself, before you get too far along in your day, the freedom you enjoy now that you are no longer caught in the habit of overeating.

Some very smart dieters start their day with a positive personal inventory. That means they stop and make a mental (written is even better) list of their good points. They give themselves credit for the many nice personality traits they have. They dwell on all their positive attributes.

Why is such a mental exercise necessary? Overweight people as a group have had a rough time of it. Many of us have been told we were self-indulgent, lacking in willpower, and heaven forbid, even immoral! And that's just what others have called us. We have called ourselves much worse in the depth of our despair. Consequently, some of us have a very low opinion of ourselves as human beings.

If there is any group of people who needs to look on the bright side, it's overweight people. And yet, despite the need, some dieters cannot seem to find much that is good to say about themselves. If you are one of these, you'll have to start giving your positive self as much exercise as you used to give your negative self.

You can begin by being more tolerant of you. Treat yourself like you'd treat a very good friend, one with which you planned to spend a lot of time today.

If you start by treating yourself in a friendly positive manner, you will be giving yourself a new and better chance to diet off excess pounds. You'd do that much for a friend, wouldn't you?

Before you reach for that extra bite today, ask yourself:
Have I been my own psychologist and offered myself positive reinforcement? Have I worked on my personal inventory, the one that lists my good points?

Who do you want to be today? You can become that person, if you promise yourself:

to be so strong that nothing can disturb your new way of eating to live or your peace of mind,

to talk of health, happiness and opportunity to everyone you meet and most of all to yourself,

to give your friends the idea that there is something in them you really love,

to treat with optimism all your daily activities,

to think only the best, work for the best and expect the best for yourself and others,

to be enthusiastic about your new lifestyle and believe in your ultimate success,

to give so much time to inner growth that you will have no time to criticize others or yourself,

to be truly cheerful,

to be too full of growing for worry about the future, too forgiving to be angry, too courageous to be fearful and too happy to permit defeat.

Doesn't this person you are trying to be today, sound like someone you'd like to know better? Often we forget that habitual behavior can be positive as well as negative. Trying to act as if you are the person you want to be will give you the practical experience of being that person. Over and over again, day after day, you can experience this new self.

You will become so busy with this more positive person you will have no time to overeat over every real or imagined problem. Dr. William Glasser, the psychologist who founded the Reality Therapy school of psychology, believes that people can even become addicted to the positive side of their personality.

Nobody is suggesting you become an addict. But it wouldn't hurt you to like your positive self a whole lot more.

Before you reach for that extra bite today, ask yourself:
Is this the person I want to be today? Am I willing to risk becoming addicted to positive living?

Most of us as children heard the Puritan admonition, "Idle hands are the devil's workshop," many times over. But few of our mothers ever advised us to keep our hands dirty! Here's one diet doctor who does just that with some startling results.

Getting a dirty hobby, is the Rx of Dr. L. Melvin Elting. Why dirty? Because washing soiled hands acts as a simple buffer between the thought of food and the act of eating. "Many fat people eat out of boredom," says Dr. Elting. "They keep their hands and mouths busy snacking. But taking up a hobby such as woodworking, auto mechanics, glass staining, pottery-making or silversmithing helps bored eaters by keeping their hands in motion." The doctor *lost fifty pounds* taking his own medicine, and won awards for silversmithing.

Many dieters would throw up their hands right here. "What! Haven't I got enough to do without getting a hobby?" But most of those who protest loudest about their hatred for hobbies, have one of the most consuming hobbies of all. They collect and pay for junk food. Almost any hobby, even one of the dirty ones, is less expensive and certainly less fattening.

Before you reach for a chocolate-covered excuse (the one about not possibly having the time or money to take on a hobby), think about all the energy, money and time you expend on your overeating hobby. And what do you get for it? Do you win any prizes? Of course not. For all that effort, you get depression, ill health and fat.

Pick a hobby that is fun for you to do, one which you'll want to pursue. The point of all this is that you should avoid mental boredom like the plague.

You can turn your old eating hobby in for one that will help you construct your new positive lifestyle. That's worth getting your hands dirty for, isn't it?

Before you reach for that extra bite today, ask yourself:
Am I willing to stop collecting food and learn a new hobby?
Do I want a hobby that will pay off in more than fat?

As you learn to withstand the anxieties of your everyday life, you are learning more about yourself. By not allowing food to come between your feelings and you, you have been rewarded with more self-knowledge. The inevitable result is that you have an increasing ability to control your appetites.

No one changes a lifelong way of reacting overnight. Growth is gradual. Each time you withstand a negative feeling over which you would have formerly eaten, you become a little stronger for the next time. The habit of withstanding anxiety is one every dieter must learn to cope with daily. It is the only way we will ever become aware of the root of our anxieties, the anxieties we have always masked with too much food

Each time you win a small battle against self-hate, hopelessness and guilt, you are stronger. Remember, no one can destroy your self-esteem like you can. When this happens it's all too easy to say, "What does it matter, anyway? I might as well eat."

Each time you accept yourself, even when you discover things that you'd rather not know, you will become more accepting the next time. No one's perfect. One of the nicest things we discover, is that we are after all, quite average in our misdeeds.

Accept yourself, get to know your feelings and what they mean. Take a chance on yourself and on your ability to grow, and get ready for a positive change.

The future may seem unfamiliar. You will see new places, have new feelings, and relate to people in different ways. But you will be ready for it, growing as you are, one day at a time, one step at a time,

---

Before you reach for that extra bite today, ask yourself:
Am I trying to use food as a buffer between me and my feelings? Am I willing to win one small battle every day until I get to know myself better?

Karl Menninger, the famous physician, says there is something symbolically motherly in eating food. For dieters, the mother-child food memories can be very strong. For many of us, food is equated with warmth, softness, security and love. Nor are all these feelings memories of childhood. We need only turn on our television to hear a jingle that says, "Canada Dry tastes like love," or "Nothing says lovin' like something from the oven."

To overweights quite often food is more than food. We use it, just like an overzealous mother, to reward or punish ourselves.

In order to lose our excess weight and keep it off, we must learn that food is not more than food — it is not love — it is just food.

Many dieters, because they discover that they have equated food with love, tend to turn in the opposite direction and think of food as an enemy. But food is not an enemy, either, it is just food.

It is common for dieters who get on a healthful, sensible plan of eating to find that they begin to enjoy what they are eating more than they ever did before. It is difficult, if not impossible, to enjoy food when it is eaten in such huge quantities and in such haste that taste buds are stunned instead of teased, "When I used to eat a half-gallon of ice cream at every sitting," recalls one dieter, "I couldn't taste it at all. After a while, my mouth froze!"

There's something very satisfying and calming about choosing a food plan that will help you live a longer, happier life. There is something very loving about eating to live instead of eating as a substitute for love. Discover your *new love* today.

Before you reach for that extra bite today, ask yourself:
Do I think that food is either my friend or my enemy, instead of just food? Have I stopped "mothering" myself with extra calories?

Perhaps you've never considered yourself a very courageous person. You may not be convinced you have the "stuff," especially when it comes to turning away from excess food as a way of life. If this is so, you will have to create more courage.

Don't begin by forcing yourself to stand on the edge of a cliff. In other words, don't try to worry yourself into a perfect diet by scaring yourself half to death with health statistics.

Take the gradual approach. You can create more courage in your life, a little at a time. The first thing you'll need to do is to convince yourself that weight loss is possible. Think about someone you know or have heard of who has lost a significant amount of weight. You see it can be done, so now you can go on to thinking that it can happen to you.

Try to see yourself mentally as a person who has lost every extra pound. See yourself as having the courage each day to say no to excess food. If your fears tell you that you don't have the courage to live without overeating, don't listen. Your fears are not very wise counselors.

Members of Alcoholics Anonymous have put fear in its place by making it an acronym for *False Evidence Appearing Real.* Remember fears of failure seldom come to pass. They seem to exist for the sole purpose of sapping the courage you need to deal with your food problem.

Make a phonograph record in your mind that says, "You can have more courage than you will ever possibly use." Play this mental record over and over again.

By creating a little more courage each day, you will be free to accept the brave new life ahead of you. You have earned it.

Before you reach for that extra bite today, ask yourself:
Am I willing to gradually create the courage I need to say no to excess food? Do I believe that if others have lost weight, I can too?

"The mass of men," said Henry David Thoreau, "lead lives of quiet desperation." He could have been talking about overweights, except that some of us are not so quiet about our diet desperation.

"Dieting makes me so irritable no one can live with me," said one dieter. She described a thoroughly unhappy person who kept up a continous stream of invective aimed at any family member who got within yelling distance.

Dr. Peter Linder, a Los Angeles bariatrician (weight specialist) says: "It's true that food deprivation makes many dieters edgy when they start a weight-losing regimen, but if their goals are strong enough, the physical discomfort fades within a few days."

While this may be true, an angry dieter is one who is in great danger of using food to push down angry feelings. In extreme cases, some overweight people get so spitefully angry at others they get even by overeating again and getting fatter. They have, in fact, a kind of fat temper tantrum.

The truth is that many of us have never learned what to do with anger. We hold it in until it explodes into an eating binge. We have never learned to accept our angry feelings as natural. Everyone feels anger at times. The solution is learning to accept these angry feelings, and to express them in a matter-of-fact way. If we don't, we will let our pent-up rage eat us up!

Try to handle desperation quietly. Ask yourself if there is any real reason for your anger. If yes, can you discuss it calmly? If not, can you accept you anger without eating over it?

The important thing is not to let anger fester until it spills onto other people, or makes dieting and inner peace an utter impossibility. Try quiet.

Before you reach for that extra bite today,ask yourself:
Am I handling my anger in positive ways? Do I believe that overeating is no way to get even with anger?

Janice has four children, none of whom are overweight, at least none are as overweight as their mother. Janice, who thinks of herself as a gourmet, cooks up a storm all day, and at night piles her family's plates high with food. Half of it goes uneaten at the table, but little of it is thrown in the garbage. Janice, mother of four and gourmet cook, is a garbage eater.

"I can't bear to throw out all that good food," she says, "especially since it took me all day to cook it." Janice, besides being a champion clean-up eater is also virtuous. After all, she reasons, she is only being thrifty by salvaging all those leftovers.

Although this game is especially prevalent among overweight women, men are also players. In one family, all the kids scraped their leftover food into their father's plate as they left the table. In this household, *he* kept the garbage pail from getting fat.

Is this an insurmountable problem? Of course not. It's simple to learn to serve smaller portions, or let people at the table serve themselves. You are just kidding yourself if you think you are actually *saving* all that food.

This is just one of the ways we overweight people rationalize our overeating. There are more. You probably have some favorites of your own.

And all the time you are eating more, you are hating what it's doing to you. Aren't you sick of it?

Ferret out all the ways you are turning the eating of excess food into a virtue. When you realize what you are doing, it will be hard to justify continuing the practice. Part of the process of self-knowledge is the painful exposure of long-held habits, some of them hangovers from childhood. But you can change life-long habits. Believe that you can.

Before you reach for that extra bite today, ask yourself:
Am I a stand-in for the garbage pail? Have I dropped all the righteous rationalizations I use in order to consume food I don't need?

February 26   Stop Listening to Your "Quack"

Many overweight people talking in different diet groups around the country seem to express the feeling that "life is passing me by."

Teenagers and young people regret the social life they are missing. "I don't get to wear the right clothes or go to parties," they lament.

Older overweights worry about job limitations, their marriages and their health. "My weight is ruining my life," they chorus.

It seems obvious to most professionals and to anyone else with an ear for human misery that overweight people are carrying an even larger burden than their excess pounds. For many, their lives are bare existence; they are hardly living in the fullest sense of that word.

One of the problems of all of us who carry extra weight is that we listen to a "quack." Not the quacks that try to sell us rubber reducing suits and jiggle treatments. We listen to the most influential quack of them all — ourselves — the quack that tells us we can't stop overeating and hope for a better life.

What you are when you are trying, is what you really are.

Repeat those words out loud. Listen to their sound. There's hope there.

Life is for the living. If life is passing you by, you must be standing still. Don't be any less today than you want to be. Trying is moving.

There is only one magic that quiets the quack in all of us, and that is the magic of emotional growth arrived at through resolving problems and building self-esteem.

Today you will have a chance to experience the joy and beauty that comes from trying to change your life from one of mere existence to one of vibrant living. If you do, you'll like today a lot better than you liked yesterday.

Before you reach for that extra bite today, ask yourself:
Do I have the feeling that life is passing me by? Have I refused to listen to my inner "quack," and become ready to experience the joy of trying?

Change, especially the change of lifelong eating habits, is at best a slow process. It takes a whole lifetime. Many of us have thought in the past that once we lost our weight, from that day on we would be thin and nothing we ate would ever make us fat again. Unfortunately, most of us have learned that there is no never-never land where we can eat whatever and whenever we want. We will always have to be aware of good eating habits.

Change, for overweights, always comes too slowly. We want it to happen yesterday. When we envision the future that a thinner more healthy body will make possible, we are so impatient.

Be patient with yourself. Change will grow out of the trying you do everyday.

The reason we seek change, perhaps more than others, is because we see that it will bring greater variety into our lives. For overweights, there are limited choices; choices limited by our bodies and by our minds.

Be conscious that change will come a little at a time.

Don't be too hard on yourself if things don't happen as fast as you'd like. We are such all or nothing people. We drift and permit ourselves to just get by, or we rush ahead eagerly attempting to force change just for the sake of change. Alcoholics Anonymous has a phrase they give to their members which helps them pace the change in their lives. *Easy does it, but do it.*

Before you reach for that extra bite today, ask yourself:
Am I willing to give myself all the time I need for changing?
Do I realize that change is a lifelong process?

There is a little of the judge in everyone, and a lot of the judge in most overweight people.

It's not the judging of others that is so harmful, but the judging of ourselves. How eager we are to point the finger of scorn and accusation. We view our every failure with such contempt.

Unlike the dispassionate judge who passes sentence objectively, we appear to find some pleasure in passing harsh judgment on our own frailties. "See there, I told you so," says our inner contemptuous voice.

Do you think your goal is ten, twenty or a hundred pounds? That is so, but not your entire goal. Your goal is also in trying and expecting your very best one day at a time. There is no failure. There is just beginning again.

If anyone needs mercy it is you. Would you have the heart to judge a friend as harshly as you judge yourself? Of course not.

You were meant to be attractive and healthy. You were not meant to carry the physical and emotional burden of extra weight (or guilt) on your shoulders. You were not meant to spend anxious days and nights.

If you consistently fall short of your goals, so that you judge yourself to be a failure, perhaps your goals are unrealistic. For example, if you tell yourself that you must lose a pound a day, the first day you don't lose the allotted pound, your self-esteem takes a nose dive.

Try to believe that each day in a small way you are changing your inner self, and that sooner or later this change will be reflected on your outer self. As you grow in this belief, you can retire your harsh judge and exchange him for one who will give you a fresh, new pardon each day.

Before you reach for that extra bite today, ask yourself:
Am I judging myself too harshly? Are my goals realistic ones?

Hope for the point of no return. Hope that today will be the day you become unalterably committed to a life without excess food, to a body unburdened with extra calories to burn, to a mind and heart free to explore the new.

This is your life. Are you unwilling to spend it in days of inner turmoil and outer stuffing? Then go beyond the point of no return. Be unable, and unwilling to turn back. The old way of using food to fuel emotional hunger cannot offer you peace or joy. The new life you seek can offer you all this and more.

Have you chosen a food plan which will change your body while you seek inner growth? Most overweights find it easier to have something written. It's more difficult to amend such an eating plan whenever whim or hunger strike. Are you committed to following a more healthful plan of eating? Have you determined as best you can that your plan is adequate to take care of your nutritional needs? If you have, then you have the physical plan you need.

What about the emotional plan you need? Psychologists claim overeaters are feeding their deepest emotional hunger, with extra food. Have you a growth plan which will satisfy your inner appetites? Have you learned that attitude is the father of action, and action the mother of confidence — the whole making up the family of your self-esteem?

Hope for the point of no return in your new life. Beyond that point, it will be easier for you to go ahead than it will be for you to turn back.

Before you reach for that extra bite today, ask yourself:
Am I unwilling to turn back to the old life of inner turmoil and outer stuffing? Am I trying to reach my own point of no return?

It's easy to have faith in yourself when you're winning. It's not so easy on days when you've overeaten and the road ahead seems too hard and long. On these days you wonder if you're brave enough, intelligent enough and strong enough to give yourself another chance.

There are times in everyone's day when they doubt their own ability, when they become discouraged. This is the time you need to fan the fires of faith even harder. Tell yourself that you can change your life a day at a time. Momentary setbacks will only give you more strength for the future.

Here is a story of faith that wouldn't quit: "I weighed well over 265 pounds," the small woman told her diet group, "in fact, I would no longer even get on a scale.

"I was only forty-two years old, but I was so fat, I had to support my body with two canes. My doctors warned me that I could have a stroke or worse unless I got rid of 150 pounds.

"It took me three years to lose that immensity, but I did. Much depended on my thinking. I discovered when my mind was clear, I just didn't have to resort to excess food for solace."

Such a feat would have been impossible without faith, a continuing, renewable resource every dieter can use. "It may be a struggle for awhile," she went on, "but you will come to a day when your feeling of exhilaration will be boundless and you will find the real you under all that weight. That is the victory!"

Not many of us have 150 pounds to lose. But no matter what the size of your weight problem, you can find within you today the faith to get the job done.

Before you reach for that extra bite today, ask yourself:
Have I got faith when the road ahead seems too hard? Do I remember always that momentary setbacks can be a source of strength, if I try again?

You have only to look at the statistics to see that you are not alone in your problem of being overweight. Some polls claim as many as 100 million Americans need to lose weight, and of that number, at least half are dangerously fat.

Why then, with so much obvious company, do overweight people tend to feel so lonely? "Nobody knows how it hurts." "Nobody can possibly understand." These are often repeated emotions in diet groups.

Perhaps the answer is that we are so busy with our own pain that we do not seek similarities in other people. It is a shock for some weight-losers to realize that other people, slim people, have similar living problems to their own. We overweights have a Cinderella complex. We tend to think that when we are thin, there will be no problems.

Relate to other overweights for your weight problem, but for the remainder of your living experience, relate to everyone you meet — overweight and thin alike. We dieters tend to divide the world into fat and thin. The world is much more diverse. It is entirely possible that we would find ourselves a good deal less lonely if we sought similarities in everyone.

It is easy to determine dissimilarity. "Oh, she's not fat; what could she know?" It's true that thin others may not be able to help us with our weight problem, but that does not mean they couldn't give us examples of their courage, strength, friendship and faith.

The next time you tend to see yourself as lonely and misunderstood, perhaps you only need look around you for the ways in which all humans are alike. You'll find that deliberately seeking similarities in others is another positive way to approach your new way of living. That sounds a lot better than going it alone, doesn't it?

Before you reach for that extra bite today, ask yourself:
Am I tired of being lonely when I don't need to be? Have I tried to look for the ways in which all people are alike?

March 4 Nothing to Worry About But Worry Itself

President Franklin D. Roosevelt consoled the nation in the 1930s economic depression, saying, "We have nothing to fear but fear itself." Overweight people, who are sometimes in a different kind of depression could say the same about worry: *we have nothing to worry about but worry itself.*

Worry about the future, worry about failure, worry about a thousand imagined and real problems is one of the greatest obstacles to diet success. And it certainly doesn't do much for your peace of mind, either.

Worry and fear go hand in hand. Neither solves a problem. But they do work to break you down both physically and mentally, making anything you attempt virtually impossible.

For some overweight people, worry has become such a way of life, the new life they are seeking is blocked by their lack of faith in their ability. "Will I measure up?" That is the biggest worry of all. For worrying, fearful people the most ready answer can be, "I won't try."

You can rid yourself of unreasonable worry by understanding fully that it is you who will determine your future. Other people cannot control you unless you allow them to. The next twenty-four hours are in your hands to do with as you will. You can build the inner power to eliminate worry.

Have faith in yourself. This is admittedly difficult for a worrier to do, but you can do it. It will take time to build faith in your own abilities, but you have the entire day to work on it.

You have one guarantee. If you spend today enhancing the faith in self you already have, you will have no time at all for snacking.

Before you reach for that extra bite today, ask yourself:
Have I worried myself into an attitude of not trying? Have I built up enough faith in myself so that I no longer need extra food to prop up my ego?

Sometimes we overweight people tend to avoid the image we see in our mirrors. We act as if what we don't allow ourselves to see isn't really there. "I only looked at my reflection," said one diet group member, "from the neck up. I could always fool myself into thinking maybe the rest of me didn't look so bad." There are many tricks that overweights use to avoid facing their outer size. Baggy clothes. Black coats. And just not looking.

If a thinner, more healthful body is ever to emerge from behind our fat cover-ups, it is important that we face our outer image honestly and realistically, and then turn to discovering our inner image.

Another dieter reported: "It wasn't until I became curious about my real size that I began to have an image of how I might really look."

What is your real size? Take a long look in the mirror of your mind and imagine what your image really is. Erase the extra flesh around your lower jaw, upper arm, abdomen and thigh. Do you have this new image firmly in mind? Hold it there. Now take an imaginary walk to the nearest clothing store. No, don't go immediately to the far end of the racks, where all the navy blue and black large-size clothing hangs. Stop off at the displays of bright, colorful styles. Mentally try them on until you find your real size.

Remember that today is another day you can give yourself to grow into your real image, if you have one in mind.

Before you reach for that extra bite today, ask yourself:
Am I avoiding the mirror of my mind? What is my real size?

The ancient Greek legend of Narcissus who fell in love with his own reflection in a pool of water has given self-love a bad press. Our social and religious teachings tell us we are supposed to be very generous with our love for others, but sparing with love for ourselves.

All too often, we overweights have been only too happy to comply. After all, it's easy to hate the too-fat, unhappy, unhealthy, and many times hopeless, persons some of us become.

Do not be afraid of self-love. It's all right to love yourself. It's not only all right, it's absolutely necessary to successful living. It is also essential to love yourself before you can possibly love another. *Real love is love between equals.*

For the dieter, self-loving is added protein for any diet. It is self-love that gives the sense of well-being necessary to seek health.

Begin today with an experience of loving yourself. Think how deeply you desire a new way of life which does not rely on the eating of extra food for security. "Each morning," says one dieter, "I experience the calmness and poise of self-love."

Are you ready and willing? You are able! The thinker is no different from the thought.

Think that you are worthy, deserving. Accept the change of attitude self-love brings. You will be able to see more value in living a growth-centered life.

If you dwell on the positive things in yourself that you can admire, and dispel the negative, you will find it easier to perform a very loving act. Today, you will follow a sensible eating plan. You will move one day closer to your goal of self-understanding. For just this one day, you will hold to it.

Before you reach for that extra bite today, ask yourself:
Am I able to love myself enough to perform the loving act of not overeating? Am I willing to experience the calm and poise of self-love?

If you've worked out a nutritious diet plan that will help you lose weight and regain health, you are halfway home. The other half of any diet is attitude. Successful dieters who have maintained a weight loss for a period of time have a remarkable attitude toward their diet. "We're partners," said one, "my diet does its share, and I do mine."

People who dare to reach deep inside themselves find something wonderful. You will find an ability you never dreamed you had. You will find that you can be a very ingenious diet partner, if you let your eating plan take care of your weight while you take care of your head.

One thing you should do right away is to begin to listen to yourself. So many times we overweight people tend to be talkers. We talk so much that we forget to listen to our own inner voices. Start listening.

What is your inner self really saying? If you have doubts, replace them with positive attitudes. If you have fears and worries, substitute reality. If you lack trust, add self-love.

The poet Dryden said, "How few know their own good, or knowing it, pursue." There is a step beyond positive thinking and that is positive acting. You must pursue the results of self-knowledge. Make it work for you; you and your partner.

You will find an attitude of partnership with a good diet plan will make the business of weight loss a richer experience. Why not get to work, today?

Before you reach for that extra bite today, ask yourself:
Am I doing my share of the work in this partnership? Have I learned to listen and respond positively to my own inner voices?

How many times have you blamed your overeating on others? "My husband (or wife) told me I should quit dieting," you say. Going even further, some of us, failing to find a handier scapegoat, blame our unhappy childhood. (Happy childhoods among overeaters are harder to find than hens' teeth.)

What people do or say has no meaning unless we agree with them.

If you don't believe this simple statement now, you should become acquainted with it. Believing will pull the pins from under all your rationalizations. If the only meaning the statements or actions of others can have is what *you* give it, then ultimately *you are responsible* for all your behavior.

Don't be surprised if you find something about this thought with which to argue. It is a disquieting notion to think for a minute that the behavior of others really doesn't influence us unless we want it to, isn't it? But take a look at this thought in a positive way. Ridding yourself of the right to blame other people means you are really in charge of your own life. You aren't trapped by the ill will of people or by the circumstances of birth. Whatever has gone before, you are in control today.

The more you think about it, the more you will see that this knowledge will set you free. It means that the next time anyone makes a cruel or slighting remark, you don't have to believe it if you don't want to. It means that when someone suggests you should do something that you know is wrong, you have the ability to go your own way. This is a great accomplishment.

Before you reach for that extra bite today, ask yourself:
Am I blaming others instead of taking personal responsibility? Do I really believe that others cannot control me unless I allow them to?

Many overweights, particularly those who have been fat from childhood, have a hidden fear of becoming thin. They think they dare not risk unfamiliar feelings, places or people. When psychologists ask what they fear most about being thin, many name "security." Said one obese man, "My security is knowing how to act. I only know how to act fat."

Behavior psychologist Dr. Richard B. Stuart believes that some overeaters' insecurities are sex-related. He calls fat "the modern chastity belt." Overweight women, especially, fear promiscuity should they suddenly become more desirable. "There is a vivacious, slim woman deep inside me," said one married woman, almost sixty pounds overweight. "How would this other 'me' handle a pass from a strange, attractive man? I feel safer when I'm fat because nobody is attracted to me, so I never have to worry about temptation."

The same woman, sixty pounds lighter, explained: "When being fat became unbearable, I was willing to run the risks of becoming thin. As my fat disappeared, I matured emotionally, and my fears about being thin never materialized."

It is true that there is little worth striving for that does not carry some risk. Becoming slender after a period of overweight will alter your lifestyle considerably. There will be a period of adjustment. Being thin certainly won't mean you have no problems at all. But you will have developed resources to deal with them, if you have concentrated on really getting to know yourself. One diet-club wit put the fear of sexual excesses in perspective and had the group in stitches when she said: "I'm not worried about becoming thin and irresistible. I'm worried that I'll get thin — and still be resistible."

Before you reach for that extra bite today, ask yourself:
Have I learned there is no true security in being fat? Am I willing to live a growth-centered life so that I will be able to cope with living thin?

There are those of us who have fought a lifelong battle against the desire for more food than our body needs. For us the problems of personal identity can be serious. "I can remember what I weighed on almost every day of my adult life," confessed a Weight Watcher lecturer to her class. "I can't always remember what significant things I did, but I can tell you, to the pound, what my body weighed."

YOU ARE NOT A "WEIGHT." Like most people, you are a paradoxical mix of all human attributes and weaknesses. You are loving and hateful, generous and greedy, courageous and fearful, energetic and lazy — but you are not just a weight.

You have the same potential talents as others. Your eyes are open to the same beauty, your mind to the same challenges. "I postponed everything until I was thin," recalls the now slender WW lecturer. "I told myself I would get a job when I lost fifty pounds, go back to school, learn to weave."

How many of us have promised ourselves we'd enjoy living *after* we'd lost weight only to find ourselves filling our empty lives with food and dreams instead of diet-action and reality?

Today is the day to stop thinking of yourself as only a weight, bound by outer conditions. Ask yourself: What action or decision will lead me to a better self-esteem? Treat yourself with the same open-minded consideration you would show a close friend. Would you advise anyone you loved to postpone happy living until his body was perfect? Of course not. But that is exactly what we sometimes ask of ourselves. Why? Psychologists believe this is our way of punishing ourselves for becoming overweight in the first place.

Not even the worst criminal receives "double" punishment.

Here's a way to stop punishing and start helping yourself. Try to get some balance into your life. You will be better able to follow a weight-losing action plan if you do. You should try to work, play and rest, including some things you really want to do. Finances and time permiting, do them *now*.

Before you reach for that extra bite today, ask yourself:
Have I stopped thinking of myself as just a weight? Do I give myself the same consideration I would show a good friend?

Jane M. was the typical jolly fat wife. "I'm shade in the summer," she laughed, "and heat in the winter." From the act she put on even in front of her fellow dieters, it was hard to guess that Jane was really hurting.

"I had to make a public joke about my weight," she recalled later, "before someone else did. I was just protecting myself with humor."

Jane is almost 100 pounds thinner now, down from a high of 250 pounds. She still has a sense of humor, but her jokes are not aimed at her weight problem "I would no more laugh about being 100 pounds overweight," she says, "than I would poke fun at a heart condition."

Overweight people, according to writer Marvin Grosswirth, are afflicted with the "good sport syndrome." We participate in our own humiliation because we think it's almost un-American not to do so. Grosswirth agrees that a sense of humor is important (especially about oneself), but that it should be *humor with dignity*. The result? You will gain in self-esteem and you will feel less ill at ease and more self-assured.

Humor aimed at our size has been one of our best cover-ups. The jolly fat man and woman is a national stereotype. "You always seemed so happy," said one of Jane's thin friends, "I had no idea you even cared about your weight."

Everyone likes happy, enthusiastic people. You should strive to become one on the inside as well as the outside. And you can.

"I just naturally see real humor in life's situations," says a smaller, happier Jane today. "The difference is that now I'm a joker and not a big joke."

Before you reach for that extra bite today, ask yourself:
Have I made a joke of my weight to cover up my real feelings? Am I ready to start laughing on the inside as well as the outside?

The bane of the dieters' existence is slipping off their diet. Although no dieter is perfect in following any weight-losing eating plan, it can be a blow to the ego to suddenly go berserk and eat every high-calorie snack in sight.

One of the causes for diet slips is a period of over-confidence after you are well into your diet routine. One dieter had lost so much weight and felt so well, she took a part-time job in a supermarket bakery. Another, a successfully dieting student, went to work in a fast-food restaurant. What happened? The bakery job turned into a nightmare of gorging. The student made A's in fast eating.

Of course, you can't spend the rest of your life crossing the street rather than walking in front of a candy store. The point is that if you want to avoid a slip, don't spend too much time in slippery places.

The two dieters who thought they could "handle" their food temptations were asking too much of themselves. It's one thing to pass up the pastry counter on your way to the vegetable bins. It's quite another to inhale "essence of donut" for four hours straight.

Know that you may always have some limitations. If you are the typical food-oriented overweight, it is unreasonable to expect that you would feel comfortable working with quantities of prepared food, some of which is not on anyone's weight-losing diet.

This may limit your choice of a paid profession slightly, but the payoff for such caution is obvious. If you stay out of slippery places, you will be far less likely to slip off the plan of eating you've chosen to mold your new body.

Before you reach for that extra bite today, ask yourself:
Am I willing to stay out of my own slippery places? Am I developing interests that aren't food-oriented?

Compliment number one:

   "You look nice today. I really like your outfit."

Response:

   "This old thing. It's cheap and faded."

Compliment number two:

   "That was a great speech you gave."

Response:

   "Oh, no, I forgot the middle part, and I got so nervous my voice broke."

Overweight people aren't the only ones who have trouble accepting compliments, but it does seem to be a real problem of ours. "I used to take compliments as guarded insults," one dieter told her group.

Many of us have so little self-regard that it is an easy thing for us to turn a genuine compliment into a personal put-down.

Sometimes we program ourselves to reject the honest admiration of others. "I can't do anything right," we tell ourselves. This negative thinking is not even rational. If we could do *nothing* right during our whole life, we would remain helpless babies.

You do many things well. You deserve the compliment you get. If you wish to become a more gracious receiver, try practicing some self-compliments. If you perform a task well, tell yourself so. If your hair/dress/suit/tie/face looks particularly attractive, give yourself a compliment.

What's the right way to respond to a compliment? Say *thank you.* That's all. Just two little words. Isn't that easy?

Before you reach for that extra bite today, ask yourself:
Am I turning away compliments because I think myself unworthy? Have I remembered the two little words, thank you?

Many overweight people feel pushed around by life. *Why me?* That is a question we ask ourselves over and over again.

You do not have to remain a helpless victim of biological and emotional programing. You can take charge of your life if you make the decision to do so.

Ask yourself: Who am I? Then identify yourself as the kind of person who makes decisions, who seeks a growth-centered life, and who follows a sensible diet.

This will take self-confidence. You already have more confidence than you realize. Do you know what it really is? Confidence is sure-footed. You will know that you can meet life and handle whatever comes along. Confidence never makes excuses. You will be able to take the hard knocks and learn from mistakes. Confidence never tries to build itself up by tearing others down. With confidence you are *already up* and need not strive to look better by making others look worse.

You have to want to make the decision to be a confident, in-control person. You will have to tell yourself *I can.* Perhaps you will have to say it more than once. But as you say it, you will begin to have a solid sense of yourself. When you do, you will no longer need to find a victim's solace in extra food your body doesn't need.

Pay attention to the thoughts that pass through your head. The first step to self-confidence is to know what is in your own mind. Cling to the confident thoughts. Reject the "I can't" thoughts.

You will find that building your own self-confidence means you won't have to play the helpless victim role. You will no longer be blown about by the daily winds of chance. You will begin to cope with life decisively. You will have no limits.

Before you reach for that extra bite today, ask yourself:
Do I feel that I am a helpless victim? Have I made a decision to take control of my life?

Behavior psychologists tell overweights that patterns, not pounds, are the culprits in the war against fat. They recommend that you discover what your patterns (habits) are in connection with certain foods, places and times.

For example, many of us relate a certain taste to a pleasant, secure memory. We seek to reproduce the remembered feelings by eating these foods whenever we are depressed. Try to discover if you are attempting to recapture the safety of childhood by overeating.

Another pattern is one of place. For most of us, the kitchen evokes instant food images because we associate eating with food preparation. "I was unable to enter my kitchen," said one overweight housewife, "without opening my refrigerator door, and getting something to eat." What are your patterns of place?

Another pattern is one of time. "When I was a boy," one man told his Weight Watchers class, "my mother had a snack waiting for me when I came home from school.

"Long after I was a grown man, I was so starved in the middle of the afternoon I had to eat." What times during your day trigger you to eat unneeded food?

Today, focus on your eating behavior. Look for patterns which satisfy emotional need, not physical hunger. Once you are aware of your behavior, you will be able to modify it, a step at a time. *You can erase behavior by simply not responding to it.* If you fail to reinforce destructive eating behavior enough times, you will extinguish the behavior forever. Certain foods will no longer mean security, certain places will not trigger your emotional hunger and certain times will not stimulate appetite. You will be free of the hidden patterns that have compelled you to overeat.

Before you reach for that extra bite today, ask yourself:
Am I giving in to a pattern of eating I no longer need? Have I become more aware of my eating behavior?

Just as if we didn't have enough trouble, some overweight people (as well as thin ones) are addicted to cola drinks. For those of us who have given up smoking, alcohol, refined sugar, or whatever else was killing us slowly, it's a blow to learn that a seemingly innocent soft drink may be harmful to our health.

Researchers at Pennsylvania State University tested people who drank between 48 and 111 ounces of cola beverage a day. They found these drinkers (they labeled them "colaholics") reported feeling jittery, having sleep problems, frequent mood changes, and headaches.

One reason given the researchers for drinking so much cola is that the subjects had "a craving." Whenever these "addicts" tried to stop they suffered withdrawal-like symptoms, including depression, nervousness and a decrease in alertness. Caffeine is a prime suspect, since up to fifty-five milligrams of caffeine are in every twelve-ounce bottle of cola.

If you have incorporated cola drinks into your diet and are feeling any of the symptoms found by these researchers, you should consult your doctor about the quantity of cola which would be safe for you. In spite of television advertising urging you to drink more, more, and still more soft drinks, you may have to cut down your intake for your health.

Instead of relying on caffeine highs in your life, try a growth-centered lifestyle. You will find that as you get to know your real self, you won't need a cola crutch to get you through the day.

Before you reach for that extra bite today, ask yourself:
Do I have a craving that is interfering with the life I want to live? Have I traded artificial highs for the real inner me?

Lasting happiness is related to what's inside the human skin. It's bound up with the ability to survive unhappiness, the ability to work and to be interested in the world around us.

Psychologists tell us that no one is born happy. Our first emotions are fear, anger and discomfort. We learn happiness. According to psychologist Erich Fromm, happiness is an achievement brought about by inner productiveness. People succeed at being happy, he says, by building a liking for themselves.

Unhappy people rarely blame themselves. Their jobs, marriage, parents, age, are at fault. Or fate. They wait in apathy for the Fairy Godmother to come and release them from the reality of their lives, the reality they have made for themselves.

You will know happiness when you have it. Happiness gives such a feeling of lightness that an exuberant doctor in 1775 declared it caused a decrease in body weight. (Dieters, take note.) But whether it does or not, the *sense of lightness* is there.

Great philosophers through the ages have tried to define happiness. Count your blessings, advised Cicero. Pause to enjoy, said Goethe. Sharpen your wits when you observe man and nature, he added. George Bernard Shaw stated, "Never fear to use yourself up." The happiest life is to be a force of nature, he went on, "rather than a feverish clod of ailments and grievances." Fromm summed it all up when he said, "Happiness is proof of success in the art of living."

Any art, even the art of living, must be practiced to be enjoyed. Practice living, really living, today. Don't sit around in the ashes of your life waiting for your Fairy Godmother to come and make you slender and happy. You do it.

Before you reach for that extra bite today, ask yourself:
Do I realize that lasting happiness is up to me? Have I started to like the self I'm getting to know a lot better?

If you are overweight, chances are you are not a slow, leisurely eater. Would you like to be? Here's how to cut down on eating speed.

"Speed kills," in this case by the spoonful. We eat in a fast, almost automated, manner. Try to break up eating behavior with a variety of activities. Dab your mouth with a napkin, speak or take a sip of water rather than taking one automatic bite after another. This technique is called "chaining" by the behaviorists. This simply means that you are linking together non-eating behavior.

Another way to slow down at the table is to divide food into three portions on your plate. At first eat two portions at your normal rate of speed. Then try the last portion on the "five second plan"; that is, after each bite, put your fork down and count silently to five. When you have been able to do this for several meals, expand this to two portions, until finally you are eating your entire meal in a slow and more satisfying manner.

If speed-eating is a problem for you, try this simple way to slow down. You'll find that what you do eat will be more satisfying and filling.

Today living is a gift to be used. How unfortunate if we smother it under mounds of food, hastily eaten and guiltily remembered.

Use your gift today to grow toward your goal of a new body, new health and new happiness. Don't minimize the possibilities in your future. You have everything it takes to accomplish your dreams.

Before you reach for that extra bite today, ask yourself:
Have I tried to break up fast eating behavior? Am I using the gift of today to accomplish my dreams?

There's a myth that dieting is debilitating. Of course, a good well-balanced diet is the most energizing thing we can do for ourselves. But nonetheless, when we are dieting and lack energy, the first thing we do is think about eating "a little something for energy."

Your problem is probably not a lack of food energy. It could be that you aren't getting enough sleep.

Individuals vary in the amount of sleep they need for health and happiness. It depends on your age, physical activity and mental stress. But if you tire too easily, don't blame your diet; you may need more sleep.

If you are having trouble going to sleep at night, the best treatment is to try not to worry about it. The more anxious you become, the longer you will stay awake. Muscles and nerves must be relaxed if the body and mind are to drift into sleep.

When you suffer from temporary fatigue because of a need for more sleep, don't eat over it. Try reading a book, watching a TV show, enjoying a quiet time in your head. Think of anything that takes your mind off your sleeplessness.

Sometimes we have trouble sleeping because we are dwelling on problems. Shift your emphasis from problems to challenges, from worrying to opportunity. There will be so much opportunity in your life today. You can believe that you are on the road to a healthier mind and a healthier body. You can believe you will have enough energy to take you to your goal and last you for a lifetime.

Before you reach for that extra bite today, ask yourself:
Why do I conclude that a lack of energy means I need to eat something? Am I sleeping enough so that my mind can dwell on life's opportunities?

Our physical body needs more than food. It needs rest. And that includes our mental processes as well. Have you programmed some relaxation time into your daily schedule?

Before you shout, "Impossible!" listen to what can happen if you allow stress to build. It can go hard with you physically — high blood pressure, ulcers, insomnia and chronic fatigue. It can go even harder on your diet plans. There is nothing that can wipe out the best diet intentions faster than too much stress and too little mental relaxation or meditation.

Effective meditation doesn't mean you have to grow a beard and live in a cave. It can be accomplished in ten minutes perhaps twice a day. Dr. Herbert Benson, author of *The Relaxation Response*, believes that the simplest method of meditation is sitting and relaxing each muscle, silently repeating a word, a syllable, a phrase, a prayer or a number. When your mind wanders, bring it back to the repetition. That repetition relieves the mind of other thoughts.

This is very similar to age-old prayers and to Eastern meditation techniques. It's difficult to understand how something so simple and easy could work. But it does. Scientific observation shows that metabolism slows, the heart rate slows, blood pressure drops and alpha brain waves slow. These physical reactions only occur when a person is truly relaxed.

Whichever form of meditation you choose, it is important for you to choose one and practice it regularly as part of your better-living plan.

Twenty minutes a day is not a lot of time to give to such an important health objective. At least you'll be doing something better for yourself than overeating.

Before you reach for that extra bite today, ask yourself:
Have I forgotten that my physical body needs more than food? Am I willing to spend time meditating so that I'll be able to better follow my food plan?

The world around you is beginning to renew itself in a cycle of rebirth that can give every overweight new hope. Outside your window, the first signs of spring will soon be followed by that wonderful, sleepy, dreamy fever that comes as the world warms.

Are you ready for your rebirth? Are you ready to relinquish the negative patterns of thinking and living which have resulted in a dreary winter of living?

Take a positive idea such as: *I am alive, alert and enthusiastic*. Become this idea of yours. Get inside it; pull it around you like a light spring coat. Make it live.

If spring's rebirth is a universal natural force, why not use this positive force to become the person you want to be. If you do not have a program of eating which will insure health and weight loss, get one today. If you do not have the positive attitudes you need to build a growth-centered life, begin them today.

Are you afraid of hunger? Don't be afraid of a life without excess food. *If you do the thing you fear, the fear will die*. Anyway, it is impossible to fill the empty spaces in your life with food. Know this. You can deal with your unhappy feelings without eating over them.

A new chance, a new life opens for you today. You need only be open to it. Take the force of the universal rebirth of nature and make it work for you. Just like every living thing, this is your season for growing, and soon, for blossoming.

Before you reach for that extra bite today, ask yourself:
Am I ready to grow with other living things this season? Have I planted positive thoughts today, so that I may reap the benefits tomorrow?

Sometimes when we despair and feel hopeless about the future we ask ourselves why we are overweight, and why we use food the way we do. Most of us know about metabolism, calorie intake, fat cells — the scientific descriptions of our problem — but those answers are rarely enough.

Perhaps one answer lies in your own mind. The mind and emotions are connected; in fact, emotions are tools of the mind. And since we have often programmed our minds and thoughts with wrong facts, these emotions can have us running around in circles.

For example, one dieter reported that every spring she could not control her eating. The rest of the year she followed a good, nutritious eating plan, but come spring, she regained much of the weight it had taken her nine months to lose.

This is the negative mind at work again, manufacturing false standards — in this case, the belief that, "Every spring I cannot diet." Because her mind had responded this way before, it responded each spring to the thought that overeating was inevitable.

Whenever your mind tries to play this trick on you, don't let it. Tell yourself that you will not be bound by what you formerly did. Today you choose a different path. Say instead, "I can and I will."

You may have to walk away from your problem a little way to see the answer. Try to step outside the mental image that insists you have to repeat destructive eating behavior over and over again. Take a good, rational look. Is there any real reason why you must overeat every spring, or on weekends or at a certain time of the month? Of course there isn't. Remember you have choices. You can choose to change. You can and you will.

Before you reach for that extra bite today, ask yourself:
Is my mind playing a trick on me? Do I believe that I do not have to walk down the same negative path over and over again just because once I did?

"I enjoy myself!" the Overeaters Anonymous member triumphantly told his group. "I went through years of my life not enjoying one minute I had to spend with myself."

Do you enjoy yourself? Could you make such a statement today and really mean it? Most of us are only vague shadows of our real selves, not sharp images. It's no wonder we sometimes have trouble living with the one person we cannot live without.

Ask yourself this question: What would happen if I completely believed in my ability to lose weight and live without extra calories?

If you weren't living in the midst of the confusion that overeating causes, you might have more opportunity to get to know your sharp image, and to begin enjoying the person you really are.

It's difficult to live with someone who is full of anger, resentment and guilt. How much easier it is to live with and enjoy the person who is positive. Demand one thing of yourself: Demand the willingness to be positive. If you are willing to believe in your positive abilities today, then you will certainly enjoy living. Sure, there may be problems. *Take the bitter with the sweet, but concentrate on the sweet.*

You can only have one thought in your mind at a time. If it is a bitter, negative one, trade it in. You have the will to replace a thought.

Before you reach for that extra bite today, ask yourself:
Can I honestly say that I am enjoying myself today? Have I the willingness to believe that I can replace a negative thought?

Don't you admire the kind of person who says no to ultra-high-calorie desserts, gets up a half-hour early to jog around the block, and seems to have a lot of self-discipline?

Disciplined people are a very attractive group of human beings. They are admired and envied, but seldom emulated. Some people never even try to become self-disciplined. To them discipline means torture and punishment and, ultimately, failure.

What's the secret of self-discipline? According to Dr. Jack Osman of Towson State University in Maryland, those who seek self-discipline have a firm set of priorities and have changed their lives accordingly.

When you decide that your top priority is health, when you really want to look trim and feel terrific, lifelong weight loss and maintenance is possible.

First, you must set up goals to help you reach your weight objective and to lead you toward a more fulfilling lifestyle. Just making the decision will give you added self-control. Then, each day as you practice the discipline required to reach your goals, you will become stronger in your ability. Discipline is, after all, a matter of practice, of exchanging haphazard habits for goal-aimed ones.

Sit down and write out your list of priorities. What are the things you want most in life? Now, number them in order of their importance to you. Rewrite your list placing number one on top, then number two, and so forth. Beside each number, evaluate the kind of discipline you will need to reach this goal. Write it down. Put your list in two places. One, memorize it so that you will always have it in mind, and two, put it in a place where you will come across it several times a day. When you do, read it over again and recommit yourself to the discipline you will need to get where you want to go. You'll make it, too.

Before you reach for that extra bite today, ask yourself:
Do I admire disciplined people well enough to try to be like them? Have I made a list of my most important life-changing goals and committed it to memory?

To tell or not to tell — that is the question for many dieters.

"Don't tell everybody you're going to take off weight," says one dieter. "If they notice you're losing weight, admit it, but don't offer the information."

That is a self-protecting approach many dieters have. If they don't tell, then they don't have to suffer the embarrassment of failure. It is not a very positive beginning to an effort which will require their lifelong attention.

Some authorities advise telling friends and family of your intention to lose weight. They will be there for support when you need it, and when you are tempted to give up the struggle. Sometimes thinking about what they might say can keep you on the track long enough to get through a crisis.

Other authorities agree with the dieter who doesn't offer too much information.

As with any problem, there is a middle ground. Perhaps it is best not to make a big point of telling everyone you meet that you're going on a diet. But you shouldn't shut yourself away from friendly help that could be vital to you later. Be selective.

After you've decided who to tell and who not to tell, you've got better work to do. You won't lose weight talking about it, so now is the time to get busy.

You need to have a *plan of eating* worked out in advance, one that with a few variations can last a lifetime. A person consumes over 100,000 meals during a lifetime. If you have a ready plan, you won't have to make 100,000 decisions. Think how much time and energy you'll save!

Before you reach for that extra bite today, ask yourself:
Have I selected supportive friends who I can tell about my diet plans? Have I decided on a plan of eating which will last me a lifetime?

Some of us are dreamers. We dream about the day when we'll be thin enough to be part of the crowd instead of the person who stands out because of size alone. We dream about the clothes we'll be able to wear, clothes that heretofore seemed to look good only on other, thinner people. We dream about the poise and confidence a slender, average-looking body will bring us in our daily lives. These dreams are good, when they lead us on to act — when they become a prelude to our striving.

There is nothing you cannot do with your creative mind. If you dream of a slender body, you can have it. If your dream of stylish clothes, poise and confidence, then you can have these, too. Keep your dreams, but start progressing every day toward what you are seeking.

You have the answers.

Ask yourself: What will give my life meaning? You know the answer. The independence that freedom from overeating brings. Ask yourself: What will result in my happiness? You know the answer — to lose weight, regain health and learn to live a growth-centered life.

You do know how to make your dreams come true. In your effort to grow, keep your memories of the past and hopes for the future, but do not let them complicate your ability to concentrate on living creatively today. Today is the day you have. Concentrate on it. Let the creative powers of your mind work for you. The human mind is the most powerful instrument of accomplishment ever created. Use it. Paint a picture in your mind of the better life you want, believe in it, and go on to achieve it. You just have to work at it one day at a time. (Members of Alcoholics Anonymous say: any day you aren't satisfied with your new way of living, your misery will be quickly refunded.)

Before you reach for that extra bite today, ask yourself:
Have I determined to turn my dreams into creative action?
Am I willing to allow the power of my creative mind to work in my life?

Fat and lazy are synonymous in most people's minds. Don't you believe it. Overweight people are far more likely to try to do too much than too little.

Some of us are "yes machines." In our desire to please other people, we forget how to say no, even to unreasonable intrusions on our time "I was the one in the back of the meeting room who volunteered every time," said one ex-yes-man. "I was really eager to help, so I took on every job that came my way, and never turned anybody down.

"The result was that I was snatching food on the run, never had time for my family, and I was constantly complaining that I carried the world around on my shoulders."

Overdoing anything (even a do-gooder role) can be a way of avoiding the long, hard look you need to take at your own life. "I thought that it wouldn't matter if I weighed over 300 pounds," said one woman, "as long as I did everything the church asked of me."

Fortunately for our health and sanity, most of us who make a career of overdoing everything cannot avoid our own reflection forever. Sooner or later, despite our frantic activity, we are forced to stop and take a look, stop and re-order our priorities. Of course, it's a positive thing to be involved with the world and other people, but our first priority is to ourselves. When we are honest with ourselves about it, it's obvious that we have to help ourselves before we can be truly helpful to others.

Put yourself at the top of your priority list. Stop saying yes to everyone else, and start saying yes to a new way of living. Think of how much energy you can give to yourself!

Before you reach for that extra bite today, ask yourself:
Am I using frantic activity to avoid taking a good look at my life? Have I made re-ordering my life the number one priority today?

There are few things in a better-living regimen that most overweights shy away from more than exercise. Why? It can be embarrassing if others are watching, and it can be downright painful as well. Muscles and tendons that haven't been stretched for years can become sore enough to discourage the most dedicated dieter. But if you want to give it a try, after checking first with your doctor, you'll soon find the benefits outweigh the aches.

Of course, exercise in any form burns calories, but you have another purpose — total body fitness. You'll help your body retain protein and minerals, increase oxygen in red blood cells, promote digestion, boost heart efficiency, increase stamina and tone muscles.

To be this effective, the exercise program you choose should give your oxygen-delivery system a good workout, be of enough intensity to stimulate heart-lung function, and, most important, be *regular*. According to some experts, "regular" translates to exercising at fifty percent of your capacity for twenty minutes three times a week.

If you're tired of being tired, of huffing and puffing, you could be living more comfortably (and it wouldn't hurt your diet a bit, either) if you exercised. Walking, bicycling, swimming, rope-skipping or even exercises by the book in the privacy of your bedroom will burn up calories and make you feel better.

That's the whole point of growth-centered living — to make *you* feel better. You've felt mentally and physically low for long enough. With a little exercise, you may find you gain more energy than you expend. You can use that extra energy to get more out of living.

Before you reach for that extra bite today, ask yourself:
Am I getting enough exercise to keep my body and mind alert? Am I tired of being too tired?

There's an old joke about the couple who are lost on an auto trip. "I don't know where we're going," the husband says, "but we're making terrific time."

If you are moving through life, "making terrific time," without a goal, you are missing most of what living is all about, and achieving only a small amount of what you could.

What can you do about it? You can write. Writing down a set of goals for yourself turns your half-formed wishes into black and white. You are forced to confront them. This is a painful process for some people. After all, if you only carry goals in your head, you don't have to analyze whether or not they are realistic or whether you are moving toward or away from them.

If you would like to confront your goals and begin moving toward them, here is what you should do. Get a piece of blank paper and put down every goal, personal and professional, you ever wished for. Be specific. To lose weight is not a goal. "I want to lose forty pounds during the next year," *is* a goal.

Now go over the goals you've written down and ask yourself if they are attainable or only wishful thinking. If they are wishful thinking, cross them out. If they are attainable, get to work on them.

You may want to make another list of short-range goals — say for the next six months. Achieving short-range goals can help you realize the long-range ones.

What good will lists do? Their mere existence will influence you to do the things that keep you moving in a positive direction. You'll not only make terrific time, but you'll know exactly where you are going too.

Before you reach for that extra bite today, ask yourself:
Have I decided where I want to go with my life? Am I setting a course which will help me to become the kind of person I want to be?

Have you ever heard sports fans say, "That team had all the breaks." Or a business colleague remark, "He was in the right place at the right time." Is it Lady Luck which rules that certain people will be lucky at sports, business, love or weight loss? No. People (and teams) make their own luck.

Studies of so-called "lucky" people have determined these people are really little different from the average, except that they *take advantage of opportunities.*

An admirer once remarked to a famous speaker that he was lucky to have so much natural ease and poise on the stage. Luck had nothing to do with it. As a young man, the speaker had been terrified to speak in public — to the point where he vomited before each appearance. But he accepted every engagement, each time telling himself that he was getting better and better and had something important to say. After a few years he turned into the accomplished performer that many people thought of as lucky.

Do you think that it is just good luck that causes some people to lose weight, while others with bad luck don't? Perhaps luck has nothing at all to do with weight loss either. Perhaps it only means that these "lucky" people take advantage of weight-losing opportunities. They have set health goals which they are moving toward. They lose no opportunity to seek a positive approach to the problems of living.

Would you like to be lucky? Try taking advantage of all the opportunities your life holds for you. You have been given the opportunity to choose a good eating plan, healthful living and positive thinking. If you stop to think about it, you're a very lucky person.

Before you reach for that extra bite today, ask yourself:
Do I envy the other person who seems to have more luck than I do? Have I taken advantage of all my lucky opportunities?

Did you know that in most cases when people have a good opinion of themselves it is deserved? Most people with high self-esteem tested at a midwestern university tended to be well-rounded and psychologically healthy.

On the other hand, the greater the discrepancy between yourself and the ideal self you feel you want to be, the lower your self-esteem.

The idea is to bring your attitudes into line with the lifestyle you want. The closer you get to your ideal self, the higher your self-esteem goes. In other words *the more you live your life as you feel you should, the more you will think of yourself.*

High self-esteem is the mark of successful, happy people. Mothers get along better with children, children behave better with their parents and other children, the sexes get on better with each other, and students even make better school grades. Another psychological study showed that the higher your self-esteem the closer you stand to people.

Think about this concept for awhile. "The more I live the way I want to, the more I will like myself." What could be more simple? If you have an overweight body but really want a slender one, then you won't think so much of yourself. If you have a negative, pessimistic attitude and you want a positive enthusiastic attitude, you won't like yourself too much.

Why not try acting as if you are the person you want to be? Eat like people who care about their weight and health. Act like people who live optimistic and winning lives. Gradually, as you move in a more positive direction your self-esteem will rise to a new high.

Before you reach for that extra bite today, ask yourself:
Am I moving my actual self and my ideal self closer together? Is my self-esteem rising every day?

Today is supposed to be a day for kidding others, in a good-natured way, just to get a rise out of them. This kind of nonsensical fun is usually followed by the merry shout, "April Fool!" Fun and games are relaxers for all of us on holidays throughout the year, as long as we remember our real priorities.

You're no fool. You have long realized that a disciplined plan of eating will spill over into the rest of your life, ending disorganization. Wonderful things begin to happen.

You will find increased confidence; you will begin to see yourself as an attractive personality. You will discover a new worthiness, a new self-love, and more love for others. You will be freed from the grip of fear and hopelessness. When people look in your eyes they will see the message: "I can make it."

Today, despite its title, is not a day for fools; it is a day full of choices. You can choose to overeat or not to overeat. You can choose to grow or not to grow.

Each day is precious material, not to be thrown away. Benjamin Franklin said, "Dost thou love life? Then do not squander time, for that is the stuff life is made of."

Today is your day for living and choosing. You can learn to use this and every other day of your life creatively and positively. The art of choosing and pursuing your life's goals will release a fantastic energy — coping power. This is the power produced by self-insight and positive thought. It means that you will not be overwhelmed by life problems to the point where you must hold yourself together with one food binge after another. You will be able to cope with events as they come along. You are no fool.

Before you reach for that extra bite today, ask yourself:
Am I sick and tired of playing the fool with food? Have I built up *coping power* through learning the art of choice?

Fatty, Fatty, two-by-four,
Can't get through the kitchen door.

If you were a fat child, chances are this sing-song chant followed you through countless play yards and school recesses. The fate of this forlorn, hapless youngster sometimes continues to haunt us in later years.

"If only I knew then what I know now, I could have spared you all that pain," is our adult response to a dialogue with the fat child inside us.

Some overweights become so upset when they think of "what might have been," they even do some sympathy eating in their depression.

If you have a fat child living in your past with all the hurts that memory implies, you can feel sad for that child, even weep for that child, but you must let your fat child go. You cannot go back and undo the pain, but you can learn to deal with the pain in your life today. And you've learned one thing over the years — a cookie won't make it better.

When you were a child, you had little control over your life. Today you can choose to have control over what you eat, over what you feel, and over what you do. You can use today to strengthen your self-image, the thin image you've carried in your mind since you were young. Perhaps the *only* thing you can give the memory of your fat child is the chance for a positive new life you can give yourself today.

Before you reach for that extra bite today, ask yourself:
Have I let go the haunting image of my fat child? Do I choose to have control, today?

There has been a lot of controversy about whether or not obesity is a disease. Many doctors have hesitated in the past to classify even severe overweight in the category of disease. Most today have no such compunction. Obesity is not only considered to be a disease, but one of chronic proportions, incurable, but, thankfully, controllable.

Do you find the idea that you have an incurable sickness a difficult one to accept? Don't worry. There is a guaranteed treatment. The Rx is weight loss. You must reduce to your natural weight to get rid of your symptoms. Although you will not be cured (since you are capable of becoming sick again through weight gain), you will have arrested your illness.

Learn to accept the reality of your disease and the even happier reality that each day you are getting better and better, simply by eating healthfully and sensibly.

Don't go so far in your acceptance of overweight as an illness that you lose your new sense of self. This disease, even though it is incurable, is only a *temporary* condition if you choose to make it so.

Overeaters Anonymous calls overweight "only the outward manifestation of our inner emotional problems." This group recognizes that dieting off extra pounds is only one step toward recovery from the illness of obesity.

Long after you have rid yourself of the "outward manifestation," you must continue to deal with your inner emotional growth.

Life holds many surprises for us, not all of them pleasant. Granted, it would be better to have no lifelong problem to cope with at all, but you *can* learn to deal with one effectively if you are developing a strong inner image.

Before you reach for that extra bite today, ask yourself:
Am I thankful that I have a disease that can be treated by simple weight loss? Am I ready to deal with my inner emotional problems?

There is an illegal gambling game called the Numbers Game. A player picks a number (often based on a dream), pays so much money, and, if the number comes up, is a big money winner. Of course, there is little chance of winning since the odds are high that your number won't come up.

Dieters have their own version of the numbers game. They set a number of pounds (usually unrealistic) that they want to lose, bet their whole diet on winning and then when they don't make their impossible goal, become "real losers" by dropping their diet altogether.

Another twist to the numbers game as played by overweights is the Comparison Game. "I'm going on the same diet that my friend Joe went on," you say, "so I can lose fifteen pounds in two weeks just like he did." You have a real problem when you play this game. Weight loss is a strictly individual process and varies greatly according to sex, occupation and glandular function. It's not surprising that old Joe's diet doesn't work for you like it worked for him. Also it's not surprising what you do about it. "Well, that proves it," you say, "I'm hopeless. Even Joe can lose weight, while I can't."

It's not important how fast you lose or how long it takes. What matters is that you reach your normal weight and stay there.

This is an age of speed, and we dieters are not immune. When the first supersonic diet is announced, the clamor for it will be heard around the world. Until that time, regular weight loss is still the very best way to reach your weight goal and to maintain it for a lifetime.

Patience is a difficult trait for overweights to cultivate, especially when our lives are daily disrupted by the extra pounds on our bodies. But try it. You're sure to become a winner at the real numbers game of living, the one that adds up to a happier, slimmer life.

Before you reach for that extra bite today, ask yourself:
Have I been playing the Numbers Game by setting impossible weight goals for myself? Do I believe that it is important to reach and maintain a normal weight?

If overweight is a disease, it receives the oddest treatment by physicians of any chronic illiness. Not all, but many, doctors tell their too-fat patients, in effect, just to eat less. As Dr. L. Melvin Elting, himself a formerly fat doctor, observes, that is like telling a person who's been hit by a truck to bleed less.

It's not because physicians lack concern for their overweight patients. It's just that they lack the extra time for counseling these patients require.

That is not to say that there aren't some doctors whose attitude toward the obese can do more harm than good. Infrequently we come upon doctors who seem to have an obvious aversion to treating heavyweights. They are sarcastic and unsympathetic ("look at yourself in the mirror naked") or even try to frighten their patient ("diet or die"). This treatment is not calculated to help a group of people already low in self-esteem.

If you have a physician, or ever encounter one, who has no time for you or who belittles you as a person, do yourself (and that doctor) a favor and take your medical business elsewhere. Check with your local medical society to see if there is a bariatrician in your town. This is a doctor who specializes in treating overweight patients with a variety of tools including specially tailored diets, psychological counseling and physical monitoring. If you needed a delicate heart operation to preserve your life you would seek a trained specialist to do the surgery. The same is true if you have a weight problem. Seek a specialist.

Every overweight person should have a doctor they can rely on to help them with their weight problem and watch over their general health. Once you do, you can go on to other things which will add to your better living program.

Going to the doctor has been a negative emotional experience for many of us in the past. There may have been times you were fearful to the point you allowed your general health to decline rather than face the doctor's disapproval. No more! Today medical guidance is an important part of your new positive lifestyle. It's just one of many things you can choose and choose well.

Before you reach for that extra bite today ask yourself:
Do I have a doctor who is concerned and sympathetic to my overweight problem? Have I incorporated health care into my better-living program?

It's no insult to tell adult dieters that they may have to go back to school and get an education in their problem. Of course, this doesn't mean they will literally have to squeeze behind a desk sized for children. It means they will have to learn what is "special" about their behavior and how to correct it.

According to diet expert Dr. R. B. Stuart, there are six things that are different about us overweights — six things that separate us from those people who have always been thin. It's reasonable to expect that if we learn our lessons well, we'll do better adjusting our food intake and losing weight. Here are your six lessons for today.

Lesson 1. Overweight people eat more food when it is *readily available*. They tend to eat less than thin people if inconvenience or work is required to obtain the food. What ways can you think of which will make problem foods less available to you today?

Lesson 2. Overweight people are triggered to eat more food when they can *see and smell it*, while thins tend to respond to hunger between four to six hours after eating a meal. What can you do to remove food (as much as possible) from your sight and smell today?

Lesson 3. *Taste is more important* to overweights than to thins. When both groups are given unlimited access to unpalatable foods, the overweight group tended to eat less than the thin group. Can you limit your choices of favorite foods today?

Lesson 4. Thin people eat until they feel full; overweights eat until there is no more food on their plate or table. Can you limit the portions on your plate and remove extra food from the table in advance?

Lesson 5. Overweight people are less aware of the caloric and nutritional value of foods they eat than slender people. Can you learn more about the nutritional content of foods today?

Lesson 6. Overweights get less exercise than non-overweights. How can you increase the amount of exercise you get today?

You can make valuable changes in your daily activities so that you will begin to act more like people who don't have a weight problem. Work on these six "lessons" today. You'll pass the course with straight A's.

Before you reach for that extra bite today, ask yourself:
Am I willing to "get an education" in my problem? Have I really tried to change my behavior so that I can act like thin people today?

Many psychiatrists have believed that obesity was rooted in emotional problems and that excess eating was a means of relieving anxieties and more serious underlying psychiatric conditions.

But the evidence against that theory has been mounting and it now appears that overweight, even seriously overweight, individuals have no higher rates of psychiatric problems than do thin people. Psychologist David Fisher says: "When the weight comes off, the depressions do too."

Quite often what passes for emotional problems in the obese is really hopelessness. We have lost and regained weight so many times, we stop believing we can keep it off for good.

Not only do you flagellate yourself for your failures, but what you see in other people's eyes supports your negative feelings. "I'm too weak to control myself," you think, "I'm just a mess."

Even thinking the way we do about ourselves, we are still members of the most highly motivated group in the world. Time and again, we overweights go back and begin again. The problem is not usually one of motivation, but one of overall thinking. We must build up self-confidence and a sense of control in our own mental environment. Then we can begin to reinforce ourselves by such things as, "Eating cookies won't solve problems" or "I'm full and I don't have to eat any more."

You can bring about a dramatic shift in the way you think if you work every day at your new mental image — the one that is in control and highly motivated. Try to forget yesterday, and all the yesterdays in which you felt weak and out of control. Success and self-loathing cannot live together in the same mind. Choose success today. You'll be glad you did.

Before you reach for that extra bite today, ask yourself:
Do I know that many of my emotional problems will disappear as my weight comes off? Have I decided to take control of my mental environment?

Food has been called the most readily available, non-prescription tranquilizer there is. Some people who are compulsive eaters become addicted to this tranquilizer. "Hooked on food," is the term used by Dr. Vivian Rakoff, a psychiatrist at the University of Toronto.

"The obese respond to food not as a way of satisfying hunger," says the doctor, "but as something that will make them feel good."

Does extra food make you feel good? If you're honest with yourself, you'll have to answer yes. But how long does that good feeling last? It is fleeting at best. A few seconds of relief, of comfort, of tasting something sweet, seem a small prize compared to the high price you pay for it.

And you do pay. It's not long after those comforting bites (that too often turn into a binge of overeating) that the guilt and self-disgust return. You look in the mirror and see an enemy — someone who has betrayed your real desire.

What can you do when you need the relief from anxiety you have always found in food? Try getting your "comfort supplies" from other sources. Tell someone about your feelings of dis-ease. They may be elusive fears that dissipate as you talk about them. Perhaps you may even need the emotional and ego support of a group of other dieters. Nothing wrong with that. Go get it.

When it comes to the bottom line, as the accountants say, there's really nothing between you and the refrigerator but your thinking. If you are thinking positively and creatively, if you have established priorities for the rest of your life, you will have "comfort supplies" when you need them most.

Before you reach for that extra bite today, ask yourself:
Have I used food as a tranquilizer today? Don't I know I can't "fix" my anxieties with any amount of food?

Have you ever been a sneak eater?

"I hid candy," said one dieter at a group meeting. "I put it under my clothes, on the shelf of my closet, even in the bathroom. And then I hid myself away so that I could eat it without being caught.

"I became so good at eating undiscovered, nobody could understand how I gained so much weight, since I hardly ate a thing in front of people."

What a tangled web of cookies and sticky, half-melted candy bars we weave. Refusing food in public, some of us stuff in private, always fearful of being caught, of being exposed to the surprised displeasure of others.

"It was almost as if what I ate in the dark didn't count," the same dieter said.

Only when she could no longer tolerate the childishness of centering life around eating forbidden food was she able to come out into the light.

Come into the light of full living. You can no longer live in the dark, hiding from the truth of what you are doing. The one person you cannot lie to, successfully, is yourself. The lie will be found out and punished — with more food.

If you are twelve it is not too soon. If you are seventy it is not too late. You have inner wealth you have not begun to tap. You are worthwhile and deserving of a happy, creative life. You are wonderful. Believe that. Think of some very nice thing you once did. Remember the tingling, the warm glow you felt at your own approval. Hold to that feeling today. This is the real truth of who and what you are. It is the root of you.

Think of it. No more hiding. No more deceiving. What a day this will be.

Before you reach for that extra bite today, ask yourself:
Have I come out of hiding into the sunlight of full living?
Am I tired of punishing myself for sneak eating?

"I can't do without that food for the rest of my life!" That angry, defiant or mournful cry is one of our alibis. Likewise, "I can't go on dieting forever!"

Of course you can't. No one can tackle a whole-life problem in one day, and that kind of thinking is self-defeating. It makes you want to give up without really trying.

But this *is* true. What you cannot imagine doing for a lifetime, you can do for one day. If twenty-four hours is too long a period to even think of going without extra food, try one hour. You can do something for an hour that you wouldn't dream of doing for your entire life. Then one hour follows another and another, until you have day after day of sensible eating, and its inevitable payoff — weight loss.

When you get that payoff, reward yourself in a new way. (Remember eating gives immediate pleasure, so make dieting do the same.)

To reinforce your staying power, try dropping a sum of money into a special bank for each day you follow your eating plan. Or find some other suitable (non-food) reward.

Now find ways to dramatize your weight loss. As you lose weight — say, every five pounds or so — fill a large empty sack with five pounds of sand. Keep adding to the bag as you lose, and when you're tempted to return to unhappy eating, heft the bag to remind you of what you will gain if you do. Doesn't that weight look better on the bag that it did on you?

Some of these efforts may seem a little silly on the face of it, but the main point is whether or not they work. And they do.

Tackle one day at a time (or one hour at a time, if you can't manage longer). Learn to *postpone* gratifying the urge to overeat. Then learn to give yourself just as much pleasure from not eating as you used to derive from extra food. You'll have more success. And the reward of success is even more success.

Before you reach for that extra bite today, ask yourself:
Do I realize that I don't have to tackle my whole weight problem today? Do I believe that I can do anything for one hour or one day that would seem impossible to do for a lifetime?

The psychological technique called aversion therapy, designed to overcome a craving for alcohol by making the drinker physically sick, has been used on the overweight as well. Researchers take a group of "hard-core over-weights," give them ipecac (a nausea-inducing compound), show them slides of fattening foods and top this off with pictures of insects crawling around on everyone's favorite desserts.

The assumption in this techinique is that these overweights will begin to associate eating the wrong foods with revulsion and begin to lose significant amounts of weight.

Of course we have been using a form of aversion therapy for ages. Much of the time we couldn't stand the sight of ourselves. One woman at the hospital weigh-in picked up her stomach and said, "Look at all these dead sandwiches." And this before she had been programmed with slides of maggoty meatloaf.

This new technique is controversial. Some patients say the effects wear off all too quickly. Others say they have been able to lose weight and change their destructive eating patterns for the first time. Whatever the case, most dieters can set up their own forms of aversion therapy on a more positive note.

You have an aversion to fat. Nobody needs to tell you that, or prove it to you. Think of some of the things you don't like about being overweight. Make a list of them. Twelve items are enough. (The list could probably go on and on forever.) Today when you think that some extra bite of this, or a piece of that, would taste good, practice your own brand of aversion therapy. Read your list over remembering all the while what too much fat has done to your life. Think how another five pounds on each hip would look!

You know the kind of living you want to do. Confident. Creative. Poised. Goal-minded. Now is the time to begin. You really can't start a moment too soon.

Before you reach for that extra bite today, ask yourself:
Have I developed an aversion to fat? Am I moving steadily toward the kind of living I want to do?

Have you ever kept a detailed written record of every bit of food and drink you consume during a day — where and when it was eaten, and under what emotional circumstances?

Many doctors are recommending such a "food diary" to their patients to help them get a handle on their eating habits. It's very rare, say the experts, for a person to be overeating all the time. A person is more likely to be eating in certain times and places and moods — and not even to be aware of it. A food diary gives a good education into your hidden eating behavior.

Food diaries aren't the only form of writing that works for dieters. Old-fashioned diary-writing or journal-keeping is a fast-growing form of therapy and discovery. Writing, in a self-searching manner, each day can bring needed insights into personal problems. Even better, you can literally write your problems away.

The therapeutic effect of writing has long been known to creative people. Professional writers write out personal problems in their books, often receiving release from the pain and frustration of unresolved situations. You can, too.

Maybe you kept a diary when you were an adolescent, writing down all your daily hopes, dreams and emotional upheavals. Remember how much better you felt after you had confided your innermost feelings? Try it again. Toward the end of the day, sit down for ten or fifteen minutes and write down how you feel about your day — what happened and how you responded to it. It will take a few days to get back into the discipline of diary-keeping, but when you do you will begin to feel the personal satisfaction that such writing always brings. You may write your way out of puzzling emotional situations, or you may find it a source of creative inspiration.

Two diaries — one for the food you eat and one for the life you live — can add up to a lot of help where you need it most.

Before you reach for that extra bite today, ask yourself:
Am I willing to begin writing my food down? Do I believe in
the therapeutic value of journal-keeping?

Supermarket shopping for a dieter is not much different from throwing water on a drowning man. It can all become too much to handle. And yet, we all have to shop for the food we eat, since the nostalgic days of grocery delivery wagons are long gone.

Here are a few tips from Dr. Robert J. Westlake, a University of Pennsylvania psychiatrist, to help make this necessary chore less painful.

"Don't shop," says the doctor, "as if every day was Thanksgiving." He goes on to suggest that it is a good idea never to go to the supermarket with more than the amount of money you expect to need. This prevents impulse buying.

Before you head for the store, make a list and shop only from the list. You won't be as likely to pick up foods which will tempt you when they sit on your own cupboard shelves.

Do your marketing after you've eaten. Hungry people buy more food. Lock your newly purchased groceries in the trunk rather than keep them on the seat next to you. You won't be tempted to snack.

These ideas seem simple enough, and will probably save you the grief of overeating due to hurry and hunger.

Incorporating these few suggestions into your supermarket shopping trips should tell you something about yourself. You refuse to admit defeat. You are always looking for additional ways to improve your eating behavior.

You can hold your head high. You deserve your self-respect. You try and keep on trying. It is as if something deep inside you will not allow you to give up on yourself. Today when you go to the supermarket give yourself a treat. (No, not one you have to hide under the rest of your purchases and hastily gulp on your way home.) As you pass through the door to the store, glance at your reflection, smile and think: "You know, you're really something. I like you."

Before you reach for that extra bite today, ask yourself:
Have I taken the necessary precautions before going to the supermarket? Am I willing to admit that, after all, I'm a pretty wonderful human being?

> *"Oh, would some power the giftie gie us*
> *To see ourselves as others see us!"*

Robert Burns, the Scottish poet, wasn't talking about us overweights, but he could have been.

Dr. Frank J. Bruno, a psychologist with a special interest in overeating behavior, has come up with ways we can see ourselves, ways which may help us modify what and how we eat.

The doctor suggests taking a portable mirror into the kitchen and leaving it there. "Watch yourself closely while you eat." Dr. Bruno counsels. "Try to observe as many details as you can such as the size bites you take, how your mouth and cheeks look during eating and how quickly or slowly you finish your food."

Admittedly, this can be a traumatic exercise. Some people can become upset and uncomfortable. But the doctor, who lost seventy pounds and kept it off for twenty years, says this exercise helped him become more conscious of his eating habits, after which he developed slower, more rational and orderly manners.

Members of the Anonymous programs have a saying: *It takes what it takes.* In other words, you have to do whatever is necessary to get the job done. If you have to eat in front of a mirror, eat in front of a mirror. If something else works better, then do that. The point is to be open to any method that might help.

Too often we say: "Oh I can't do that. It's too embarrassing." Since when were we strangers to embarrassment? It is impossible to live overweight in a country that glorifies the slender, youthful body without suffering mountains of embarrassment almost daily.

Be willing to see yourself as others see you. There is no shame in trying to change, by facing yourself as you really are.

Think of it this way. When hearts are irregular, doctors sometimes implant a pacemaker. And so when your eating is irregular, you have to implant a pacemaker in your head to help you regulate a function as vital as your heartbeat.

Before you reach for that extra bite today, ask yourself:
Do I see myself the way I really eat? Am I willing to implant my own eating pacemaker?

Self-mastery is the goal of almost everyone, thin or fat. Without the resources to cope with the experiences of daily living, we can lose our way.

Most overweight people feel there is something lacking in their lives. If you feel that way, don't be sad, be glad. This may be the beginning of really important life changes.

There is a whole new way of life for you to discover. A positive, creative life which you can challenge, instead of merely rolling over and allowing life to happen to you. If you have started to turn your thinking from negative to positive, from the impossible to the possible, you have a new means of expression. You are no longer hooked on certain foods. Perhaps you find yourself exploring talents which you only dimly knew you had. Maybe you can paint, write, make music or business decisions that are really creative.

With an inner-directed life, you will be able to overcome the discontent, the vague feeling of uneasiness, because you will discover that the answer lies within you.

You will feel real self-satisfaction because you will be, at last, living up to your potential.

You will come to understand the power you have in your own mind, the power to change, the power to express, the power to feel and .the power to act confidently.

You will live each day more fully than you ever dreamed you could. The desire to quiet yourself with extra portions of food your body doesn't need will be under control because you believe you will be able to do it.

With self-mastery, most of the guilt will go. We fat people have had a corner on the guilt market; we have had what amounts to a *vocation for guilt*. No more.

With confident, positive inner direction, your life today will be a delightful adventure. Just want it.

Before you reach for that extra bite today, ask yourself:
Is self-mastery my goal? Am I living today as fully as I can?

You are more than a body.

You are a human being with feelings. The answer to every feeling is not more eating, it is feeling. The answer to anger is to be angry. Don't eat. The answer to sadness is to feel sad. Don't eat. The answer to disappointment is to begin again. Don't eat.

You are not all flesh.

Growth-centered living is the process by which you uncover your real self. You have been in a state of being out of touch with your own nature. You have not seen the positive aspects of your personality for which there are a thousand new connections you can discover.

You are becoming aware of the ways you use food in your life, and how often a wall of cookies goes up between your feelings and your ability to act on those feelings. You will have to see what it is you *do* with extra food before you can *undo* it.

You can be your strongest feeling. If you hold back any part, you suppress that much energy and potential. Don't hold back today. Express your feelings to continue a sensible eating program with great energy.

If you never try to modify your eating habits, you never learn. Without risk, you stay where you are. But if you go ahead and do it, really do it today, that makes your feeling of energy stronger for tomorrow. As author Hugh Prather would have it: "It's not that 'today is the first day of the rest of my life,' but that *now* is all there is of my life."

Have you decided what kind of life you prefer? Have you become a little more open to change? You are more than a body; you are a creative mind, with the solutions to your living problems. Your only job is deciding when to begin. Why not today?

Before you reach for that extra bite today, ask yourself:
Do I know that I am much more than body and flesh? Do I want to grow and uncover more of my real being?

Every overweight is waiting for a miracle cure, a penicillin for fat. That is why some of us fall prey to the desire to hurry up and get off the pounds as quickly as we can. One way to do this is by fasting — eating no food at all. Before you try such a drastic step, even if your head tells you you can do it, read on.

Fasting, according to the medical men who should know, is definitely not a do-it-yourself project. It requires constant monitoring, even hospitalization. Even with this kind of professional supervision, many fasters suffer weakness, headaches and nausea. Others whose kidneys cannot cope with the increased breakdown of protein show high uric acid levels which can lead to kidney and bladder problems. The list of medical problems goes on and on, culminating in the biggest problem of all — death.

In some cases, such as people who weigh upwards of 500 pounds, fasting may be a quick way to save their lives or prepare them for surgery. Even then it is risky. You certainly don't reeducate eating habits during a fast. One veteran who fasted at the Los Angeles Veterans Hospital and lost 100 pounds remembered crying after eating his first meal in three months. He rapidly regained the weight. Fasting may be fast, but it doesn't last.

For most of us overweights, calorie control, plus exercise coupled with re-ordered mental priorities, remain the only realistic way to take off weight permanently and safely. No one but someone who's been through it knows the agony of losing 100 (or 50 or 20) pounds only to regain it. *Think permanent.*

Before you reach for that extra bite today, ask yourself:
Do I accept the fact that there are no easy miracle cures? Am I willing to start thinking about losing my extra weight for the last time?

For so long we overweights have been told we need will power. What we really need is will (or desire) — the will to give ourselves the chance to lead natural lives not covered with a thick layer of extra food.

Try treating yourself like a child. In other words remember the good advice you give to children:

Try to play down the delights of sweet foods and praise the goodness of wholesome protein foods.

Never use food as a penalty or reward for yourself.

Keep yourself active(you wouldn't let a child you cared about lie on the sofa all day).

Have professional health checkups, especially while you're dieting.

You'd do at least that much for a child. Do that much for yourself. It's no fun to go up and down the scale like a human seesaw. To see that needle zoom up to your former weight (and most often beyond) can be the most discouraging and heartbreaking experience any dieter ever faces.

Protect yourself from having to suffer this disappointment again. Keep constantly in your thoughts today the physical image of how you really look. You already have this size and shape, if you will just uncover it. You are already what you want to be, but you must strip away the outer fat, covering the real you.

If you hear a negative voice telling you that an extra piece won't hurt, don't believe it. You can let your positive, creative thoughts drown out that voice. It has lied to you often enough. Look where you got listening to negative advice?

Listening to your will, the positive thoughts that fill your head, will give you the illusion of not being alone. You're not.

Before you reach for that extra bite today, ask yourself:
Am I answering the child in me with good advice? Have I suffered enough seesawing up and down the scales?

"I rationalize away almost everything I eat," said one fortyish diet-club member. "It's almost as if I'm not an adult when it comes to food."

The search for honesty begins with a willingness to recognize the areas in our lives where we have resisted growing up. All of us make alibis for our behavior that have a plausible ring. "Well, wouldn't you be mad, too?" we ask, excusing anger. Or, "Experience has taught me not to trust people like her," is a good-sounding excuse for a suspicious nature. But nowhere in our lives do we have more alibis than for our eating behavior. "I need this because I'm tired/sick/unloved/nervous/anxious/rejected/frightened" or any number of other feelings.

It sometimes takes a tragedy to help us realize that we are still reacting to emotions in a childish way. For us overweights the moment of tragedy comes in front of our mirror when we must confront ourselves honestly.

Nobody says the confrontation is easy. But your survival demands that you begin to make more mature choices, especially in your way of eating.

It won't be difficult to take the first step. You only need admit your need for a change in your life. That should be easy enough.

Next you will have to begin a search for honesty and self-understanding, for a rational diet program and new emotional habits.

You won't have far to look. You have the basis for honest, mature thinking patterns already. Peel back the layers of alibis and excuses and allow your mind to grow and guide you in new and more honest directions. Good luck in your search!

Before you reach for that extra bite today, ask yourself:
Have I become willing to recognize the areas in my life where I have refused to grow up? Am I willing to take the steps necessary to find self-honesty?

Do you have one certain food or a certain type of food over which you have no control? Over the years, diet-club members have reported that specific foods (mostly of the sweet variety) were beyond their ability to handle. These foods, called "binge foods," were ones in which one bite was too much and the whole box not enough.

"I can't have anything chocolate in the house," said one dieter who called herself a chocoholic." "Even if I have it locked in a kitchen cupboard out of sight, it sings to me until I answer."

If you have a binge food, whatever it is, most dieters find they have better diet success if they simply don't keep it around. That doesn't mean you can never again have a bite of this food. It means that you'll have to wait until other, more positive things have become sweeter to you than any chocolate drop.

It is a paradox that we overeaters fall in love with certain foods. Most of us have tales of sick bodies and unhappy lives brought about in part because of our dependence on binge foods. And yet, year after year we have surrounded our favorite foods with a mystique which gives them magical and even curative powers.

The only thing we get from binge food is fat.

Replace the feelings of discomfort in your conscious mind, the feelings that have you reaching for your binge food. Joy, confidence and hope are feelings which will relax your body. Think about how good it is to be alive and to be losing weight.

Learn to recognize the storm warnings your body sends to your mind, warnings that have, in the past, sent you straight to your binge foods.

Alcoholics long ago found out they could control their physical craving for alcohol if they just didn't take that first drink.

You can overcome your craving for any binge food. Just don't take that first bite.

Before you reach for that extra bite today, ask yourself:
Have I identified my binge foods? Am I willing to substitute positive feelings for the feelings of discomfort which feed my craving?

Clock-watchers have a bad name in our society. But they are doing the right thing if they are watching their own internal clocks which monitor body rhythms.

Have you had this experience? For some reason you got to bed much later or got up much earlier than is usually your habit. The next day you feel disoriented, unable to concentrate, tired, even flushed. All these physical reactions merely remind you that your internal clock is ticking, and that you have disturbed your natural body rhythms.

Dieters should be internal clock-watchers. Our bodies like to stick to routine — sleep at the same time, eat at the same time — every day. Our rhythms even influence our moods. We can become depressed and inefficient if we don't pay attention to our inner ticking. Both depression and inefficiency can be especially hard on the dieter.

Researchers know that eating can greatly affect body rhythms. When volunteers at the University of Minnesota ate only one meal a day, their carbohydrate control systems were altered.

Find the sleeping and eating rhythms right for you. If you need eight hours of sleep every night, try to arrange to get them. If you need to eat meals spaced five (or four or six) hours apart, arrange that schedule, too. It won't take a lot of experimenting to determine what will make your internal clock keep the best rhythm for you.

This is just another way we overweights can become aware of our bodies. For too long, we have tuned them out. Not listening can cause unnecessary physical and emotional problems. Tune in to yourself today and really listen.

Before you reach for that extra bite today, ask yourself:
Am I watching my internal clock? Have I found the sleeping and eating rhythms that help me live best?

There's a joke that apple pie is synonymous with mother and the American flag. Unfortunately for people who have a problem with their weight, this is all too often the case. Apple pie, or whatever other favorite you might have, can come close to being sacred.

Why is this? Because we overweights have not developed our X-ray vision so that we can see apple pie for what it really is. Dr. Frank J. Bruno, a psychologist, suggests we don't look at our favorite confection for what it emotionally represents to us. "Pretend you can see right through the crust," he says. "You'll see refined sugar, white flour, hydrogenated fat, artificial flavor and color, and a lot of calories."

Are you bewitched by the way certain foods look? Try developing your X-ray vision and it will break the spell you're under.

Perhaps you will have to reach into new areas of enjoyment. There are more feasts for the eyeballs than just apple pie. Try looking at the skyline, the ridge of a nearby hill you'd really like to climb. It would be unreasonable (even silly) to weigh yourself down with other items in our American triumvirate. (You wouldn't carry your mother on your back or a heavy flag over your shoulder.) Why then should you carry long-eaten pieces of apple pie disguised as added pounds?

Open your eyes to more than food. There is a whole world to enjoy, and you will need a whole body with which to enjoy it. The rewards of your effort will be great. Just use your X-ray vision and begin to really see what you are doing.

Before you reach for that extra bite today, ask yourself:
Do I look beyond the visual appeal of foods and see what is really there? Am I ready to feast my eyes on the whole world beyond my plate?

Do you do a lot of eating standing up? Well then, sit down. Overweights who have become successful dieters report that eating while standing up, near the refrigerator or over the kitchen sink, is a way to avoid knowing how much food they are really consuming.

Most behavioral psychologists agree that the best way to diet is to have one place in your home where you allow yourself to eat. Knowledgeable dieters choose their dining table as their "eating place." They make it a rule *never* to eat food in any other place. If they are going to eat, even nibble a piece of celery, they go to the table and sit down before they eat it.

There is no way to control portions if you eat out of containers by refrigerator light. And portion control, as we all know, is important to weight control.

Removing the food from its source, carrying it to the table, getting utensils and plates, sitting down at the table — all these actions act as buffers between your desire for food and the point of eating. You'll have much more time to be reminded of the good eating habits you're trying to form if you don't grab and eat food right on the spot.

All habits are learned. But they can be unlearned, too. If you refuse to feed (that is reinforce) your overeating habit, it will eventually disappear.

Write a new script for yourself. You, not food, are the star actor, playing the main part. Imagine yourself learning to control your stand-up eating habit. Imagine your new image, the way you want to appear on the world's stage. Set a scene which shows you climbing on a scale which registers your goal weight.

You alone possess the possibility for your personal fulfillment and happiness. It is there, already a part of you. Act the role.

Before you reach for that extra bite today, ask yourself:
Have I stopped eating standing up? Have I written a life script which will help me find my thin self?

The ability to relax is vital for dieters. Too many times we overweights have reached for extra calories because we needed something to quiet anxieties. We have decided that food was the only thing which would get rid of the lump in our throats.

Do you know what tension can do to you? If you are subjected to stress over an extended period of time, you will begin to experience tension, and prolonged tension can make it impossible to follow a disciplined way of eating.

If you have a tape recorder, get a blank tape and record the following statements in a soothing voice. If you don't have a recorder, write them on a white sheet of paper. For a healthier mind and body, first get comfortable, then play back or read aloud these suggestions when you feel yourself becoming tense:

1. You are a very composed person.
2. You avoid worry about things you can't change.
3. You have control over negative feelings.
4. You avoid tension-producing situations.
5. You avoid tension-producing people.
6. You are breathing deeply and regularly.
7. You are seeing yourself as your thin ideal.
8. You think of yourself as a person with self-control.
9. You are able to relax.
10. You trust yourself.

After you have listened to your own voice outlining these positive, creative steps, you are ready to try some mental imagery. Imagine yourself in an unavoidable situation or argument which produces a lot of tension for you. But, this time, instead of reacting stressfully, watch yourself (in the theater of your mind) playing the part of a poised, calm and relaxed person. Practice this exercise whenever you feel tension that might cause you to reach for a food pacifier. In a short time, you'll be more relaxed and weigh less, as well.

Before you reach for that extra bite today, ask yourself:
Do I allow tense moments to trigger my overeating? Am I willing to reprogram myself so that I will become a more relaxed person?

Long before we overweights find out what it is like to be thin, we learn what it is like to be fat.

First there is fear. The fear of ridicule, social disapproval, being lectured and not getting the job/boy/girl. Is it any wonder if we grow "thin-skinned" under our burden of pounds?

Second, there is the loneliness of being different from others, and even more, of being different from the person we really could be.

There is so much misery, discrimination, recrimination, that many of us end by rejecting ourselves.

We learn the lessons of fat all too well. When it comes time to learn to be thin, to live in a new, creative way, the experience is alien to us.

What is it to be thin?

You will touch the earth lightly; nothing will rattle or shake as you pass by.

You will be able to pay attention to the world outside your body; every mirror will stop reflecting defeat.

You will not have to hold yourself back, to trade opportunity for acceptance.

Alone will not be as lonely, because you will be with an inner friend who is helpful.

You will be in balance with life. Food will have a place, but not every place.

You will wake and find your dream of losing weight is real. You will believe that it is eternal this time.

You will feel quieter inside, a kind of rich silence calories could never allow.

You will be eating less for health and vibrance; just to do it, not to have it done.

Before you reach for that extra bite today, ask yourself:
Now that I know what it's like to be fat, am I willing to discover what it's like to be thin? Am I willing to concentrate less on my fat misery and more on the joys of becoming slender?

Are you hungry? If you recently ate something, but still have gnawing pains in your stomach, chances are that's not hunger, but the *fear of hunger.* "I don't really know how true hunger feels," said one overweight at a therapy session. "I'm afraid to get hungry."

It takes from twenty to thirty minutes for the food you eat to signal your brain so that your brain can decide you've had enough to eat. If you finish your meal in a few minutes, then reach for more food saying, "I'm still hungry," it could mean you haven't given your brain the chance to catch up with your stomach.

"My family was dirt-poor when I was a kid," explained another dieter in the group, "so I never got enough to eat. Maybe that's why I eat more than I need. I still remember going to bed hungry."

It's sad to remember a hungry child, especially if that child was you, but eating for that hungry child can only make the adult you've become too fat. You can't erase the past with any amount of food.

Why not try to live with a little hunger? If your doctor has not diagnosed a chemical imbalance which requires you to eat more frequent meals, try to get beyond your next hunger pang. If it is true hunger and not just your emotions playing tricks on your stomach, you will know that each rumble is the sound of more fat being dragged out of storage to give you the energy you need to wait for the next meal. Fat is stored energy. Why not use some of it today?

Before you reach for that extra bite today, ask yourself:
Am I afraid of hunger? Do I eat so fast that my stomach doesn't have a chance to signal my brain that it's full?

Whatever our fears, most of us can learn to deal with them. That doesn't mean you should ignore excess fear. You may be ill or have the beginnings of hypoglycemia, a low blood-sugar condition. If, however, your physician finds no physical cause, then you can stop blaming your body and look to your anxieties.

Why not try sharing your feelings of fear with others? If you are afraid of diet-induced hunger or of any other conflict you may have, talk it out with someone who'll understand — perhaps another member of your diet group or an intimate friend.

Try not to be overconcerned about the fact that you are afraid. This can only intensify your fear. Remember, reasonable fears are a natural and normal response to living.

Live in the present. Many fears are of the unknown future, and most of them never even happen. Can you remember what you were afraid of last week? Did your fear ever materialize?

Try to put fear in perspective. Sometimes we overweights tend to dramatize. Everything becomes a catastrophic tragedy, when in reality *most ordinary fears are merely inconveniences.*

Perhaps you are trying too hard to do a perfect job. You can work yourself into an absolute frenzy of perfection (and fear of failure) when you place this burden on yourself.

Have you learned how to relax? It's impossible to be a fearful person while you are relaxed.

Ask yourself if you have a good idea about the meaning of your life. Do you have goals? Are you inner-directed or dependent on the opinions of others?

For dieters as for others, the test of bravery is one of endurance. Alcoholics Anonymous members have capsuled this character trait as succinctly as they have so many others. They just say: KEEP ON KEEPIN' ON.

Before you reach for that extra bite today, ask yourself:
Am I brave enough to face my fears without more food than I need? Do I have a good idea of the meaning of my life so that fears cannot harm me?

Are you one of many overweights who think exercise will only make you hungrier? Do you believe that exercise is really counterproductive to weight loss?

Dr. Brian J. Sharkey, an exercise expert, says this is one of the greatest diet myths. He has found that *exercise before a meal can dull the appetite* and cause calorie intake to decrease.

As little as one half-hour of exercise every day can take off as much as twenty-six pounds a year if you keep your calorie count the same. (Does that sound like a waste of time?)

The fallacy that you would have to exercise to exhaustion in order to lose weight is just that, a fallacy. *Regular exercise*, rather than exercise intensity, is more important.

Perhaps the most important reason for overweights to exercise along with their new eating plan is this: *The average person burns up to twice as many calories following vigorous exercise as he or she does normally.* After a twenty-eight minute run, for example, you'll burn double calories for up to six hours.

Of course, you should consult your doctor before embarking on a course of exercise. Usually the more overweight you are, the easier you should take it in the beginning. (You're not Tarzan or Jane!)

Sure you can lose weight without exercise, but you'll be missing a marvelous body experience. After only a few sessions you are likely to feel more limber, and more alive.

If you've lived fat for very long, you've lost touch with your body's capabilities. You don't know what it can do. Maybe you even mistrust your body to the point you think it can do nothing.

Don't believe it. Your body can have new spring, find new balance, have muscles and tendons and joints that work without creaking — in fact, you can have a whole new sense of physical well-being with a little exercise effort on your part. Why not try it today?

Before you reach for that extra bite today, ask yourself:
Am I willing to drop my old ideas about exercise and give it a try? Do I trust my body?

Four years ago, Anna had her first baby. She's still wearing the same maternity clothes. "I'm too embarrassed to buy new clothes," she confesses. "I'd have to try them on in a dressing room, and I never know when a saleslady will peek in and see me in all my fat.

"I did go once, and tried on an orange knit suit. Orange, for God's sake! And the saleslady had the nerve to tell me I'd better grab it because that was all they had in my size."

Anna went home and ate for two days, avoiding her mirror, hiding from her body, running from her fat.

"When I have the courage to look in my mirror," she says, "I know I've got to lose weight. I've got to!"

Anna's story, admitted tearfully at a diet-group meeting, is the first evidence that she is willing to come out of hiding.

Food is the great cover-up. For Anna, as for many of us overweights, being too fat took her out of the mainstream of life, and gave her a ready-made excuse to cut off involvement with the rest of the world.

We all know the traps of too many pounds — they can create enormous physical and emotional barriers, and, of the two, the emotional barrier is the higher.

When you begin to think that there is hope, when you begin to stop hiding from yourself and your weight problem, you are ready to let your creative mind get to work. The idea that you are capable, positive and worthwhile is the latchkey that opens your prison door. Your are no longer locked inside a hostile body.

Come out of hiding. Turn the key to your physical prison. You will tap reservoirs of strength you never knew existed. You will begin to hope that, at last, you will lose this weighty burden — and, oh, how sweet it will be.

Before you reach for that extra bite today, ask yourself:
Have I had enough of hiding from myself? Am I willing to unlock the door to my prison and come out into the world?

What a surprise to climb on the scale after a period of dieting to find that you are pounds lighter! Now, deliberately walk to the mirror and take a look at your face. What do you see? The face of a winner. There, watch the satisfaction in your eyes.

Have you also been practicing better grooming? Sometimes when we overweights are without hope, we may allow our appearance to deteriorate. "Why bother," we think. "Nothing could make me look any better." Of course that's not true, and we quickly become more conscious of our looks the more we follow a plan of eating to lose weight.

Have you accomplished a good deal more work lately? When we stop overeating, when our world stops revolving around food, we can concentrate on other aspects of our lives. Keeping ourselves busy is a good way to put dieting into perspective as just a part (though an essential one) of daily living. Remember you're a human being first, not a professional dieter.

Have you started forming some new habits? Since you have more time (overeating is *so* time-consuming), you have spare hours for new hobbies, social get-togethers or just for getting to know yourself better.

It's no wonder that as the scales inch down, our self-esteem soars upward. So don't forget to go to the mirror after you weigh in at a lower weight. You have a right to see the excitement and happiness on your face. What's more, why not give your reflection a conspiratorial wink? After all, the sweet taste of success is better than anything you've ever tasted before.

Before you reach for that extra bite today, ask yourself:
Have I seen the face of a winner in my mirror today? As I lose weight, is my whole life changing for the better?

"Where does it say," asks Joyce Fabrey, "that a woman should feel she has to wear an overcoat in the hottest weather just to hide her figure?" Joyce is an officer in the National Association to Aid Fat Americans (NAAFA), and she's talking about pride. "There's no reason," she adds emphatically, "why heavy people should not have pride in themselves."

NAAFA members resist the idea that they must lose all their weight *before* they feel self-worth. And you can, too. It won't be easy in an era that makes a cult of thinness. But while you're on your way to a more desirable and healthful weight, there's no real reason to hide behind a shield of cloth. One day at a time you can serenely face warm weather, wearing cool, appropriate clothes, until you reach your weight goal.

And the goal *is* worth working and waiting for. No one but someone who's been through it can possibly know what it's like to become thin again after a period of fighting overweight. It is one of the loveliest experiences in life.

But the struggle leaves more than a new figure in its wake. It teaches you to like yourself, to take good care of yourself, and, above all, to enjoy your life.

Let go of any limiting attitudes about yourself, as you are today. Of course, you needn't hide extra pounds under extra clothes. You know (whether anyone else knows or not) that one day at a time you are growing toward a new image. You believe in your ultimate success. You are happy and enthusiastic. To paraphrase Abraham Lincoln: You can be just about as happy today as you want to be. Honest Abe never had a weight problem. So don't take Abe's honest advice lightly.

Before you reach for that extra bite today, ask yourself:
Have I given up my shield of cloth for comfortable clothes of the season? Am I enjoying each day on the way to my goal weight?

Being too serious about taking off your excess pounds can sometimes lead to a feeling of "carrying the weight of the world" on your shoulders. But you can slim down without taking yourself so seriously. In fact, that's the number one rule for happy weight loss: Be determined and serious, but not "deadly" serious.

Try, just for this day, to walk on the "funny" side of the street. It works. Most world-famed humorists have paved their own road to success with a fantastic ability to laugh at themselves. And laughter, according to modern-day psychologists, is a better therapeutic release than tears. Even most of the religions of the world tell us to *act as if* we're happy, and we will be.

When you think about it, it's not so difficult. There is so much joy in losing weight, in revealing the new person underneath that excess flesh. When clothes begin to droop and sag, when rings fall off *that's fun.* And what holds greater glee for the successful dieter than walking into a department store and buying a smaller size in the latest fashion?

But that's only the beginning of the real fun. No longer will tender, sensitive feelings block out the comedy of life, the sheer delight of living in a body that is really alive.

Tune into this day and let the pleasure in it spill over into every minute. Be free from all feelings of heaviness, of burden — of the weight of the world. Your sense of well-being and ease with yourself will be apparent to everyone you meet. Take a look in the mirror. See? A brighter more zestful you looks back where before was only a negative, humorless reflection.

So day by day *don't take yourself so darn seriously.* Enjoy every moment. And by the time you uncover your real image, your mind will be in perfect harmony with your new body.

Before you reach for that extra bite today, ask yourself:
Do I see the fun side of life? Have I decided to *act as if* I'm a happy person?

The ancient Roman warning "Let the buyer beware!" goes double in today's supermarket, especially for dieters. If you're trying to lose pounds or keep off already-lost pounds, you should learn to read package labels. Granted, that will slow down your food shopping just a bit, and nobody is suggesting you make shopping a full-time career, but you will be able to learn much more about what you are putting in your mouth by simply reading labels.

By law, all ingredients must be listed in the order of predominance. That means if sugar in any of its forms is listed above the fourth or fifth ingredient, there may be too many sweet and empty calories in the product for your weight-losing diet.

Checking the ingredients can help you save money, too. Products with the same or similar ingredients may vary drastically in price.

Supermarkets are filled with a dizzying variety of foods, all of them attractively packaged and within easy reach. As you walk down a supermarket aisle, you'll pass 250 food items every minute. It's no wonder that sometimes we forget the Roman warning and join the grab-and-snatch school of food shopping.

Your life is changing for the better. In many ways you are becoming more attuned to things you formerly took for granted. *Less food intake equals heightened mental awareness.* That is a universal diet equation which never fails to add up.

You can use a brain which has not been made sluggish by carbohydrate calories. You can use it to see inside yourself more clearly, to develop an inner sight that is really a sixth sense.

Today, use your sixth sense to keep the other ones (taste, touch, sight, smell, hearing) under control, especially while you are shopping in the supermarket.

Before you reach for that extra bite today, ask yourself:
Am I learning to read labels so I'll know in advance what I'm putting in my mouth? Have I developed my inner sixth sense?

"I'd rather have somebody point a gun at me than a camera." Ever heard another overweight say that? Ever thought it yourself?

There is almost nothing more traumatic for us than to have our "real" bodies forever enshrined on film for ourselves and our posterity. And we have developed a hundred tricks to help us avoid Mr. Kodak's sadistic invention.

"I always held one of my children in front of me."

"You could always find me in the back row or behind a tree during a family photo session."

"I wore the biggest dress I could find, thinking I could hide behind folds of material."

"Whenever I could, I always managed to be the one *taking* the picture. In our family album, I'm like the man who isn't there."

If one of these photo-dodging tricks didn't work, the next best thing was to get the negatives first, destroy them and then facetiously lament that our pictures never seemed to turn out.

What can you do about photos? Just one thing — you can't learn to deal with your problem until you are ready to face the truth. After all, you can't hide from yourself. It's a good idea to take a good (revealing) photo when you begin your new healthful eating regimen, and others after losing each twenty pounds. Be honest. Get a good profile and full front. Look at it. Yes, that really does look like you.

It doesn't matter what you do with the photos once you have them. You can put them in a drawer, paste them to your refrigerator or show them at your diet-group meetings to encourage others not as far along as you. What matters is that you will have a visual image of the change in your appearance. As you go down in size you will be approaching the ideal image you have been carrying in your mind for so long. Finally there will come a day when the picture you take and the one you have in mind will be a perfect match.

Every day you follow your weight-losing eating plan brings you closer to that day. Before you know it, you'll be there.

Before you reach for that extra bite today, ask yourself:
Do I hide from the camera so that I can hide from myself? Am I willing to record my weight loss on film so that I will know how far I've come?

God, grant me the serenity
To accept the things I cannot change,
The courage to change the things I can,
And the wisdom to know the difference.

The Alcoholics Anonymous Serenity Prayer is spoken in dozens of languages daily by millions of people thoughout the world. The point of the prayer is simply the desire to see things clearly and realistically. It is both spiritual in nature and very practical.

The AA Serenity Prayer (also used by other Anonymous programs) is a perfect antidote for self-pity. By repeating these words, most alcoholics and overeaters find it impossible to cover up feelings of guilt or aggression with self-pity. They often find the comfort in those words allows them to replace negative, destructive feelings with positive, constructive actions.

The word serenity used here is not a nothingness but a stillness within. So many of us overweights carry on a ceaseless dialogue within ourselves about what, when and how we are overeating. *We need the stillness of serenity.*

Many of us are confronted daily with problems that seem to have no ready solution. Sometimes we try to force a resolution with little success, and we eat over it. Sometimes, when we could change a thing for the better, we don't do it, and we eat over that, too.

When you have a problem, ask yourself: Is this a problem I can solve? Can I take action today? If so, what action?

If you make a decision to act, then do so. If you decide that action is impossible, then do nothing. The point is to make decisions based on constructive thinking. Vacillating has led to more food binges than any other kind of behavior.

Make a decision. Act on it. Don't look back.

Before you reach for that extra bite today, ask yourself:
Am I seeking serenity through decisiveness? Have I ceased looking back and second-guessing myself?

"I *only* lost seven pounds this month," the dieter said with a wry self-knowing grin. "Of course, I'm never satisfied with my progress."

We overweights *are* hard to please. No amount of weight lost in a given period is ever enough. A more positive way of looking at our weight loss is to mentally double it. That's right, count what you lost this month and what you didn't gain. The dissatisfied dieter who lost only seven pounds in one month didn't gain the five she had been averaging for some months prior to her diet. Added together this makes a very respectable twelve pounds that she is lighter than she would have been had she not started an eating plan for weight loss.

If you are honestly following a new eating-to-live health program, your excess weight will come off. We may not always lose as fast as we want, but our bodies lose as fast as they should.

Learn to accept the weight loss your body gives you. If you are farther down the road today than you were yesterday, that is Progress with a capital P.

Think to yourself: As the days come and as the days go, you will travel farther along the road to complete health. Food will no longer rule your body and mind.

Self-pity (because you didn't lose as much as you wanted) is a luxury you cannot afford. Replace destructive self-pity with the recognition of true progress.

If you look hard enough, you can find all you need in today. You will move toward better health, more happiness and greater self-understanding. What more is there to progress than this?

Before you reach for that extra bite today, ask yourself:
Am I learning to be satisfied with the weight loss I achieve?
Do I know what true progress is?

The way we Americans consume sugar is a crime. We eat as much in a week today as we ate in a year around the turn of the century. Of course, those figures are for average Americans, and no overweight can assume that the statistics apply to him or her. We probably consume two, three, or even more times the national average.

Refined sugar is implicated not only in obesity, but in dental decay, heart disease, hypoglycemia, diabetes and even infection.

"Sugar in the form of candy and pastries did crazy things to me," admitted one dieter to her group. "About one half-hour after consuming a lot of it, I would get dizzy and very drowsy. Sometimes I would go to bed, sleep two or three hours and wake up feeling drugged or hungover.

"My mood was awful. I was easily agitated and bad-tempered over everything."

Not every overweight has this reaction to consuming too much sugar. Some of us just get fat. But if you have physical and mood changes in addition to gaining weight, you'd be wise to consult a doctor.

Overweights who have had negative reactions to refined sugar may have to decide to live without it. Many people who have eliminated white sugar from their diets say this is surprisingly simple. After about seventy-six hours, the craving for sweets leaves and does not return unless it is fueled again with more sugar.

You may think eating without sugar means a return to a Stone Age diet. Perhaps that wouldn't be a bad idea. Mankind evolved and developed the master brain of the planet without refined sugar. Still, you may not have to go that far.

Your main task will be to make a decision about the foods you want to go into your body and what you want them to do for you. You've got too much living to do to spend even a small portion of it in a sugar stupor. Now, that *would* be a crime, wouldn't it?

Before you reach for that extra bite today, ask yourself:
Do I have a bad sugar reaction? Am I losing any time to overeating that I could use really enjoying life?

Studies have shown that overweight people tend to drink too much coffee. Excessive amounts of caffeine in your system can cause too much insulin to be produced from an overstimulated pancreas. The insulin uses up too much sugar and may cause a low blood sugar condition. If you are already predisposed to hypoglycemia, extra caffeine can become a problem and make it more difficult to stick to a weight-losing diet.

Other symptoms, such as fatigue, nervousness and headaches, often accompany heavy coffee drinking. If you feel that caffeine is causing you discomfort, you may want to cut down or consult your doctor.

How much coffee should you drink? A person's intake must be based on the drinker's own reaction to coffee. If you're concerned about caffeine consumption, don't forget to decrease the amount of tea and cola drinks, even diet cola, in your eating plan. Tune in to your body. It will tell you if you are getting too much caffeine.

Excess caffeine, like too much food, is a crutch we sometimes use to prop up our personalities. But no matter how firmly rooted is our need for a crutch, we can replace it if we face ourselves and study our strengths.

Get a strong image of yourself as someone who doesn't have to reach for "a little something" whenever you need a release from care.

Plant a picture of health in your mind. See yourself as healthy and free from all crutches. You can throw away your caffeine crutch, your food crutch and all the others that make you feel better momentarily, but do nothing to solve your problems.

You have an ability to think and to make decisions based on the facts. If any substance you are taking into your body is causing you health trouble, you have the power to take control and remove the source of your trouble.

With this positive attitude you cannot help but make steady progress in the direction you want to go.

Before you reach for that extra bite today, ask yourself:
Do I drink too much coffee? Have I been able to throw away all my crutches and walk on my own two feet?

Overeating is no less an addiction than alcohol or gambling. In some ways it is a worse addiction. Life for food addicts is a powerful network of stimuli, reminding them constantly of the urge to overeat. What can you do about your addiction?

1. The most important first step is to make an honest assessment of yourself, and the ways you use food to cushion your life against stresses and strains. Do you try to work out your problems, or do you take the all-too-familiar escape route of overeating?

2. Have you tried to defuse the trigger mechanisms which set off your addictive responses to food? Do you eat when you are angry or sorry for yourself?

3. Do you avoid people and situations which set you off? This may involve keeping "goodies" out of the house or having lunch with people who are trying to watch their weight rather than those who will tease and tempt you.

4. Have you tried to develop other interests and projects to which you can enthusiastically commit yourself?

5. Keep in mind that your course is not an easy one. You will be tempted to give in at times and overeat. But if you wait, lost pounds will be a bigger reward than food ever was.

6. If you can't resist the pull of old habits alone, perhaps you should consider a group of like-minded people. Diet groups have helped when all else has failed.

Remember, food has always offered the *illusion of escape.* It seems to give you a remedy for your problems. But when food becomes an addiction, you must realize that you have a chronic, crippling disease. And you must fight against it.

You shall overcome.

Before you reach for that extra bite today, ask yourself:
Have I made an honest assessment of myself today? Am I ready to resist the illusion of escape for the reality of freedom from addiction to food?

Overweight people can become very depressed, We can feel "down" or "blue" or "in the dumps" when we are having diet problems. To paraphrase psychologist M. E. Seligman, depression is the common cold of dieting.

There are no magic remedies, but there are some practical ideas for what you can do to overcome mild depression so that you can get on with the fun of living

Dr. Seligman believes that depression is simply the conviction of one's own helplessness. Once you begin to think of yourself as an effective human being, you cease being depressed.

For most of us, the mood of depression is not too intense and does not require professional help. Self-help can often work. Here's what you can do for yourself:

Try some activity. Depressed people often have the tendency to wallow in their negativity and find it difficult to stir. Dr. Seligman suggests this is because your thinking is distorted. You can only remember the bad and not the good. *Try not to color everything black and remember the things that give you joy.*

Stop talking depressed. Once you've talked it all out, it does little good to go on repeating and repeating. The tendency is just to become more depressed, and this kind of talk drives your friends away.

Fight against helplessness. Try to achieve something. Get moving, performing chores or acts that are important. Function. As you begin to achieve some satisfaction you will exert more control over your life. It's just like learning to walk. After the first, few timid steps, you're off and running.

It is most important that dieters arm themselves with some action steps against the times when they are "down in the dumps." What you are doing is much too important to be left to chance.

Building your new life, one that is healthier, happier, and thinner, is more than just a hobby. It is survival.

Before you reach for that extra bite today, ask yourself:
Do I get busy when I get blue? Do I consider building a new program of living the most important thing in my day?

None of us can go through life without the approval of others. But problems occur when we constantly need others to tell us that we are capable, intelligent — or even thin enough. Moreover the need for the continuous approval of others never seems to come in the quantity or quality we want. Soon it becomes an intolerable situation to always postpone making decisions about ourselves until others have commented.

The truth is that we don't really seek honest evaluations, we usually seek agreement. When we don't get it, our whole day can be ruined, and as a result we tend to overeat.

Some of us choose a path which seems to guarantee a continuous stream of approval from others. We try in every way to please them. Of course, this generally means we are false to ourselves. Our aim is *to forestall any chance of rejection.*

People-pleasers are doomed to disappointment. They eventually become obsessed by the idea that other people wouldn't like them the way they really are.

The art of getting along with other people has received a great deal of attention over the years. Only recently has much thought been given to the art of getting along with oneself.

The simple fact is: You can't please all of the people all of the time. You should begin to think more about pleasing yourself. How do *you* feel about a given situation? What do *you* want to do about it? Although it may seem a contradiction, you will find that the more you please yourself, the more independent you will become and the more you will please others.

Independence and decisiveness are two tools a dieter can use every day. There is a good feeling that comes from being responsible for yourself. You will find you can do a better job for yourself than anyone else. Do it today.

Before you reach for that extra bite today, ask yourself:
Am I tired of being a people-pleaser? Have I decided to take responsibility for my own decisions?

"Hurry. Hurry. Hurry. Step right up folks. Eat all you want and never go hungry. Just watch your fat melt away painlessly in two short weeks."

Like the old-time medicine man selling snake oil cures, there are an ever-increasing number of diet gadgets promising almost instant relief from fat. The long list includes vibrating belts and tables, rollers, rubber suits and "tummy bands," candy and pills, rubbing creams and sure fire "plans" by the dozens.

It's not hard to understand why we overweights can be so easily bilked out of millions of dollars a year. No one but someone who's been fat can understand how desperately we want to lose weight. Sometimes we go to ridiculous lengths.

We overweights cannot rely on gadgets to help us lose weight. If we are to lean on something, we must lean on ourselves. Actively seek self-reliance. You alone determine your destiny through your own efforts. Do you want to lose weight? Then establish a master plan for eating to help you lose weight. Do you want to change your emotional pattern? Then establish a master plan of inner growth, too.

Change, according to Dr. Ari Kiev, involves the discovery of alternative paths to objectives, using resources in new ways. Most people resist change, acting from habits reinforced by old beliefs.

Success in changing your life-style results when you *combine adaptability with activity.* If you are not losing weight on your present eating plan, get another. Only if it works is it good enough for you.

Progress comes step by step. Trying to hurry progress with expensive diet gadgets (which don't even work) will not add to your master plan for future success. Day after day, you're moving toward your goal. Today is just another step, but a long one.

Before you reach for that extra bite today, ask yourself:
Have I relied too much on reducing gadgets and not enough on myself? Am I moving toward my goal of a thinner body and a happier life, one long step at a time?

You are good. Once you accept this premise, you'll be better off.

Of course, this doesn't mean you don't have faults, things you have to work on for future improvement. What it does mean is that you are not the worthless slob you may have been telling yourself you are.

Have you made a realistic assessment of your abilities and your potential? For example, you know that you have the ability to diet off extra pounds and to live in a healthy, happy body. You know that the goals you have chosen to work toward are possible ones and they can be reached by taking one step at a time, one day at a time.

Never be afraid to aim high. Being realistic does not mean you should approach life with goals that are too easy. Quite the opposite, you must strive toward goals that will demand your best. Remember, also, that your best is good enough.

Today concentrate on developing a winning self-image. Dress as if you were a success. Act as if you were a success. If possible, try to spend some part of the day with positive people who have changed their lives in ways you want to change yours.

Do you have some nagging task that you have been putting off? It can be anything from a basket of overdue ironing to a new business merger. Whatever it is, do it today. If possible, begin the job and complete it today. At least go as far as you can with it. No matter what the task, when it is done, you will experience the sensation of success. Accomplishment will walk with you. You will be able to say, when today is over, "I have had a successful day."

Do you like the feeling of success? You can repeat the feeling over and over again, if you repeat the action.

When we feel like failures, like meaningless blobs of flesh, it is a short step from feeling to feeding. But when we feel that we are *good*, that we have the ability to succeed at life's tasks, then we can go on to do more for ourselves by eating less.

You are better than you think. Remember that today, and act on it.

Before you reach for that extra bite today, ask yourself:
Am I thinking well of myself today instead of putting myself down? Have I concentrated on developing a successful self-image?

Do you feel great? When we overweights are not eating excessively, when we are following a weight-losing diet for our health and bodies, we feel great.

Most of us in the past have eaten ourselves into a state of lethargy. Every task was too much for our meager store of energy. Every step required our last bit of strength. It seemed as if our insides would burst out of our skin. In our extremes, we vomited and fell into bed sick.

"It was as if my body were allergic to the quantities of food I ate," said one dieter. "I had all the symptoms of allergy — my face and body puffed out. I was half-sick all the time.

"I can remember hearing my daughter tell a visitor that her mommy had the flu, when, in reality, I was in bed with a box of candy under the covers."

Not all of us have gone this far. But most of us have had some of these symptoms of overeating, and we are certainly capable of them.

How much better it is to feel free of the compulsion to overeat. Within a few short days of starting on a moderate eating plan, we find ourselves with new spring in our step. We begin to take on more, and feel like doing it. There is a sense of bodily well-being. Of being whole.

Does your body feel well? Do you feel like you could tackle any physical task today and conquer it? If you are eating for health, your body will respond with health. It doesn't take long. The difference is just amazing. Most dieters report that by the third or fourth day they show a marked inner physical change.

How do you feel? If you are following a sensible nutritiously-balanced diet today, you will feel just great. And that's a guarantee.

Before you reach for that extra bite today, ask yourself:
Am I willing to do what is necessary to feel physically good? Does my body feel alive and responsive today?

According to Judeo-Christian tradition, the first man and woman on earth got into trouble because they indulged in forbidden food. Their descendents are still banished from Eden because of this dietary indiscretion.

But we can't blame our early ancestors too much. Overeating to store fat, whenever possible, was a basic survival mechanism. Two million years ago, early mankind spent most of its short, brutish lifetime hunting food in order to feed insatiable bodies.

Dr. Abraham Weinberg, a New York City psychiatrist, thinks the reason people store excess weight in the twentieth century is due to a folk memory of the days when we used our bodies (instead of our refrigerators) to store food. "Fat meant survival," Weinberg says, "and deep down we still remember."

Despite this cellular memory, other psychiatrists complain that mankind's predisposition to store fat, a predisposition that saved the species millions of years ago, could very well be our undoing today.

The fact is that most of us do not live in a feast-and-famine economy. Food is almost always readily available, so to store it in our bodies against the time of some dimly possible catastrophe is dangerous.

The problem of overeating today is that we store and store, but never use the stored energy. We have to diet off the fat in order to get rid of it. Our ancestors may have walked, fought and swung through the trees to stay slim, but most of us get little if any exercise unless we go out and deliberately seek it. Our ancestors would be amazed — not only to see us so fat but to see us using our bodies so little.

In order to survive as a species and as individuals, we must work to change our lifestyles. We no longer need to store food in the form of fat. We no longer need energy saving devices. We need energy expending ones.

Your ancestors did what they had to do to survive. You have to do what you have to do to survive. It's that simple.

Before you reach for that extra bite today, ask yourself:
Am I still storing fat like my Stone Age ancestors? Am I determined to survive today, eating nutritiously but sensibly?

Dieting is a lone venture. There is ultimately nothing that stands between dieters and the refrigerator except an enormous desire to lose weight and regain self-respect. Still, lone does not have to mean lonely.

There are a variety of diet groups to help you take off weight through the buddy system. You may want to consider joining, just for the ego support you'll get.

TOPS (Take Off Pounds Sensibly) is the oldest national diet group, organized in 1948 and still going strong with groups in almost every community. It's a folksy organization with lots of good cheer and singing, national conventions and awards that can keep you going.

Overeaters Anonymous was formed in 1960 and is a carbon-copy of Alcoholics Anonymous except that they substitute the word "overeating" for "drinking" in AA's famous Twelve Steps to Recovery. OA has a spiritual base and a system of sponsorship for new members which gives great strength when you need it most.

Weight Watchers is a more commercial organization for dieters but because it is, it has a great many helpful products to offer. Meetings are inspirational, the diet allows a compulsive overeater to satisfy the compulsion to eat with low calorie foods. The principles of behavior modification are used to help dieters reeducate their living habits.

In addition to these three nationwide (even international) organizations, every community has diet therapy, exercise and nutrition courses connected to the local school system or sponsored by the Y's.

If you feel that a group would give you the strength, hope, and guidance you need to change your eating habits and your life, why not visit each available diet group until you find one you feel is compatible with your personality.

Groups are not for everybody, but most dieters will find that it's better to share this part of their lives with others who are attempting to turn away from food-centered living.

Before you reach for that extra bite today, ask yourself:
Am I a lonely dieter? Have I really given diet groups a chance to help?

A tourist came upon an old man living in the desert next to an encampment of whirling dervishes. There was a deafening commotion which prompted the tourist to ask the old man: "What on earth do you do about those whirling dervishes?" The old man replied quietly, "I just let 'em whirl."

How many times have you been tempted to take responsibility for the actions of others? Sometimes we take on the problems and failures of our families, our friends and our coworkers until the burden is too great to bear. Have you ever overeaten because others didn't do as you thought they should? "If I were in their shoes, I would know how to do that, " you think to yourself. In a way this is a giant conceit. Far too often, when we spend too much time living through other people, we are avoiding our own problems.

Peace of mind comes only after we let go of any desire to "manage."

Recognize that the responsibility for change is only to yourself. If you do a good job of living *your* life, it will take all the effort and time you have.

The poet/philosopher Kahlil Gibran says, "Let there be spaces in your togetherness." Live with others but not so closely that you invade their space of responsibility. That does not mean you should ignore others. It means that you should *tend to your own house first.*

Nobody can stop worrying about everything, but if you constantly seek to replace worry with positive priorities, you will come to realize that other people's behavior is outside your "self."

Remember the old man's advice: "Let 'em whirl."

Before you reach for that extra bite today, ask yourself:
Do I get so involved in the affairs of others that there is no space left between us? Am I less interested in changing the actions of other people, and more concerned with changing my own in a positive way?

"You won't believe this," said the tearful newcomer to the diet group, "but I gained four pounds today.

"During the last year I've gained thirty-six and I dieted most of the year! I can't imagine what I would weigh if I hadn't.

"It seems food is the only source of enjoyment I have. But every day, with every pound gained, I'm more unhappy.

"And I'm scared, too. Where will it end? I consumed 20,000 calories one day — I counted them — and I still didn't quit. I just kept stuffing.

"There's nothing wrong with my glands. I just had a complete medical check-up. Now I have no excuses left.

"What can I do? There's no future for me."

The members of the group not only believed the young woman's story, but they, each in turn, got up and told similar ones. "I thought I was the only one who did such crazy things with food," the newcomer said after the meeting. "I see I'm not alone, and I believe if you can do it, so can I."

Don't be scared. If you overeat, sometimes to the point it frightens you, you are not alone. Most of us have been where you are.

Be thankful that you have heard the warning bell, that at last you have an overpowering urge to do something. Don't feel sorry for yourself. Try to see the thin person which is really you. Set your sights on becoming that person on the outside as well as on the inside.

Today you will be happy; you will enjoy life while eating moderately. Who needs 20,000 calories? Four football players! You need much more than calories can ever give you. You need to use your positive, creative intelligence to become the person you want to be. And there is only one way to become that person. Stick to your eating plan today and let it stick to you.

Before you reach for that extra bite today, ask yourself:
What is my true story? Have I heard the warning bell, the one that calls me from unhappiness to a new life?

If you've been fat (plump, overweight, heavy, chunky, whatever your word for it) for as long as you can remember, there may be a special reason you've had so much trouble with diets.

Research seems to indicate that there are some long-time overweights who developed more fat cells as a child than thin children. Unfortunately these fat cells have become a permanent part of the adult body. In addition to the added cell count, a metabolic change takes place which requires fewer calories to maintain a weight level than a slim person of comparable size.

All this can be downright depressing and frustrating. It hardly seems fair to be saddled with a problem you developed as a child, during a time when you may have been overfed. Is this just another rotten thing your parents did to you? Maybe not. This aspect of overweight, as with most others, has its positive side effects.

You can stop feeling guilty. True, because of your extra fat cells your thin friend may be able to eat more than you do and maintain a normal weight. Nevertheless you have got to look at your problem realistically. Sure you don't need to feel guilty, because fat cells are not your fault, but you *do* need to face the reality that you will have to learn to eat less. Excess fat cells may be indestructible, but bad eating habits aren't. You can absolutely destroy them by replacing them with a good eating plan based on positive principles of good nutrition. (Being fat may not be your fault, but getting thin is your responsibility.)

It will take time to alter food attitudes you've held all your life. But if you take it a day at a time, you'll defy those fat cells and be healthy and slim.

Before you reach for that extra bite today, ask yourself:
Am I blaming extra fat cells for my weight problem? Do I accept the idea that I can't get rid of them, but I can get thin?

Sid Caesar, the star of television's classic *Your Show of Shows*, works out first thing every morning and eats a high protein diet of his own devising that even includes soup for breakfast. "I go to a lot of parties," says the comic, "but I don't eat the rich food. I'd feel uncomfortably full." Caesar has lost fifty pounds (and that's no joke) and is thinner today than he was as a young movie star of the 1940's.

It's not very funny to be fat. It's not amusing to find life slipping by while you spend your days grappling with a weight problem.

What are you doing about your life today? Have you cultivated at least one friend who has a diet problem, someone with whom you can share your thoughts and feelings?

What do you do when you get a compulsive urge to overeat? You don't give in to its demand. Do anything to take your mind off your compulsive hunger, but do not yield. The first extra bite is often the beginning of a series of extra bites.

Are you letting your fantasies run away with you? If you have a picture in your mind of yourself enjoying a binge, erase it. This picture is a delusion. Your guilt will be almost immediate and it will follow you through your day.

The best antidote for the compulsion to overeat is the compulsion to be thin, to live in a healthful and happy body. It is absolutely true, as Sid Caesar says: if you overeat you will feel uncomfortable.

Aren't you sick and tired of the discomfort of overeating, of being fat, of constantly having to deal with your fatness?

Today, you will not yield to the impulse to overeat. Your mind will not delude you. Your body will feel comfortable the whole day. You and Sid Caesar will make quite a happy team.

Before you reach for that extra bite today, ask yourself:
Have I done everything I can to take my mind off the urge to overeat? Am I keeping my false fantasies under control?

There is a personal joy that comes to all of us overweights as we progress toward a beautiful body and mind. This joy is not something we can rush. We must learn to wait for it.

But there comes a day (perhaps today) when you say to your inner self: "I know you." There is joy in knowing that from the depths of uncontrollable eating, you can rise to such self-knowledge.

It hasn't always been easy. No one said it would be, and yet you secretly hoped it wouldn't be too hard. You were surprised when you stumbled and learned to pick yourself up and begin again.

You found friends who gave you extra help. And loved you. When you were afraid, somehow you found you had courage. When you felt guilty, you found forgiveness, too. When you felt self-pity, you also found perseverance.

As you progressed along the road to your happy destiny you dropped your alibis, and one by one lost your faults.

You learned to live in the Eternal Now called today. The futility of yesterday and tomorrow you recognized, as if seeing with new eyes.

You have a powerful dream that is coming true a piece at a time, a day at a time.

You no longer live in a vacuum with food. You have a relationship with life. You are not the same as you were yesterday. Today you are as much mind as body, and with more feeling.

Perhaps today is your day to comprehend the possibilities there are in being you. Joy.

Before you reach for that extra bite today, ask yourself:
Am I willing to wait for the joy I know will come? Have I got a powerful dream?

It's only good sense to keep those tempting delicacies out of your way whenever possible. You can't eat them if you don't have them.

That good advice works two ways. *Always have on hand the foods your eating plan calls for.* It's just as true that if you don't have them in the house, you won't eat properly either. You usually just grab something else which isn't on your diet. The excuse that you don't have the proper foods available is just that, an excuse. Buying the right foods and stocking them in your home should be high on your list of priorities.

Not keeping the proper foods on hand is, in a way, a form of cheating. Don't kid yourself that you are saving money. When did we overweights ever save money on food?

Do you have a mental image of your thin self? "I think of myself wearing white pants and having almost no hips," said one woman dieter, "I would never dare wear white until I lose weight."

What is your thin mental image? Can you see yourself thin? What are you doing that you can't do now because of your weight? Maybe you want to learn new dance steps. Imagine yourself thin and dancing beautifully. Perhaps you want to take up sky diving, horseback riding or gardening. Whatever it is that fat is keeping you from doing, imagine yourself thin and doing it.

Your mind, not your mouth, does most of your overeating, so reprogram your mind to eat for a slender person. While you are busy doing this, be sure you keep a supply on hand of the foods your eating plan calls for.

Today you may be hungry, but you will be able to control what you eat or do not eat. Your desire for a healthy, thin body is becoming stronger. You are aware of what you eat and buy it in advance. But, happily, you don't think about food as much as you used to. Isn't that a great feeling?

Before you reach for that extra bite today, ask yourself:
Have I stocked the proper foods for my eating plan? Do I have a mental image of myself as thin and doing something I really want to do?

Dr. Jean Mayer, the famous nutritionist, says overweight men are apt to be "fat blind." He thinks more men than women have weight problems because they can get away with being fatter in our culture.

It takes a twenty-five pound gain to cause a change in pants size for men. Mayer suggests this causes more complacency about the first few critical pounds.

Parents are more apt to think their daughters are too fat than their sons, even though they may both be the same percentage overweight. Somehow there is a sexual bias dictating that "bigness" (translate that into fat) is masculine.

There's nothing masculine about fat. It's just as deadly for the male of the species (and maybe more so, since fifty percent of all men die of cardiovascular diseases) as for the female.

The social burden is no less for a man. Too-fat males end up as water boys instead of making the team and they stand, embarrassed, in the endless stag lines at dances. Just like overweight girls, they are not as apt to be chosen for top colleges, and later, on the job, they are less likely to make it into top executive ranks.

Fat is not fun for anyone — male or female. It saps your energy, steals the joy from your youth, robs you of career choices and, finally, tarnishes your golden years with a variety of fat-related physical ailments.

Fat can also drain your psychic energy. It takes up your thinking and feeling time. It costs you money. It frustrates your sex life. It's a damned nuisance.

Make today the last fat day of the rest of your life. Sure you may still be physically overweight tomorrow, but if you begin a positive, creative mind change today, and couple that with a sensible eating plan, you're going to *feel* thinner. Put thin in your head and let it spread to the rest of your body.

Now get going, and good luck.

Before you reach for that extra bite today, ask yourself:
Have I taken off my fat blinders and seen myself as I really am? Am I tired of being fat?

Millions of people have lower back pains, particularly those of us who weigh more than we should. One of the major causes of backache, according to orthopedist Dr. Edwin Guise, is overweight. "Fat builds up in places like the abdomen and the buttocks," he says. "This causes a posture abnormality and an increase in the curvature of the lower back. Soon the muscles go soft and fail to support this weight, adding to the curvature of the lower back and the strain."

Dr. Guise says the simple cure for most bad backs is weight loss and exercise. Where have we heard that one before?

Are you still resisting getting the proper exercise for your weight and physical condition? If so, perhaps you need to add a little spice to your exercise regimen. (After all, we overweights have spicy appetites.)

Sometimes fitness advocates play favorites. One will tell us tennis is the answer to all our problems. Another will swear by jogging. Still others will extoll the positive virtues of bicycling, walking, bowling, or croquet. See, the same old all-or-nothing attitude. No spice at all.

So here's what you could do: everything. That's right. Open your mind to every sport or exercise that catches your fancy. *Versatility is the spice of exercise.* Don't try to concentrate on one sport alone — you'll never make the Olympics, anyway.

Branch out. Try as many exercises as you can while you enjoy yourself. Before long your bad back (and the rest of your body, too) will be in pretty good shape.

Paint this picture on the palette of your mind. You are exercising and having fun. You back feels great. Your muscles are getting stronger and stronger while you are getting thinner and thinner. Wow! What a picture.

Before you reach for that extra bite today, ask yourself:
Is my weight putting a strain on my back? Have I put a little spice in my exercising today?

One of the most amazing diet stories is that of former circus fat lady, Dolly Dimples. After miraculously surviving a heart attack in 1950, Dolly (really Celesta Geyer) dieted off 430 pounds. It was literally "diet or die" in her case.

"I guess I was lucky," says Dolly about her heart attack, "because it changed my whole life. I never dieted with a gimmick; instead, I patterned a new way of life, carefully eating the proper foods in the proper balance, and doing it with a will to live."

As with most very large weight losses, the story ends with the admonition, "if I did it, with my problem, certainly you can do it with yours."

She's right, of course. Most of us, if faced with immediate death, would be able to diet off excess weight and keep it off. But most of us are not faced with our immediate demise, so we can postpone a diet without too much fear.

What we can't postpone is life. The reason for dieting off excess weight is not that we'll die if we don't, but that we won't live, really live.

Is your excess weight changing your life? Would you live in any other way than you do now, if you were slender? Of course you would. Fat is limiting. It limits your choices, forces you into negative behavior patterns, gives you a one-dimensional life. When food comes first, anything else — love, job, adventure — runs a poor second.

Dolly Dimples had a strong will to live. So do you. But you don't have to be threatened with death as she was. You are already threatened with half-a-life.

You can make your life whole, give it rich meaning and fill it with choice. Here's the first choice you can make: Today you're going to eat the proper foods in the proper balance and you're going to try to grow in at least one area of your mental life.

There's no stopping you now.

Before you reach for that extra bite today, ask yourself:
Am I ready to live, really live? Have I had enough of a life built around food?

So you've hit a weight plateau and you have a bad case of the diet blues. You begin to wonder if it's all worthwhile.

What can you do?

In the first place, be careful about writing diet scripts that may not play well. For example, you decide that by a specific date you will have lost so many pounds. Now, there's nothing wrong with goal-setting if the goal is realistic. But examine your goal to be sure it's possible and not just a future emotional booby trap you've set for yourself to trip over.

Here are some other antidotes for diet blues:

1. Carry around a picture of yourself taken when you were slim, or if you have never been slim, a picture of the way you think you'll look. (Some dieters search magazines and clip out photos of slender people that have their approximate features and coloration.)

2. Remember, don't weigh yourself every day. Dieters go through long periods when they seem to be losing weight very slowly. You'll eliminate some of the frustration if you stop hopping on the scale every five minutes.

Still need a lift?

3. You could try checking your measurements instead of your weight. Nobody seems to know why, but bodies that aren't showing a weight loss on the scale can actually show loss of inches on the tape measure. If you have been keeping a record of your measurements, you may find that your body has been busy reshaping itself even though you haven't lost weight. Sometimes just knowing that change is happening can help you get over the emotional trauma of a diet plateau.

If these tonics fail to make the doldrums bearable until the scale inevitably begins its downward march, there is only one thing you can do. For heaven's sake, don't eat. Go to an extra meeting of your diet group or see your doctor instead. The doctor will check to see if all your working parts are still in order, or if your diet plan needs a minor adjustment.

It's always only a matter of a short time until you begin losing weight again. How many times have you given up just short of your goal? Not this time. You can't be stopped now.

Before you reach for that extra bite today, ask yourself:
Am I going to beat the diet blues this time? Have I determined never to stop short of my diet goal again?

"I never eat a whole meal," a very overweight woman told her doctor. "I can't imagine how I gained so much weight. I want you to check my glands."

A complete physical showed no endocrine abnormalities. Was the woman lying? No. She was suffering the symptoms of a painful disease which primarily attacks housewives — snack sneaking. She ate a mouthful here, a bite there. While serving a meal to her family, she "tasted" all of it to make certain it was properly spiced and heated. She "didn't have time" to sit down and eat a full meal, so she grabbed and snatched food all day long, kidding herself all the time that she wasn't really eating very much at all.

The doctor told her to go home and, instead of eating her usual bite, taste, or piece of food, to put it in a container on her kitchen counter. "I could only do it for part of one day," the woman later admitted. "I was so shocked when I ended up with an enormous bowl of food. I had no idea I ate so much."

This dieter was not only surprised at how much she ate, but how often as well. Like other snack sneakers, she lost weight rapidly once she changed her eating pattern to three meals consumed at a table.

All of us overweights are great self-deceivers. We can cover up the worst eating habits by just *not paying attention.*

Pay attention today to what you are doing with food. Be honest with yourself. You can take control of your eating and the rest of your life today. It can be done. And you can do it!

Before you reach for that extra bite, ask yourself:
Am I sneaking a bite here and there without being aware of it? Have I decided to quit being a human garbage pail?

Excuse Number One: "I can't diet at work."

Excuse Number Two: "I can't diet if I stay home near the refrigerator all day."

Both of these excuses (actually two sides of the same coin) are the ones many overweights use. The truth is that you can integrate a weight-losing eating plan into any lifestyle, if that's what you want to do more than anything else in your life.

There are lots of studies around to show that overweight men and women in the business world are less likely to be successful than their trimmer counterparts. Unfair though it may be, our society puts so much emphasis on being trim that thin people are considered more intelligent, harder-working and more productive than fat people.

If you've ever been up for a promotion you know that an overweight has to continually prove worth, while a trimmer coworker will be granted the benefit of the doubt.

According to a survey by business writer John T. Molloy, here's how successful business people get thin and stay that way:

1. Most regularly choose low-calorie meals when eating out.

2. Almost half the sampling did not drink alcohol with meals.

3. Ninety-three percent weighed themselves regularly.

4. Many used part of their lunch time to exercise.

5. Business dieters used all the tricks of the diet trade — drank water or low-calorie soda before meals, and used slow-down behavior modification techniques.

So many of us overweights have made our eating plans a separate part of living. To be really successful, we must learn to integrate a way of eating to lose and maintain a normal weight into our total life style.

In the past, food has kept you in one place like a hermit. If you dieted, you could do nothing else. If you did anything else, you couldn't diet. That is "mind garbage" — negative thinking. Today you will turn a positive corner by taking some positive action.

You've got what it takes.

Before you reach for that extra bite today, ask yourself:
Have I made up my mind to lose weight no matter what else I may be doing in my life? Am I ready to join the ranks of successful men and women?

Gestalt psychologist David Katz has found that chickens given a larger pile of food will eat more. When a group of chickens was given 100 grams of grain, they ate half of it. When these same chickens were presented with a pile twice as large, containing 200 grams of grain, they still ate half the pile.

These studies suggest that appetite is in large part controlled by visual stimulation. That's why it's easy to overeat at buffets, picnics and at holiday time when large quantities of food are spread out on a table. Further proof that our eyes are responsible for our stomachs is the low incidence of overweight among blind people.

To further test these theories, overweight subjects in scientifically controlled experiments agreed to eat all their meals with their eyes closed. They reported later that they found eating to be far less exciting. They enjoyed their food less and quit eating sooner, because they couldn't see how much was left on their plate or table. *They considered the meal finished when their hunger was satisfied, whether or not the food was gone.*

Of course, nobody wants to serve or to eat unattractive meals, but it might be interesting to see how much visual stimulation has to do with your own eating behavior. It shouldn't be too difficult to test. Just close your eyes, or even blindfold yourself while you eat.

The important point is to avoid piling your plate or your table with more food than you want to eat for good health.

We human beings all too often find it difficult to believe what we read. We have to make the experiments ourselves. If you want to test your visual response to food, go ahead and be your own scientist. But be honest with yourself about your findings. You know there's more to life than a feast at every meal.

Before you reach for that extra bite today, ask yourself:
Am I able to stop eating when my hunger has been satisfied, whether or not all the food is gone? Do I gladly accept my food limits in exchange for a happier new life?

Did you know that exercising tones up the brain? Famed heart specialist Dr. Paul Dudley White told his patients: "The better the legs, the clearer the brain."

Studies have shown that almost anyone who takes up a sound exercise program will experience in some measure one or more of the following benefits:

1. more positive work attitude
2. improved work performance
3. less strain and tension
4. greater stamina, strength, endurance and coordination
5. increased joint flexibility
6. reduction of chronic fatigue
7. an improved and more efficient circulatory system.

Overweight and underactive in today's society seem to go hand in hand. Our immediate ancestors walked and worked from sun up to sun down. They didn't have to worry about proper exercise. It was built in to their daily lives.

That's not true today. Whether you're an executive, a housewife, or an astronaut you're a great deal smarter if you exercise. Your goal should be twofold: to improve the condition of your body's vital organs and limbs and to build up the efficiency of your heart and lungs. This will add to your muscular strength and endurance, your balance, flexibility and agility.

You need to help your body so your body will help you. If you feel physically bad, it's going to be that much harder to build a new more positive lifestyle, one that does not depend on extra quantities of food to get you through the day. But if you feel physically good, you are going to know more about the joys of a body that functions the way you want it to. You are a physical creature, not a blob.

Whatever method of exercise you choose, don't delay the good body experience. Start exercising today and you will have a long series of happier and healthier tomorrows.

Before you reach for that extra bite today, ask yourself:
Am I clearing my brain with exercise? Have I built a program into my day for my physical self?

Every man, woman and child in the United States eats an average of one teaspoon of sugar per minute, mostly in the form of snacks. Are sugar-loaded foods just good sources of quick energy? No, say an increasing number of health specialists. Sugar is public nutrition enemy number one.

Refined sugar is suspected of contributing to everything from arthritis to impotence. Nutritionist Dr. Carleton Fredericks, the high priest of natural sweeteners, claims refined sugar is the cause of hypoglycemia, a disease which he thinks may afflict as many as twenty million Americans. (Hypoglycemia, or low blood sugar, can cause dizziness, irritability, anxiety, insomnia, depression, loss of sex drive and even nervous breakdowns.) It's not just the body that succumbs to sugar. For years, dentists have blamed sticky cereals, chewy candy and syrupy soft drinks as cavity-causing culprits.

Why, then, knowing what we know, do we continue to eat more and more white sugar each year? "Our tastes are conditioned from the day we're born," explains Dr. Eleanor Williams, nutrition professor at Buffalo State University. "Sugar is a hidden additive in baby food, vegetables, processed meats and bread and predisposes us to crave even more highly sweetened foods."

One of the best ways to determine whether your sweet tooth is being tweaked by hidden sugar additives is to read the labels on products you buy. If they have a high sugar content, you may want to think twice before buying them.

We overeaters have been told so many times that we have to *reeducate our eating habits* that many of us just tune out when we hear that phrase again. But in the case of the hidden additive, we would be wise to take a good look at what we are eating so that we don't trigger our craving for sugar unnecessarily.

Today you will feel your confidence grow, you will let go of anything which will limit living. Your life will be so sweet today, that no confection will be needed. Or wanted.

Before you reach for that extra bite today, ask yourself:
Am I watching the foods I eat for the hidden additive? Do I find that the less sugar I eat, the sweeter my life becomes?

A long, hot summer with vacations, children underfoot, and relatives dropping in for a week or so is enough to make any overeater think of heading for the cool comfort of an open refrigerator. But cool it! This summer will be different, starting today. No more stuffing yourself while watching the rest of the world spring to life and laughter. This summer you have the strength, hope and courage to stand in the sunshine, without a food crutch.

Describing the dark days of his out-of-control eating, one man in a TOPS (Take Off Pounds Sensibly) group said: "Summer was the worst season of all. I was always an observer of life, never a participant."

Whether you're near your natural weight or just beginning a weight-losing program, you can participate in living this summer to its fullest. So often, we overweights tell ourselves, "When I'm thin I'll go swimming" or "When I look fantastic, I'll buy new clothes." We make the simple pleasures and even necessities of life dependent on how much we weigh.

Get rid of this negative thinking. Thoroughly reject "postponing" as a way of life, and commit yourself to living each day as fully as you can — just the way today finds you.

Remember your value as a human being is not measured by how tall you are, how rich, or *how much you weigh.* You are as worthy as the next person on the beach. You deserve those new clothes. You have a right to the most exciting summer you can imagine.

Go ahead. Join the world.

Before you reach for that extra bite today, ask yourself:
Have I stopped postponing the simple pleasures of living?
Have I decided to become a participant of life?

If you were raised to think that the world was a pretty good place and that most people would play fair, then you have been preconditioned to positive thinking. But if you were brought up to believe that the world was unfair and most people unkind, then you have a very negative outlook on life. This outlook has probably meant you have developed a good deal of self-pity, but worst of all, you have probably found the negative world you expected to find.

The first step to becoming a positive thinker is to get rid of all preconditioned negative thinking. When you were a child, you believed the concepts fed to you by adults. But you are no longer a child to be led like a sheep. If negative thinking is destroying your life, then begin to use your mind's potential to change things.

For example, you may have been told, "Oh, you're just a fat slob and there's nothing you can do about it." Or you may have been given an even more destructive message, "Because you're fat, the world owes you a living."

Either one of these, or other negative attitudes given to you by others, can cause you untold misery. Sadly enough, long after the old influences are gone, your preconditioned, negative thinking goes right on controlling your actions, so that every day the world becomes what you think.

Why not make an about-face today? Eliminate negative thinking. Think and act as if you can do the things you want to do. Nothing can hold you back if your mind is set on a positive, creative path. Get out of the old ruts and move onto the high road, the road that will carry you to a healthier, thinner and happier life.

There, that's more like it!

Before you reach for that extra bite today, ask yourself:
Have I reexamined old, negative concepts given to me as a child? Am I ready to do my own thinking?

"The devil made me do it," is a comic rejoinder some dieters use when they overeat. Don't you think it's about time that tricky old devil got a taste of his own medicine? O.K. Here are some ways you can trick *him*.

1. Buy the kinds of food in your supermarket that require preparation —such as unsliced bread and wedges of cheese. In other words, dispense with easy-to-eat foods.

2. Try to organize yourself so that you do all your grocery shopping in one trip each week. If you plan carefully, there should be no need to keep going back every other day. (If some items won't keep for a week, send someone else back to the store to buy them.)

3. Don't store your food so that there is a tempting array of leftovers and potential snacks every time you open your refrigerator or kitchen cupboard. Pack them in nontransparent plastic containers or wrap them in aluminum foil. The point is to build in a delay between wanting and actually getting food.

These are just three ways you can trick the ol' devil. You can probably come up with your own tricks. Just make it as hard as you can for the old boy. *Success is defeating the "food devil" and becoming boss.*

Have faith in your ability to think. You can think through your weight problem in a rational, nonemotional way and come up with solutions that work. Get your mind working for you. You have all the answers necessary to help you lose weight and lead a new life without being deviled constantly by a desire for more food than your body can handle.

You are mentally stronger than you think. Use your strength to change your life.

Ask yourself, "What kind of life do I want for myself?" Then start living it today. Nobody, not even the devil, can stop you once you really get going.

Before you reach for that extra bite today, ask yourself:
Am I willing to use every trick in the book? Have I gone to work for myself so that I can change my life?

Have you ever wondered how your emotional attitudes affected your eating habits? Many of us overweights have been aware that there was an umbilical cord stretched between our emotions and our stomachs. Researchers are now busy proving our suspicions were right.

Dr. Robert Plutchik, at the Albert Einstein College of Medicine, found that there are consistent patterns in people who are overweight. They are generally aware that they eat excessive amounts of rich and starchy foods. They also acknowledge that they eat more when they are depressed and nervous.

Particularly evident was the relationship between overeating and emotional difficulties in three areas: depression, anxiety and impulsiveness. Frequently, these overweight research subjects would report that they had trouble controlling quantity, and that they found themselves nibbling all day.

Another point of interest in Dr. Plutchik's research is that he noted a direct relationship between an individual's degree of being overweight and the number of overweight relatives in the family.

The results of the research suggest the following actions you can take.

1. If you tend toward overweight you should watch the amounts and kinds of food you eat, changing to less starch and snack foods. (Heard that one before?)

2. Try to identify what's behind your depression or anxiety and deal with these problems more effectively by other means than eating.

3. Try to minimize the opportunities you have to eat impulsively, primarily by keeping busy in some challenging activity.

4. Recognize the influence of any relatives who may serve as a model for eating habits. You can't change genetic tendency, but you can try to reduce the influence of overeating relatives.

You can change your life. Cut out new patterns for yourself to use. Refuse to be trapped in the old ways of responding. Find other means of expression — don't let food do your thinking, feeling and acting for you.

There's no time like the present. Start today.

Before you reach for that extra bite today, ask yourself:
Am I ready to cut the umbilical between my emotions and my stomach? Have I decided to change the old negative patterns of responding to positive, new ones?

The famous English poet, Lord Byron, wrote in his poem *Don Juan,* "I hate a dumpy woman." And yet, paradoxically, Byron, himself, the romantic ideal of his time, once had a fifty pound weight problem. He tackled dieting with his customary intensity. "I wear seven waistcoats and a great coat," he wrote a friend, "run and play cricket in this dress till quite exhausted by excessive perspiration, eat only a quarter of a pound of butcher's meat in twenty-four hours, no supper or breakfast, drink no malt liquor but a little wine..."

Although no overweight today would want to follow Byron's personal slim-down-program, some of us share his anti-fat attitudes. Many diet group members have been heard to say that they don't like other overweights. "When I associate with another fat person, it's as if I'm admitting that I'm fat," said one. "Other fat people remind me of how I must look," said another, "and I hate the look of fat."

Because overweight has been considered weak, immoral and ugly, many overweight people, like Lord Byron, do not like their own kind. It is, in a sad way, a method of rejecting ourselves — certainly of rejecting the reflection of a hated image. Even chubby five-year olds, when shown silhouettes of fat, medium-build and slender children, chose the slender ones as the shape they liked best.

Stop hating yourself for the shape of your body and begin changing your life (and your shape) in a positive way today. Love yourself for all the creative things you can do.

There's an old cliche which goes: Every fat person has a thin person inside, screaming to get out. That's not true.

You are a thin person, with a fat person outside screaming to get off.

That's a basic difference in thinking. You are already thin within. You just have to peel back the layers of destructive fat to get to the real you.

Think well of yourself and your fellow sufferers. Help yourself today, and help them, too. You can do it — sure you can.

Before you reach for that extra bite today, ask yourself:
Do I love myself? Am I willing to change my life so I can change my reflection?

"I decided to forget about my diet during my vacation," said a dieter, retelling a too-familiar story. "I ate my way clear across the country and had to buy a new dress, in a bigger size, to wear home."

You can't take a vacation from a normal, healthful way of eating, because your craving for excess food never goes on vacation. Do you leave your extra pounds at home? Of course not. Well, then, you can't leave your eating plan at home either.

A vacation is a time to get away from your surroundings, your job or school. It's a time to relax and recharge your coping batteries. You may be planning to go to the most exotic place in the world, but there is no magic which will allow you to stuff yourself without gaining weight.

You must try to let go of the idea that the only fun in living comes from eating. The same is true of vacations. You can have more real fun sticking to your good-living diet than by eating any amount of rich, high-calorie treats. "Having to buy new clothes just so I could get home ruined my vacation," remembered the dieter. "When I think about it, I only remember how angry I was with myself."

Some vacation! Overeating, humiliation, self-castigation — sounds like a depressing itinerary.

The great and wonderful things you desire for yourself will not come easy. Sometimes, for example, when you are on a vacation you will be tempted to return to your old destructive urges. Don't do it. You will have a vacation to remember, all right, but it will not be a happy memory.

Each day, wherever you may be, you are practicing the principles of positive living. No matter how far from home you are, your urge to live without excess food is growing stronger. Look out, world, here you come!

Before you reach for that extra bite today, ask yourself:
Am I packing my new way of life right along with other vacation essentials? Have I integrated good eating practices until they are a normal part of my lifestyle?

A popular poem, *Desiderata*, suggests that negative people are vexations to the spirit. You know the type. How many times have you had this scene repeated? You are feeling enthusiastic and positive, when a Gloomy Gus says, "What! You're on another diet? This must make the hundredth one this year." What happens? Your high, good spirits plummet to the dust.

You don't need negative people. You are, in every sense of the word, fighting for your life. Being around negative others is like taking an enemy with you into battle.

And that goes for your negative self, too. Try to look on the positive side of every situation yourself. Remember the worthwhile goal you seek of lifetime good health and slimness. Remember the new image that will stare contentedly back at you from your mirror.

Do not be afraid to make mistakes or to have temporary setbacks. They're not negative. This is part of the process of growth. Trial and error are major components of everyday living.

When you make a mistake, forget it. When you win a victory, no matter how small, remember it, so that you can go on to imitate it over and over again.

Learn to trust your creative mind, and to respond to it positively. Never have you reached for a compulsive bite of food that your mind hasn't issued an immediate danger warning. Learn to listen and to trust.

Relax while you learn to live without excess food. Practice relaxing (or meditating) every day as often as you can. These sessions, no matter how brief, will give you a little positive jolt when you need one most.

Negative people are a great energy drain. That is why you should concentrate on positive thoughts, positive actions and positive people. You're going to need all your energy to live thin in a thin world. Peace.

Before you reach for that extra bite today, ask yourself:
Am I allowing negative people to exert too much influence on my life? Have I learned to imitate my own victories over and over?

"I don't understand why I eat so much," the newcomer confessed to the diet therapy group. "I'm almost constantly miserable.

"I've tried to join other diet groups, but after a while, I can't stay with it. I never seem to get along with the people.

"My doctor says my problems are all in my head. And he may be right. The more I eat, the angrier I get with myself, until lately, I'm always in a bad mood."

There are overeaters who have such serious emotional problems they need professional psychiatric help to find out what is at the root of their compulsive eating. Many of us are obviously trying to deal with problems of frustration and anger by constant nibbling on the wrong kinds of food.

Sometimes we invent reasons for not stopping, such as not being able to get along with others at a weight-reducing group. But that needn't be. There is such a variety of groups and the people in them are so diverse that anyone seriously interested could find someone with whom to identify.

Compulsive eaters are essentially lonely people. Dr. Joyce Brothers, the psychologist, suggests that we may eat to gratify a need for contact which we won't allow ourselves. We find it difficult to relate to people, because we're afraid of being hurt. Overweights, for good reason, don't see people as particularly friendly.

If you are stuck in the unhappy cycle of eating and hurting and eating some more, you must begin to deal with your feelings of anxiety on a less hand-to-mouth level.

Allow yourself to seek strength from within, from a psychologist, or through a group of other dieters. You'll find more strength than you knew existed. You just have to try. No matter how many times you've tried before, you must try again. There, that's better.

Before you reach for that extra bite today, ask yourself:
Do I know what's really eating me? Have I given myself, my psychologist, or my diet group a real chance?

It seems that as the twentieth century progresses the world moves at an ever-faster pace. All too often, we get caught up in speeding from one activity to another and forget to take time to really live. Here are a few things you can do today to slow the pace of your life so that you will have time "to smell the roses."

Take time to eat so that your food will be truly satisfying.

Take time to read something inspirational about a personal problem you may have yet to conquer.

Take time to help an overweight friend, who may not have the strength you have today.

Take time to do some unselfish service for others that will not be discovered.

Take time to meditate so that you will have a source of hope throughout the day.

Take time to appreciate your good qualities and to reward yourself positively.

Take time to have fun. It doesn't have to cost you money.

Take time to say thank you to someone who has truly helped you in the past.

Take time to remember your successes and to be ready to repeat them.

Take time to give thanks for the great good fortune that put you on the path to health.

You will have to slow down your life just like you must slow down your knife and fork. You won't miss much if you do, but you are guaranteed of missing out on a great deal of living if you rush through today.

Isn't this nicer?

Before you reach for that extra bite today, ask yourself:
Have I taken time to "smell the roses"? Have I taken time to really live today?

Successful people have a variety of psych-up techniques. Pitcher Mark Fydrich speaks to the ball before he pitches. Television correspondent Leslie Stahl says she puts a wall around herself to shut out pandemonium on the set. Right before she goes on, she takes deep breaths to calm down. Herbert R. Sand, a toy company executive, says he focuses only on the job when he gets up in the morning, blocking out all other thoughts.

A certain amount of stress is actually good for you. Dr. Tobias Brocher at the Menninger Foundation says people sometimes worry too much about life's stresses. "It's a question of the amount," he says. "Everybody has to find his own balance between the rat race and boredom."

We overweights live in a world of almost unlimited stimuli. When we get out of bed in the morning, we face a day which will include food stimulation of our every sense. Let's be ready for it.

What is required is total concentration. Spend the first few minutes of every day thinking intensely about your schedule — the people you will meet, the stress situations you will face which might tempt you to overeat. Work out a few techniques in advance which will help you cope with potential problems.

Later, at the end of your day, psych down. Review your activities and see how you might better handle the same problem situations when they come up again. Let go of any inner stress.

If all this sounds like the Scout motto "Be Prepared," you're right. You are taking simple precautions and at the same time you are learning to recognize and work with your deepest feelings. You are actually walking hand in hand with your emotions, instead of being led by them. That's true balance.

Now you've got the idea!

Before you reach for that extra bite today, ask yourself:
Did I psych up for today? Am I prepared to spend a few minutes concentrating each morning so that I can face food temptations?

More than anything, overweight people value freedom of choice. We feel we should have the right to determine our future just like thin people do. Perhaps no one values freedom of choice more than we overweights — *because we have so little of it.*

Every time we give in to the compulsive urge to overeat, we lose a little of our freedom of choice. If we give in often enough, the time comes when we no longer have any freedom at all. Many centuries ago a philosopher said, "Don't do as you want, then you may do as you like."

It is frightening to think that we could continue indulging ourselves to the point where we lose all our freedom. And yet, we know people become so fat they lose their freedom to walk, to love, to work and, eventually, to live.

If you are gradually losing your freedom of choice because of the urge to overeat, you must get to work to regain the freedom to live as you like. You may have thought in the past that true freedom was being able to eat anything, anywhere, anytime, in any quantity. Now you know it is not. You have been exercising such "freedom," and you have ended up chained to food. Look what you have given up, to keep on eating what you want.

Sure, it's hard to deny yourself. You feel deprived if you have to say no to dessert or an extra cocktail. But when you've learned to say no to others (and most especially to yourself), you are on your way to regaining your real freedom.

Are you a slave to food? Does your mind tell you that you can't escape? Don't believe it. You can. You can help yourself and you can get a great deal of help from others — doctors, diet groups, psychologists, friends — and on and on. Just make up your mind that you want your freedom back and you want it back today.

Now, get going!

Before you reach for that extra bite today, ask yourself:
Am I unwilling to give up my freedom for a momentary pleasure? Have I decided to get the help I need and to get it today?

Certain attitudes are vital factors in continued and contented dieting. They seem to separate "the men from the boys," the successes from the drop-outs. See how many of these seven success attitudes you can actively use in your life today.

1. *Honesty* — Today you will be free of self-deception and sneak-eating.

2. *Willingness* — Today you will be willing to admit a mistake, take firm steps to correct a diet error and to deal fairly with yourself.

3. *Courage* — Today you will deal with the problems and realities of life without relying on an extra snack to "pull you through"; you will have determination to stick-to-it no matter how angrily your body cries out for more food.

4. *Appreciation* — Today you will appreciate your healthy mental attitude, the one that urges you to change your life.

5. *Openmindedness* — Today you will be open to all suggestions which will help you live without excess food and build a positive and creative new lifestyle.

6. *Humility* — Today you will be willing to face facts, to recognize that you have lost control of your eating and that you are not too arrogant to accept help from every helpful source.

7. *Service* — Today you will express your gratitude for the help you have received by passing it on to other dieters whenever you possibly can without hurting them.

When you take a good, close look at this checklist, there are not many time or money consuming demands on it. They benefit you far more than they benefit others. You haven't much to lose by giving them a try, and a lot to gain. And by gaining in positive attitudes, you'll lose weight. Are you ready to give it a try? Go to it!

Before you reach for that extra bite today, ask yourself:
Have I given the seven success attitudes an honest try? Are the risks of overweight so great that I am willing to try anything?

Anger is one of the most destructive emotions. But for overweights it can be an absolute killer. Nothing can make us hungrier than anger, unless it is the even more hunger-inducing *righteous anger*. Both kinds can make us fat.

If you're angry, settle it as soon as you can — certainly before you get around to eating over it. If you don't, it can become a destructive force and take on an energy all its own. It's dynamite!

Why don't you do as members of Alcoholics Anonymous do and make up a grudge list. See, on paper, who it is that you hate. Decide why it is that you hold them within this circle of resentment. Ask yourself: Has my life become better for this anger? Were they the only offenders?

The point for alcoholics (and for us) is that we refuse to grow to the extent we hang on to anger. But, you may ask, what about a case where you were definitely in the right and were the injured party? Somehow it doesn't seem to matter if your anger is righteous. Alcoholics have found that they can get just as drunk over righteous anger as any other kind. They say it's best to let go of all anger as quickly as possible. That sounds like good advice.

It is plain that a life holding deep anger or even several petty resentments is an unhappy futile life. And if you happen to also be an overeater, it can only mean that feeding this negative emotion will make you fatter and fatter and madder and madder.

Take a good look at your grudge list. Is there anyone or anything on it that is worth gaining weight over? Is there anyone on your list who would change if you got fatter? Of course, the answer to all these questions is a resounding NO.

Today, you will remember that anger is the most destructive thing you could do to yourself, and avoid it like the plague. You're much too busy for anger. You've got a beautiful life to live, weight to lose, and work to do.

Before you reach for that extra bite today, ask yourself:
Am I harboring an anger which is making me hungrier? Do I know that being right and angry will still make me fat?

Do you think that after a certain age you won't be able to lose weight? Not true. Take, for example, Kate Smith, the famous singer and television personality still going strong after fifty years in show business. She's seventy-five pounds lighter today than when she started her original radio program on May 1, 1931 — her twenty-third birthday.

What is Kate Smith's advice to dieters? "Be true to yourself," she says, "don't sneak to the refrigerator for a snack."

She adds that there are certain enjoyments inherent in eating whatever you want, that you must sacrifice to trim weight. "But," she says, "it'll be worth it."

Surely Kate Smith, who has already won the accolades of nations and the adoration of millions, wouldn't have much to gain in a material sense by losing weight. Her secret is evident. *She is being true to herself.*

You are, in every sense of the word, being *true* to your inner self when you make sensible eating a part of your master living plan.

Ask yourself these two questions: Do you think, in the innermost recesses of your mind, that you can lose your excess weight once and for all? Do you think you can turn your whole life around? Your answers must be YES.

Treat yourself to a new thought today, the thought that you can have the kind of life you yearn to live. If you hold this thought for just twenty-four hours you won't return to total negative thinking. As Oliver Wendell Holmes said: "Man's mind, stretched to a new idea, never goes back to its original dimensions."

You can expand your mind today so that it will hold all of your dreams. Just do it.

Before you reach for that extra bite today, ask yourself:
Am I being true to myself? Do I have firmly in mind the thought of a new kind of life, one without excess food?

So you've been losing weight, reordering your priorities and, in general, setting your life straight. Marvelous! Enjoy living today and every day, but be alert to negative thinking which can come creeping into your mind when you least expect it.

You'll want to keep the freedom you've gained. In order to stay free of the compulsion to overeat, watch for these danger signs along the road.

1. *Watch out* when you begin to think that no matter what you eat you'll never get fat again.

2. *Watch out* when complacency lowers your guard and allows anger and resentment to make a new appearance.

3. *Watch out* when you find yourself being dishonest about your diet with your friends, your doctor or yourself.

4. *Watch out* when you become cocky about weight loss.

5. *Watch out* when you drop out of your diet group because you don't need them anymore.

6. *Watch out* when you demand praise for losing weight.

7. *Watch out* when you become bored with your eating plan and decide to spice it up a bit.

8. *Watch out* when you again attempt to solve problems with a "little something."

If you come upon any of these danger signs in your path, reactivate your memory. Remember what it was like before you found a way of eating to live a more healthful, happy life. Remember what it was like to go from dark day to dark day without hope or help.

No matter what path you travel, danger signs are not meant to make you get off the road entirely, but simply to warn you of bumps ahead. You can then make a choice to go around them, or go straight ahead but with much more caution.

The life you are building is worth protecting. Take it easy. Study the map you've drawn for yourself to make sure you're still on course. You'll make the trip all right. Hang on. Nothing can stop you now.

Before you reach for that extra bite today, ask yourself:
Am I watching for any danger signs in my thinking? Have I charted a course which will take me to a new life?

Sometimes we overweights have found that our emotions can rule us. That is why it is so necessary to find a way to use them constructively instead of destructively.

Experience shows us that feelings of hate, criticism, resentment, jealousy and self-pity have not helped us become the thinner, totally healthful people we'd like to become. We have used the enormous energy in our emotions to negative ends, especially at the table.

And yet, none of us can do without emotions. Without them we would be bedridden blobs, unable to carry on the smallest task of living.

Harness your emotional energy. Use it, instead of allowing it to use you. How? Love is human energy in its most positive form. Today, instead of allowing your negative emotions to hold you in an enervating grip, try to use your positive emotional energy. Love yourself and others. Love life enough to give it to yourself, now and in the future.

With the positive energy forces of love you will begin to make right decisions about how to proceed with living. The negative force of hate, criticism, resentment, jealousy and self-pity kept you on a collision course with disaster. Guided by these destructive forces you made very bad diet decisions, indeed.

You are the one who must activate your own positive energy force. No one, no matter how much they may want to, can do this for you. But once you have decided to use love, the positive emotion, in your life, you will find that you have a great deal of help from a dozen different quarters. The love of living is the most attractive force in the universe.

Today there is a miracle waiting to happen to you, if you will let it. Get rid of all the negative emotional forces that are draining your energy, the energy you need to find a sanctuary from the pain of being fat and unhappy. Allow the positive energy of love to open your mind and heart to real living.

Now you've got the idea!

Before you reach for that extra bite today, ask yourself:
Am I allowing negative forces to rule my life? Have I become willing to turn on the positive energy of love full force?

The international diet group, Overeaters Anonymous, lists some interesting personality traits which they have found to be present in overeaters to some degree. How many of these are yours?

1. *Low frustration tolerance* — This is an inability to endure for any length of time an uncomfortable circumstance or feeling. The most common trait of all seems to be impatience.

2. *Anxiety* — This trait is exaggerated in compulsive eaters and drives them to escape into food. Most of the time, overeaters don't know what they are anxious about.

3. *Grandiosity* — The big "I" is usually a cover-up for low self-esteem.

4. *Wishful thinking* — This is the art of arranging to eat what we want to eat, then making it appear logical. Rationalization and half-truths are the glue that keeps this behavior from falling apart.

5. *Isolation* — Overeaters are insecure loners.

6. *Sensitivity* — Sometimes we interpret "not being asked to the party" as meaning "Everybody hates me." We dwell (and swell) on these snubs until they grow into permanent hates.

7. *Impulsiveness* — The overeater is intense to the point of emotional exhaustion. Long-term jobs are not our cup of tea. We prefer a burst of effort which quickly dissipates when the fun is gone.

8. *Defiance* — Many overweight people tend to reject society before society rejects them.

9. *Dependence* — Beyond the obvious food dependency, overeaters usually are emotionally dependent on others.

Not all of these personality traits may contribute to making you overeat. But if you have problems with any of them, it would be wise to do something about these characteristics.

Of course, you can't change overnight. But just following a healthful eating plan and living a growth-centered life will help reduce the effect of these personality traits a little each day. This will bring you great peace of mind, which will make it easier for you to follow a healthful eating plan in the first place. Now that's the kind of cycle you'll love being caught in.

Before you reach for that extra bite today, ask yourself:
Have I assessed my personality to see how many negative traits I have? Am I ready to get on a positive path?

Stan was born with a spoon (and a knife and fork) in his mouth. By the time he was nine years old he weighed 200 pounds; 300 pounds by the time he was sixteen, and so on up the scales until at thirty-two he weighed 520 pounds. He had to weigh on a meat scale, and search all over town for size seventy-four pants.

"When I was a kid," Stan says at his Weight Watchers class, "other kids in my New York neighborhood followed me down the street calling me fat in three different languages. And even though I could hit a baseball nine miles, they'd never let me on the team because I was always out at first base."

Stan never dated, couldn't go to the movies because the seats weren't wide enough and soon was only able to sit, talk and eat. He cried in his sleep. Finally, after trying every diet known to man, he joined Weight Watchers and lost 328 pounds which, for a dieter, is something like hitting the winning home run in the World Series.

Today Stan is playing in a whole new ball game. The old one was, he says, "called on account of pain."

Do you know how it feels to buy a huge size of clothing without a choice of colors and styles? Do you know what it's like to be refused service in a restaurant because you're too fat for the chairs?

Whether your weight problem has ever been the size of Stan's or not, you know something about the pain he suffered. You share it. Every day.

A life that has control is *order versus disorder.* Everything makes sense when you are eating sensibly. Do you want to turn your life around, lose your weight and live with dignity? Do you really want it?

To truly achieve the potential within your grasp, set a goal and make a resolution today. You have the intelligence; you have the enthusiasm; you have the commitment. Now you will have the results as well.

There are many good diets and many good diet programs around for you to choose from. Choose one. Today.

Before you reach for that extra bite today, ask yourself:
Do I remember the pain I caused myself with overeating?
Have I decided to make a good choice for myself today?

There's not a dieter alive who doesn't ask, "How long will it take me to lose the weight?" It's a natural question. We wouldn't be trying to lose weight if we weren't anxious to start a new life in a new body.

What so many of us tend to forget is that a "diet," in the sense that we overweights use the term, is not a plan of eating for a few days, weeks or even months. The word diet comes from the Latin *diaeta* and the Greek *diaita*, both meaning "way of life." And that is exactly the interpretation most of us overweight people must put on the word — we are entering into a new way of life which must last us all of life.

Now about the question of how many pounds you'll lose. Since each person's body reacts individually, we all lose at our own rate of speed. It stands to reason that if you're very much overweight, your initial loss is likely to be greater. It's not unusual for a 250-pounder to lose nine or ten pounds the first week of moderate eating. The important thing for you to remember is not to watch other people's weight loss. Watch your own. You'll soon see that there are patterns to your loss. For example, you may lose very little one week and much more another, even though you're eating the same foods. Check to see if you were exercising more the week you lost more, or weren't taking some fluid-retaining medication the week you lost less.

Before you've gone too far, you'll develop an intuition about the rhythms of your body so that you can almost tell before you get on the scales how much you've lost.

But while all of this is interesting and the excitement can keep you going through a crucial period in your new regimen, what's really important is reaching your weight goal — and staying there — not how long it takes.

Remember the old saying: It Takes As Long As It Takes.

Before you reach for that extra bite today, ask yourself:
Am I discouraged because I'm not willing to give it as long as it will take? Have I developed a sense of my body rhythms so that I can tell when my body is changing?

If you've been in the overeating habit for some time, you may need to go through a period of reeducation. Here are some get-smart tips which will help you lose weight and, best of all, keep it off.

1. Reeducate your eyes by measuring your food. Get to learn what a proper portion looks like so that you can train your brain not to overeat.

2. Never skip a meal. It's not the way to lose weight faster. Chances are you'll just get so hungry you will eat twice as much at the next meal.

3. If you feel like having a snack and you can't talk yourself out of it, get a kitchen timer, set it for ten minutes and relax. Lie down or do some simple meditation exercises. When the timer goes off, you may realize you are not that hungry after all.

4. Learn to ask yourself "how" questions instead of "why" questions. For example, don't say, "Why can't I ever stay on a diet?" Ask yourself, "How can I stay with my weight losing plan?"

5. If you start to slip off your diet by eating a slice of high-calorie cake, don't allow yourself to fall down completely by eating the whole cake.

6. Plan for success. Be on the lookout for new tips and ideas that might work to help you lose weight.

7. Try to lead a less food-oriented life. Do everything possible to divert your attention from food and the so-called pleasures of eating.

The point is that you must be ready, even eager, for change. Your old ways of doing things haven't worked very well. Look for creative new ways. There's no better time to start looking — start today.

Before you reach for that extra bite today, ask yourself:
Is my mind wide open to new diet techniques? Am I always looking for creative new ways to live my life?

There are three major effects of weight loss which every dieter hopes to experience. Did you know you could look forward to changing physically, mentally and cosmetically? Here is what these changes will mean to you.

Physically, statistics show that weight loss extends life and makes a great deal of difference in the state of your health during your entire life span. Freeing your body from its prison of flesh can make you feel physically alive for the first time in years. Some dieters describe a sense of "free-floating" which a large weight loss gives them.

Mentally, and emotionally, every study shows an improvement. What can compare to the feeling that you've achieved a fantastic goal you never thought you'd reach? You like what you see when you look in the mirror, and this makes you glow with self-esteem inside, too. Of course, just because you're thin doesn't mean you have no problems. But at least you don't have one *big* problem anymore.

Cosmetically, you will look absolutely sensational to yourself, your mate and your friends. Nothing can beat that top-of-the-world feeling when you walk out of the store wearing a new, smaller size. Dieters tell stories about the discovery of bones they didn't know they had — and of the pure joy of being in a body they can use to live fully.

Plato said that the first and best victory is to conquer self. What Plato didn't say was that it could also be very rewarding.

Today, give yourself a new chance to change physically, mentally and cosmetically. Take a little time to think through your day so that you can move in a positive direction. Wouldn't it be wonderful to be further along your way by the time this day is over? And you can do it, too — like no one else.

Before you reach for that extra bite today, ask yourself:
Do I yearn to get the three rewards of weight loss? Am I working today so that I will be further along the way to my goal weight by tonight?

June 22   More Aversion Therapy (But With a Twist)

Aversion therapy, a type of behavior modification technique, tries to make the overeater hate his or her favorite foods by showing pictures of them full of maggots and slimy worms — sometimes with the added help of a nausea inducer.

But the Center for Behavior Modification in Minneapolis has come up with an ingenious new twist on aversion therapy. Here's how it works. Each dieter makes a "contingency contract," and leaves a pad of checks for amounts ranging from fifty cents to $100 each made out to some cause. The twist is that the checks must be made out to a cause the dieter finds repugnant — the American Nazi Party, the Ku Klux Klan, the Democratic Party for Republicans or the Republican Party for Democrats. For every pound gained, out goes a check, but weight-losers get all the checks back at the end of the course.

Does this method work? It sure does. "It gets a person over the rough spots," explains Frank R. Quale, the system's inventor. "Anyone who has made a contract is not about to eat that chocolate cake if he thinks it will help the Nazis.

"This is one way to put the lid on overeating behavior," Quale adds. "While the lid is on, it gives people a chance to try out sensible eating programs."

You may not want to write checks to your most unfavorite cause, but you could work out a positive system of your own. Why not reward yourself for every lost pound by putting aside some money for a mini-vacation, a new item of clothing or just to do something nice for yourself?

It's not selfish to reward yourself for a good job. And every time you lose weight it means you've done just that — a darn good job.

Congratulations!

Before you reach for that extra bite today, ask yourself:
Do I recognize real growth in myself? Have I forgotten to reward myself for a job well done?

There is an old saying, "Eat like a king for breakfast, a prince for lunch and a pauper for dinner." This is not just a bit of folklore, but for some moderns, an essential key to dieting.

It has been found that Americans eat most of their food *after* 6:00 p.m., getting little or no exercise after the biggest meal of the day. The next morning it is very easy to go without breakfast, lunch is a normal-sized meal and dinner is again huge.

But what if you turn your eating upside down? If the most substantial meal is breakfast and you reduce your intake throughout the day, your good sense tells you that you will use up more food as energy and lose weight. And there's an added bonus. Studies have proved that dieters who reverse their eating habits (especially if their breakfast is full of protein) will have a better disposition, be less tired, be more productive and in better control of emotions as the day wears on.

One dieter reports after simply reversing the amount of her dinner and breakfast that she went from a size fourteen to a size nine and lost twenty-one pounds.

Of course, the benefits of losing weight are not just in looking better or even feeling better. You'll also be more active which will help you lose even more weight or stabilize the weight you've already lost.

If you have a large weight problem, you may have to take other measures as well. The point is to take a look, really take a look, at what you are eating, how much you are eating and when you are eating it.

An Arabian proverb says: He who has health has hope, and he who has hope has everything.

Today, you have everything.

Before you reach for that extra bite today, ask yourself:
Have I been eating most of my food after 6:00 p.m.? Do I see the hope everywhere in my life?

Living every day to its utmost means putting in everything you have. You can't get all until you give all.

Sometimes we hurry too much. We fail to stop and allow ourselves time to feed our inner needs. For only when we can pay attention to something we really love can we concentrate and find real answers.

Why do you want to lose weight? It's not hard to think of a dozen obvious reasons. There's another not so obvious. Peace. Some call it contentment, consciousness or God. With all the stuffing of food, overweight people have an emptiness, a strange blank spot food never fills.

When you undertake your quest for the priceless treasure of a healthy body, the search itself will give you a kernel of peace and contentment. Growing each day, the small seed will expand until you experience life more directly because you will be more aware of yourself.

You must have a sincere desire to experience your positive inner self more fully — your truth, love, joy, and beauty.

When you are drowning in repeated acts of overeating, you block deep positive experiences. You are only capable of feeling pain, suffering, disgust and tension. There is no way you can get to your creative inner self until you remove the stumbling block of food.

Today try to function on an inner level. When you feel positive, try to become as one with the feeling. Let go of the inhibiting blocks of fear, doubt, reservation, self-criticism. They only act as brakes.

Today you will establish a positive dialogue with life, and you will live beautifully.

Before you reach for that extra bite today, ask yourself:
Have I put everything I have into today? Have I thought to slow down and get in touch with my deep inner self?

Unpleasant emotions are commonly accompanied by tightness in the skeletal muscles and the muscles of the internal organs. Keep up this muscle-tensing long enough and you begin to hurt.

The stomach is one of the primary organs afflicted by negative emotions. You might even call it, with apologies to the heart, the most emotional organ you have.

When the stomach muscles tighten because of emotional upheaval, the feeling is that of a lump in the upper abdomen; some people describe it as a "stone." When the stomach muscles squeeze down really hard, a pain is produced, sometimes a very severe one, which can feel a lot like ulcer pain.

How is this pain translated by overeaters? "I'm hungry," they think. "I'd better eat a little something."

Instead of feeding an overemotional stomach, there are other more effective treatments you can use:

1. *Keep it short and simple.* This is called the KISS technique, and never fails to work. Overeaters have an uncommon ability to complicate their lives. If you find yourself taking on more than you can handle (since you're already concentrating on your eating plan), take a minute to remind yourself of the KISS principle.

2. *Avoid waiting for disaster.* Some overweights are so negative in their outlooks that they actually spend much of their time thinking something terrible is about to happen.

3. *Learn to like work.* If you like to work, and enjoy the simple pleasure of doing something well, you will not have so much time to spend churning up negative emotions.

4. *Make today an emotional success.* This day is the only pleasure you have. It's fine to anticipate pleasure, but today is a fine day for living. In fact, the future is absolutely dependent on how emotionally successful you are today.

Remember to dwell on the positive emotions you are certainly going to have. But if some small problem does arise, don't let it go straight to your stomach.

Before you reach for that extra bite today, ask yourself:
Am I overeating because I'm emotionally tense? Have I remembered to KISS?

Overweight people have been talked at, preached to, and yelled at so often that some of us have developed two deaf ears when it comes to our weight problem. You can bet that we want to do something about our eating all right, but we have forgotten how to listen. Studies have shown that the average person is only a half-listener and gets only half of what is heard right after hearing it.

One of the techniques proved effective in a classroom is to give the simple command "pay attention!" before teaching something important. Why not try it out on yourself? Before you visit your doctor or weight group you might find it helpful with your weight problem to tell yourself: "Pay attention!"

But good listening demands that you do more than just pay attention. You have to participate, too. *Actively listen.* Think to yourself how the information you are hearing can benefit you. Ask yourself if the facts are accurate, and if you could safely apply them. Try to involve yourself by being *interested.*

Good listeners learn to concentrate on the theme (the intent) of the message and not get sidetracked. The main question is: What am I hearing that I need to know?

You have to learn to fight distraction, too. Noise and your own desire to interrupt are two big distractors.

Being a good listener has another important effect on you and the person to whom you are listening. Intelligent listening on your part changes the way speakers relate to you, and even helps them give you more information. It stands to reason that a good listener will encourage talkers to be more outgoing.

Don't make up your mind in advance that you know it all or have heard it all before. That may even be true, but each time you hear a diet idea you hear it for the first time. You have become a different person since you heard it last. This time you may be able to put it together with another bit of diet information and make it *change your life.*

You wouldn't want to miss that chance, would you? Learn to listen.

Before you reach for that extra bite today, ask yourself:
Have I opened my mind and my ears to what people are trying to tell me? Have I tried to become an involved listener so that I get every bit of help I can?

Ask yourself: "Am I becoming easier to live with?" and "Do I care as much for the feelings of others as I do for my own?"

Most of us overweights have to admit that we are sometimes hard to live with. When we are eating compulsively, when all hope seems to be gone, we can feel so miserable that we are not very good companions.

Sometimes in our own deep hurt, we lash out and hurt others who are innocent.

But when we find a plan of eating we can live with, and begin to grow in a way excess food wouldn't allow, then we can become the vibrant, joyful people others seek to be with.

There are some dieters who use dieting as an excuse for self-pity — both their own and others. This attitude soon goes if they honestly yearn for diet success. Unless they change from self-pity to self-responsibility they soon return to unhappy eating habits.

If you are feeling good about yourself and your life today, let it show. Try to look as good as you can. Dress neatly and attractively. Speak in a low, well-modulated voice. Treat others with courtesy — especially members of your own family. Try not to criticize, improve or regulate the behavior of others. Today, you can spend the entire twenty-four hours criticizing, improving and regulating yourself. Now that's something you can really get your teeth into.

You are a considerate person. Today, you will be very easy to live with.

Before you reach for that extra bite today, ask yourself:
Am I careful of the feelings of others? Am I so busy with myself today that I don't have time to manage anyone else's life?

We've all come across a person we don't like in almost every activity of life. There's the office snitch, the neighborhood gossip and the family moocher, and some people who seem to have no outstanding faults, but still arouse our dislike.

Of course, one of the best ways to conquer our frustrations about other people is to be so goal-oriented, others don't seem to matter very much. It takes a certain amount of idle time to work yourself up into a really good snit. If you're too busy, you won't have that extra time.

But sometimes, nothing works. You're angry and frustrated and that's it.

Try writing your frustration away. If someone has angered you until you are tense and unhappy (and hungry), sit down and write a letter to that person. Tell him/her exactly what you think about his/her irritating habits. Really lay it on. Now, put it away for twenty-four hours.

The next day retrieve your letter and read it again with renewed satisfaction. You feel better, don't you? You're finished with this exercise. Right? Wrong. Now, sit down and write yourself a letter *from the other person.* Give a thorough explanation of the other person's frustrations. While wearing his/her shoes, write out the problems that have him/her baffled and furious.

Read both letters again. You don't have so much satisfaction in your first one, do you? Now, tear them both up and throw them in the wastebasket. Nobody's hurt, your frustration's gone, and you probably have a deeper insight into your own and the other person's feelings than you had before.

Spending a little time with pen and paper today can save a lot of frustration on your part — deadly frustration which adds unwanted, unhappy pounds on your body.

You could say that with this writing trick you come out a winner *without* getting your "pound of flesh."

Before you take that extra bite today, ask yourself :
Am I willing to do anything to overcome frustration? Would it help to put myself in the other person's place?

"There is no more miserable person," wrote William James, "than one in whom nothing is habitual but indecision, and for whom everything is the subject of deliberation."

Repetition, doing the same thing over and over again, can be a help to dieters. Some diet-group members report that to deemphasize food, they try to eat the same things every day. Such repetition appears to relieve them of their former preoccupation with food, its preparation and menu decisions.

Diet groups, especially Overeaters Anonymous, seem to have rituals that are repeated each meeting. Overeaters Anonymous is perhaps the most ritualistic of all the groups. They spend about one-third of their meeting time reading the same material aloud for emphasis. The structured time, far from being boring, seems to add to the group strength. An OA member from California can visit a group in New York and feel right at home.

Repetition, in a slightly altered form, can become discipline — the trait most overeaters can use in abundance.

Society today encourages us to reach for variety of experience, and that may be delightful advice for sometime in our future lives. But for now, while we are trying to create an atmosphere of positive action, it may be to our advantage to build a repetitive rhythm into our day.

Leading a more structured existence will give you more time to spend building up your self-image. Search around in your mind today for the successful memories you have of yourself. See yourself forming new habits and dropping old, self-indulgent ones. Find pleasure in the rhythm of your life. Make pleasure the same daily habit that overeating used to be. Repeat it and repeat it and repeat it all day, today.

Before you reach for that extra bite today, ask yourself:
Have I built some repetition into my day so that I am not troubled with constant, small decisions? Am I building a successful self-image in my free time?

Today ends the first half of this year. It's time when business budgets are overhauled to make sure that the money will last through the rest of the year. It might be a good time for you to take a good look at your own diet "budget" to see where you are.

You are halfway along the road between the beginning and ending of the year. Look back. What has this year meant to you so far? Have you grown, matured, lost weight?

These are questions to answer honestly to yourself. But they are not questions on which you should dwell. Today is more important than all the past days of this year. It is the day you can make new progress, if you really want to.

Take the trouble to do something for yourself today. If yours has been a half-lived life for the first half of this year, determine to live fully from this day on. You don't have to tackle your whole life problem today, you must just make a small beginning. You can do anything (even eat moderately) for one day.

Try to make your mind stronger today by learning one thing about overweight that you didn't know before. Then put that knowledge to good use.

Trust yourself in the here and now. The mistakes you made in the past are dead. The future is not yet born.

Don't play tricks by trying to manipulate yourself into an eating binge: "I've had a rough year, I deserve to eat!"

You are ready to take the high road to good health, weight loss and self-esteem. You are ready to look and listen wholeheartedly to yourself and others. You will become the master of your life, instead of its puppet.

You are really all the positive things you think you are. The thin person you yearn to be is already part of you. You have only to *become yourself.* Remember the philosopher Kierkegaard's affirmation: "To be that self which I truly am."

Before you reach for that extra bite today, ask yourself:
Do I believe there is no end, only a new beginning? Am I ready to set foot on the high road?

So many overweight people play a sad game called "If Only." Have you ever said, "If only it weren't for my job/spouse/age/education/sex/income, I could get thin and stay that way?" If you have, you are looking for an external answer to what is, essentially, an internal problem.

Try a new concept. Free yourself from the idea that you can diet when and if your environment is absolutely right. *Begin your new life from where you are.* Of course, you may need to make some changes in outer conditions as you progress. Losing weight may give you the courage to change an unsatisfactory job, or go back to school. But these changes will not automatically help you to diet off excess weight unless inner change has already begun.

Once you begin to build a new master plan of living which includes healthful eating and positive attitudes, you will be moving toward a goal. Your life experiences will expand, and so will your opportunities. Pitfalls which you once fell into readily will vanish. Difficulties which formerly stopped you cold will be transformed into challenges.

Mystics claim there is a spiritual force that remains dormant in each of us until called upon. How can we overweights activate it? Easily. The *first step* toward a more positive living style causes it to awaken and urge us onward.

This force gives us a sense of expectancy. It changes despair to hope. You will find yourself thinking less and less about external changes and more and more about internal ones.

When you stop playing the "If Only" game, you will discover your capacity for love increases. When your mate is no longer responsible for your weight, when your job stops "making" you fat, then you can find more happiness with them.

Finally, you must let go of the limiting belief in luck. If you believe you are a victim of fate, you can wait a fat lifetime for Lady Luck to smile on you. But if you believe in your own spiritual force, you won't have to wait. You can activate it today.

Before you reach for that extra bite today, ask yourself:
Have I stopped saying "If Only" and taken action? Am I willing to awaken my own inner spiritual force by starting a positive eating plan today?

What you think is how you feel.

Since 1959, psychologists Aaron Beck and Maria Kovacs have studied the patterns of thinking of depressed people, finding that they almost always describe themselves in negative terms.

They can't even escape in their dreams. Depressed people more often than not dream of situations in which they are frustrated, humiliated, rejected, deprived or punished. What overweight child hasn't dreamed of being ridiculed by classmates? Dreams are mirrors of the way we think about ourselves.

Most fat people distort their own lives, describing themselves as losers whether or not they truly are. Even if they are only performing at a slightly less than top creative level in their work, overweights tend to consider their performance *all* bad.

Therapists often hear radical distortions of reality. Janet receives a call from Hal breaking a date due to a work problem. When she hangs up the phone, she is sure Hal no longer cares for her and this rapidly becomes, "What's wrong with me?" It was not the broken date that upset Janet as much as the meaning she attached to it. She becomes convinced that she is unlovable, and completely loses her objectivity.

How often have you exaggerated the meaning of a telephone call or conversation? The result can be that a potentially good relationship is lost because of pessimistic thinking.

How often have you told yourself: "I am dumb, I am lazy, I am fat, I can't finish anything." If you tell yourself often enough, this is exactly the kind of person you become.

Set up an internal dialogue with yourself. When you say, "I am dumb," ask yourself how you have managed to hold down a responsible job for so many years. When you say, "I am fat," answer with the positive things you are doing to lose weight. Continue with this internal dialogue until you have reached realistic conclusions you can believe and feel.

When you think positive thoughts about yourself, you'll have positive feelings about yourself. Doesn't that make a lot of sense? And isn't that the way you really want to live?

Before you reach for that extra bite today, ask yourself:
Am I focusing on positive things about myself? When I feel pessimistic, does my internal dialogue set me straight?

Psychologists have a number of interesting ways to help overweights look at themselves objectively. One is a Pleasure Diary in which you write down all your living activities as they occur, and decide on the spot whether they constitute an accomplishment.

Quite often, people who have formerly been very negative in their personal outlook will discover that they do a number of things quite well. It becomes increasingly more difficult to make such sweeping statements as: "I can never do anything right."

Start a Pleasure Diary today. It will not take too many days before you discover that you are having more pleasant experiences than you realize. You will soon note that your low moods are directly related to negative thinking and that your Pleasure Diary will help you change from pessimistic to optimistic. After all, it is difficult to continue thinking negatively when you have proof of real accomplishment right there in your diary. (You'll also get rid of what psychologists call "selective recall," which means you will lose your tendency to remember only negative experiences.)

You will also think better of yourself if you get rid of negative premises. For example, "If I'm not popular with everyone, I'm a total failure." No one can be universally loved. There are always those who will dislike you no matter what you do. That doesn't mean you're a flop. Lower your expectations and don't aim at unattainable goals.

Do aim at a goal you can attain; that one is a healthier body and a happier life. One day at a time you can approach a new way of looking at yourself. Each day you can improve, finding hidden strength you didn't know you had. "Can't" won't be part of your vocabulary. More and more you will fill your Pleasure Diary with happy experiences which you will dwell on. They are proof positive that your life is getting sunnier every day.

Let the sun shine in!

Before you reach for that extra bite today, ask yourself:
Have I added to my Pleasure Diary so that I have proof that life isn't all bad? Am I concentrating on the sunshine instead of the rain?

The Fourth of July traditionally has been a time for celebrating in the United States. Families get together, citizens spill onto main streets for parades, and fireworks culminate the day's events.

This year you can set off your own fireworks — not the kind that light up the sky, but the kind that quietly illuminate your inner mood.

Once you thought you had lost everything, but today you know you have a future without limits. Once you believed that excess weight would lead to an eternity of dark days; now you know that ridding yourself of fat is a challenge that will help you grow to be the kind of person you always admired.

Be interested in yourself. Awaken to your inner needs. Whatever you have to do, do it now, and do it well. Then take time to celebrate your own progress with some inner fireworks.

No one will tell you it's easy to eat less today than you want. It's not easy — but it's possible. You may only have to have the willingness to stay away from those foods you can't handle. We all have certain foods we think we can't live without. They are usually just the tidbits mankind has lived without very well since the beginning of existence. We overweights have to be especially cautious on holidays like today. It's so easy to get carried away and end the day wondering, "How on earth could I have eaten the whole thing?"

Set off your own inner fireworks and light up the truth hidden within yourself. You are all the positive things you think you are. Now, look in your mirror. See the pounds disappear and your positive inner self emerge. Isn't that a nice reflection on you?

Before you reach for that extra bite today, ask yourself:
Have I celebrated my new way of living? Am I gradually exposing my inner self so that the happy truth shines out?

Picture this. It's a hot and humid July day. An overweight woman bathed in perspiration struggles up to a bus stop, laden with packages, wearing a large black coat. Why? In an (unsuccessful) effort to hide her extra pounds, she is making herself miserable.

You have the "right to bare arms," to wear cool, comfortable clothes, appropriate for this summer season. You need only give yourself that right.

Look forward to the physical self you will soon have, but don't deny yourself the right to comfortable dress until you reach your goal.

Dr. John Schindler points out six basic needs every human being has:

1. The need for love.
2. The need for security.
3. The need for creative expression.
4. The need for recognition.
5. The need for new experiences.
6. The need for self-esteem.

For overweights, the need for self-esteem should head their list. With a little self-esteem, the woman at the bus stop could leave her winter coat at home, she wouldn't need to attempt to hide her body.

If you are working on a master plan for inner growth, which includes a new way of eating for better living, you won't want to hide yourself from others. "I knew I wasn't covering it up," said one dieter. "It was my shame I was trying to hide."

You have nothing to be ashamed of. You are moving forward toward your goal. You are building a winning personality, one which will help you achieve success in spite of every obstacle. You are sick to death of hiding. You are becoming more positive every day. "I can see it through," has become your motto.

Aren't you proud of yourself?

Before you reach for that extra bite today, ask yourself:
Am I dressed appropriately for the weather today? Have I stopped hiding, and started moving toward my goal?

Dr. John H. Renner, a medical doctor interested in how patients treat themselves, says the real medical malpractice problem in this country today is not the one described on the front pages of daily newspapers, but rather the malpractice that people are performing on themselves.

The health crisis today is a crisis of lifestyle, according to Renner, particularly when it comes to diet and exercise.

Here are some of the ways people "malpractice" in their own lives:

1. Overeating which leads to obesity and its consequences.

2. High-fat intake which contributes to arteriosclerosis and coronary-artery disease.

3. High carbohydrate intake which contributes to dental caries.

4. Fad diets that lead to malnutrition.

5. Lack of exercise that aggravates heart problems and obesity.

6. Malnutrition which leads to any number of health problems.

7. Lack of recreation which contributes to stress.

Even the most conscientious physician can't do very much for us if we don't practice some self-help health care.

The first, obvious move we can make is to eat a nutritiously balanced diet. In order to do this, most of us will have to take a good long look at our destructive eating habits and let them go one by one. Once we have success with one habit, it is easier to have success with the next and so on. The experience of succeeding is the way human beings build confidence. Remember when you were a child, and learning to ride a bicycle. The first time, you fell down; the second time, you were wobbly; but the third time, you took off down the block. The same is true when you begin to relearn good eating habits — you build on success. You may not make it the first or second time you try, but sooner or later you will take off.

It doesn't matter how many times you have failed in the past. It only matters that you succeed today, and remember it. Don't destroy self-confidence by remembering failure. *Remember success.*

Before you take that extra bite today, ask yourself:
Could I sue myself for malpractice? As I unlearn destructive eating habits, is my confidence soaring?

One of the most common reasons for diet failure is a simple anxiety over hunger. Because most of us overweights have eaten whenever we felt real or imagined hunger, we think that not eating is impossible. Whenever we have tried to control eating bouts between meals, the fear of hunger has gripped us until we were compelled to eat again to quiet it.

These anxiety attacks are real, but they can be stopped. Arnold Lazarus, Ph.D., and Allen Fay, M.D., have a simple solution. "Talk to your anxiety as if it were a naughty child," they suggest. "You can say, 'Now you stop that this minute!' or 'Now you start behaving yourself!' "

Many people find that this causes the anxiety to weaken and disappear. Although this sounds like a very simple-minded technique, it may not be necessary to go through years of psychoanalysis for emotional problems. Telling your unreasonable anxiety to "Stop that, you hear!" may be all that is necessary.

After all, if you have eaten a full meal only to find yourself, after an hour, driven to eat by the fear of being hungry, it is safe to assume that you are not on the verge of starvation or anywhere near it.

Who knows how such anxieties start? Parents, teachers, peers, society in general are all makers of hunger myths. Nevertheless, the important thing for us overweights is to know how to control hunger fears.

You have the capacity to change, to solve problems. Sometimes the biggest problems have the smallest answers. So remember when the urge to quiet the food anxiety comes, you may only be dealing with the unruly child within you. Feeding this fear will never stop it; it only adds fuel.

Today you will not be ruled by myths or destructive emotions. You will be a self-manager.

Isn't this better?

Before you reach for that extra bite today, ask yourself:
Am I allowing my fear of hunger to rule me? Do I really believe that I have the capacity to change, starting today?

Most of us are grateful for the new way of life we're finding. To be free of the compulsion to overeat, to gain in health of body and spirit, all these mean a great deal to us. It might be interesting to sit down today and find out how much your new way of living is worth.

What are the benefits of sober eating, a body gaining in vibrance and agility? What are the benefits of opening up to the world and watching as it opens up to you? Try hard to make an honest evaluation. How much is it worth to you in dollars and cents?

"I'd give a million dollars if I could lose this weight." Remember how many times you've said that to yourself and others? Add to this sum what you've gained in mental, spiritual, social and health benefits, and you can readily see that your new life is priceless.

There is almost no fortune imaginable to the human mind that can determine what a life well-lived is worth. And that is exactly what you are aiming for — a life lived to the utmost.

At this point, it might be interesting to remember just how you got to be worth so much. You took four simple, yet giant, steps forward. First, you admitted you had a problem with food; second, you began to believe you could do something about it; third, you expressed a desire to change; and fourth, you became willing to work for that change.

That's it. Four simple steps which led you onto a new life path. But your work isn't done. Sane eating and continued inner growth is a heck of a big job, one that will last a lifetime. Work on it a little every day.

Before you reach for that extra bite today, ask yourself:
Is any food worth the loss of my priceless benefits? Am I willing to put out a little effort every day to continue growing?

Many of us become veterans of the unpublished war against fat when we are still in our teens. TOPS (Take Off Pounds Sensibly) even has a Teen TOPS competition with their own weight-loss queen. The ceremony would make the Miss America Contest seem drab by comparison. The annual crowning, in true Bert Parks style, is an emotional series of shrieks, cheers and a standing ovation for the most successful dieter. "Isn't she beautiful? Isn't she beautiful?" resounds through the hall while the winner, having the time of her life, smiles and waves for photographers.

Not all fat teenagers resolve their problem so happily. The social and psychological scars of growing up fat are immense. You are always haunted with the idea that people are laughing at you. Hiding from others, or the opposite side of the coin, deliberately becoming the butt of their jokes are two well-used responses by adolescents to social pressures.

Parents can't help much, if they're overweight, too. Many bariatric doctors think it is useless to treat the teenage overweight without treating the entire family.

Diet therapy groups such as Teen TOPS, Overeaters Anonymous, Weight Watchers or Y classes have proven more and more successful with today's mature young people. It used to be thought that young overweights "hadn't suffered enough" to be able to discipline themselves for life change. But today's successes tell a different story. These teens don't need to "hit bottom," or spend half-a-lifetime overweight before they are ready to turn their lives around.

The process is the same for the young, the adult, or the senior citizen. Make a decision to spend the rest of your life healthfully thin. Draw up a master plan of action which includes a moderate diet and regimen for inner growth. Then get going.

Before you reach for that extra bite today, ask yourself:
Have I suffered enough without hitting bottom? Am I ready to hear someone say, "Isn't she beautiful?"

If someone offered you $100,000 to lose weight, would you do it? If someone threatened to kill your child if you didn't lose weight, would you do it? If the answer to either of these questions is "yes," then why won't you lose weight for your own happiness and peace of mind?

Drs. Arnold Lazarus and Allen Fay say that there are very few things in life you "have" to do. When you think you *have to* or *must* do something you are really meaning, "I choose to do it."

Do you, then, choose to remain fat? Perhaps. But if that is true you can just as easily choose to lose weight, since the choice is up to you.

It's obvious you are motivated and have made a decision to do something positive with your life. The next step is to choose a goal and begin to move toward it, one day at a time. Specific diets can be very helpful, but if you know how to lose weight (and most of us do) you won't need to search and search for the perfect diet. Just begin putting into practice what you already know to be healthful eating.

Once you have followed a weight-losing regimen to your goal, the rewards are so enormous someone could offer you $100,000 to get fat again and you wouldn't take it.

Doesn't being thinner please you? Practice doing more things to please yourself. Ask yourself today, "What would be nice to do for me?" Then do some of those nice things today and everyday. Too often, we overweights have become adept people-pleasers because we felt the need to be awfully good to make up for our lack of physical beauty. It's inappropriate to put the needs of others constantly before your own. Learn to say "No" or "I'll think about it" when others intrude on your time.

Use your time to become better acquainted with the exciting new person you're becoming.

Before you reach for that extra bite today, ask yourself:
Am I willing to lose weight for the sake of my own happiness? Have I learned to say *no* to demanding others and *yes* to myself?

During the hot summer season, most of us look for a cold drink many times a day. Unless we subsist on diet beverages (often too carbonated for constant use), we can drastically increase our calorie intake just by satisfying our thirst.

There is only one beverage that does not contain a single calorie, but it doesn't rank very high on the average dieter's list of favorite drinks. You guessed it, the beverage is WATER.

Too often, we dieters drink carbonated sodas until we are uncomfortably bloated, or juices that have too many calories to be used as hourly thirst quenchers.

To encourage yourself to drink more water, try putting an insulated water jug or cooler in your refrigerator — one with a spigot to make it handier to use. For a real treat, try filling it with bottled spring water, which often tastes better than tap water.

For another hot-weather treat, try freezing diet drinks in ice cube trays. Remember when you were a child and your mother gave you a piece of ice wrapped in a paper napkin? Use frozen diet drink cubes the same way or add them to occasional diet soda drinks for an undiluted, tasty, thirst quencher.

During the hot summer months, it's not unusual to consume sixty-four ounces of liquid a day or twice that amount if you are exercising. As you can see, if all your liquids contained calories, hot-weather dieting would be more difficult than it need be.

Don't be surprised if you discover that ice-cold water is as tasty as anything you have in your refrigerator. Go ahead, take the plunge!

Before you reach for that extra bite today, ask yourself:
Am I willing to find substitutes for high-calorie beverages?
Does my new way of eating have priority in my life?

"Happiness," says Dr. Wayne W. Dyer, "is the most natural feeling of all." Most of us overweights would quarrel with Dr. Dyer's statement, but let's stop to think about it first. As young children, we were spontaneous and happy, until we *learned* self-defeating behavior. It follows that if we unlearned such behavior, we could return to our natural state of happiness.

Dr. Dyer offers these seven suggestions to help you do just that.

1. Stop playing roles that you think you're *supposed* to play. If you're acting out the "jolly fat person" role, get rid of it and be *you.*

2. Have the courage to take risks in life. If you want to make a change, don't let anxiety stop you from making it. Most change involves some fear but little personal danger.

3. Don't blame others. Stop saying, "My mother made me fat," or "My boss makes me feel bad." Replace blaming others with self-responsibility.

4. Assert yourself. You're a grownup. Don't ask others how you should lead your life. Decide for yourself.

5. Stop analyzing so much. Several times each day, allow your brain to rest.

6. Stop looking to others for validation of your own self-worth. Ironically, the less you ask for approval the more you'll receive it.

7. Associate with positive people. Expect to be happy yourself and it will work out that way.

Remember, happiness is the most natural way of life you can choose. It belongs to you. You have a right to it. Go get it!

Before you reach for that extra bite today, ask yourself:
Am I unlearning all self-defeating behavior? Do I move toward my natural state of happiness?

Those of us with weight problems sometimes have a great sense of dis-ease within ourselves. We are uncomfortable with silence, and with our own thoughts — a mental monologue that repeats again and again, "You've got to do something about your weight." On top of this inner stress, we are also victims of our world's frantic pace. What can we do? We can meditate instead of reaching for another high-calorie snack. Here's how.

Find a quiet place and sit down in a chair which will keep your back straight. Close your eyes. Bring your full attention to the movement of your breath as it moves in and out your nostrils. Keep your focus at your nostrils.

Each time your mind wanders to how much weight you've got to lose, bring your attention back to the simple, natural rhythm of breathing.

Don't try to control it, simply be aware of it. Give it your total attention. If you have trouble keeping your mind on each breath, count up to ten breaths, then start over.

Set a timer and meditate for twenty minutes, twice a day, in the same place, at the same time. There, that's all there is to it.

It might be a good idea to meditate *before* you encounter something stressful. For example, if you're going to the doctor, the weighing-in process may worry you. Try meditating before your appointment. The same holds true for an unfamiliar social situation, a job interview or any other potentially threatening situation.

Scientists have discovered that this simple, safe meditation technique can help you become more relaxed the more days you do it. At the same time, you become more alert and have an increased attention span. You'll do better at whatever you try.

For us overweights, losing weight is the most important thing in our lives. Wouldn't it be great if you could use meditation to help you reach your diet goal? Try it. It will give you more ease within yourself and with your world.

Before you reach for that extra bite today, ask yourself:
Have I given meditation a chance? Am I willing to try anything that might help me reach my goal?

You're having an energy crisis. Dr. Thomas G. Skillman, an endocrinologist at Ohio State University, says fat people tend to be so energy efficient they pile up energy in the form of pounds. It's not that you don't have enough energy, you have too much!

How can you get rid of all this extra energy? Exercise is one answer. And for the overweight, no exercise is better than swimming. When you get into the water, along with 100 million other Americans this summer (according to a Nielsen survey), you'll be in *your* element. You may not be able to jog, walk or cycle on a par with the skinnies, but the buoyancy of water is a great equalizer. You'll be able to swim as well as anyone.

There's only one drawback — the anguish and humiliation of appearing on the beach in a bathing suit. But take a good look around. How many wonderful bodies do you see on anyone over the age of twenty? Not many. Remember you have as much right to exercise as others. Remember, also, that you are a beautiful person, trying hard to change your life. Don't drag yourself around a pool or beach as if you have something to be ashamed of. Strut!

Once in the water, relax, keep your legs straight and "grip" the water. Swimming pros suggest you think of the water as Jello, grab hold of it and push off with your body. Work on endurance — a smooth stroke which will carry you some distance. Don't just float in the water. You'll get no more exercise than in your bathtub.

Sometimes, we overweights, short of breath and body-tired, think of ourselves as having very little energy. Just the opposite is true. We have so much stored energy, that getting rid of it automatically means we'll feel better.

Wouldn't you like to feel better, today?

Before you reach for that extra bite today, ask yourself:
Am I allowing what others may think to keep me from the healthful exercise I need? Have I been kidding myself that I really don't want to swim, when I'm dying to get into the water?

A woman in Milwaukee, Wisconsin, died not long ago. She was a wife and mother, only forty-six years old. This woman was not a celebrity, and yet her death made all the newspapers. Why? Because she weighed 880 pounds at death, which made her the fattest woman in the world. Eleven firemen carried her on a tarpaulin when she was taken to the hospital with kidney failure. "She gradually gained over the years," her daughter told reporters. "Here lies the world's fattest woman" is not a fitting epitaph. It doesn't tell of the lifetime of hurt and failure, of living in an immense body in a world engineered for small ones.

It doesn't tell of a woman in a darkened room gradually escaping from the world as much from its beauty as from its pain.

Simultaneously, in Milwaukee, another woman is being honored by TOPS (Take Off Pounds Sensibly) for losing over 100 pounds in a year. "I attended my husband's Christmas office party for the first time in seven years," she says. "I didn't mind a bit that people didn't recognize me."

What is the difference between these two women? What makes one "gradually gain over the years," and one lose so much that people didn't know her? One difference is persistence. Nothing else in the world can take its place. Talent, genius, education, wealth — all of these together are not as helpful to the overweight as persistence and determination. They can literally make the difference between life or death. Try expanding your own store of determination everyday. You can do it. Just hang on, and don't let go.

Before you reach for that extra bite today, ask yourself:
Am I sick of gradually gaining a little more weight each year? Do I have the persistence to become a winner?

Lifting weights has always been a favorite way for men to turn flesh into muscle, but not women. Not until Dr. Jack Wilmore, an exercise physiologist at the University of California, discovered that weight lifting was good exercise for females and would not give them bulky muscles.

Why don't girls develop muscles like men do? The answer is hormones. Female hormones just don't allow muscles to mass like they do on men, so women can use weights to tone and firm their body into an even more feminine shape.

Weight lifting is also a good way to build strength and stamina along with curves in the right places. Dr. Wilmore measured a twenty to fifty percent gain in strength. The women in his research program found they also began to improve in other areas of exercise. Their swimming, bicycling and tennis performances increased and they had energy to spare.

Here's what Dr. Wilmore recommended for beginning female weight lifters.

1. Warm up with push-ups, sit-ups and other basic exercises for about ten minutes.

2. If you don't have professional weights, fill two bags (with handles) with sand until they each weigh ten pounds. Now, holding the bags, do some side bends from the waist.

3. At an auto-wrecking yard, you can pick up some old gears to make your own barbells. Attach thirty pounds of them to a bar, and lift these weights overhead.

Make sure you can lift the bags or bars easily ten times. If not, lighten the load and work up to the suggested limit.

There are commercial weight lifting kits on the market for both women and men with complete instructions. Some dieters find weight lifting more challenging than plain exercising. It's just more satisfying, because you can see progress in the increased poundage you can lift. That alone keeps you interested, and maintaining interest is what many people find the hardest part of any exercise routine.

There's no argument that exercise is important to weight loss and good body tone. Any way you do it, with weights or without, you're bound to get a lift.

Before you reach for that extra bite today, ask yourself:
Am I willing to try a new exercise to help build my new body? Wouldn't it be wonderful to have extra energy instead of feeling all dragged out?

For far too many overweights, maintaining a good eating plan — never an easy job — seems to be harder each year. Millions start and stop, other unknown millions are too overwhelmed by past failures to even try again. And yet, the steps to successful weight loss, permanent weight stabilization and new life are deceptively simple.

Decide to make your eating plan work. You must make a conscious decision to stick to your diet, and even try to improve it as you go along. For many years, words like "decision" were unpopular with dieters. But without a daily commitment to make your diet work, it won't. Begin each day with a silent or written renewal of your decision.

Establish a dialogue. Eating less is often eating better for your body and its health, but it can be a very lonely business as well. Open lines of communication with other dieters — either friends, family or a diet group. In this way, when problems arise, you will have a sympathetic and knowledgeable person to share with.

Become aware of what you do to make dieting unpleasant. Just as you want to establish a dialogue with others who have eating problems, you don't want to dwell on diet until you would do anything to get away — including overeat. There's a fine line between sharing and complaining. You'll know when you've crossed it.

Let your diet "breathe." Get away and dwell on other things, when you feel that you've concentrated enough of your day on your eating plan. Work with a hobby, visit friends — get busy in some fascinating new area, so that your diet will not grow stale with too much concentration.

Day after day you are trying to eat for health and grow as an individual. The initial flames of your exciting new life often die down into a mellow glow. But this maturing can bring a great deal of comfort as you put one good day after another behind you. Healthful, growth-oriented days are the most richly rewarding days we overeaters can spend. But such success requires self-understanding, time and careful handling.

Discover it for yourself.

Before you reach for that extra bite today, ask yourself:
Have I given my eating plan the necessary first aid? Am I willing to allow my new way of life to mature naturally?

"Didn't you used to be Shirley Kerns?" a passer-by asked the slender woman. "Yes, and I still am," came Shirley's good-natured reply. She's used to having acquaintances, even old friends, pass her by or hesitate to speak. It's no wonder. Svelte Shirley Kerns looks nothing like the Shirley Kerns who weighed 342 pounds six years ago.

Now a lecturer for Weight Watchers, Shirley is a prime example of someone who has lost a great deal of weight and maintained the loss. "Anybody can lose weight," she says. "I did it time and time again, dropping forty pounds and gaining back fifty. Keeping it off is the challenge."

In eighteen months, Shirley reduced nineteen dress sizes, nine bra sizes and five shoe sizes. "I even had to buy a padded bra this year," she laughs.

To keep 200 pounds of flesh from creeping back on a receptive body requires courage. Courage is the ability to survive defeat, disappointment and loss, without looking for that old destructive drug — food.

Weight maintenance also requires a good memory. Shirley Kerns will never forget that she was struggling to stay in a size sixty dress which she could only order from a catalogue. She'll never forget that a short walk was exhausting, a longer walk, impossible. Nor will she ever forget that her children worried about her health and in the silence of her room at night, the sound of her own labored breathing frightened her.

You have the courage to maintain your weight loss, and the determination. You certainly have the memory. Who could forget?

Before you reach for that extra bite today, ask yourself:
Why can't I use just a little more courage like Shirley Kerns? Am I remembering what it was like to live in a fat world without hope?

"The wonderful part of self-honesty," the dieter told her Overeaters Anonymous group, "is not having to hide anymore.

"I hid from my body by never looking in a full-length mirror. I hid in the bathroom to eat my cookies, and then hid the wrapper at the bottom of the clothes hamper; I even hid the chocolate on my breath by brushing my teeth before I came out.

"Worst of all, I hid the truth of what I was doing to myself, from myself."

It's strange that people who wouldn't dream of lying, stealing or cheating where others are involved, are able to lie, to steal from and cheat themselves and rationalize it all away. "I'm nervous and sick," we say, or "It's hereditary or glandular." We rationalize the most irrational eating behavior so that we can continue doing the very thing that is making us so unhappy.

One of the reasons we continue to fool ourselves is that we're hiding the guilty secret of our behavior. We think we're the only one in the world who ever ate in the bathroom and hid the remains in the clothes hamper. Joining a group of other overweights soon enlightens us. We discover that we are not alone. Other overweights eat in the bathroom, steal their children's Hallowe'en candy, buy two cakes — one for the party and one to eat beforehand. You'll find others have kept such eating secrets, too — secrets that can only be shared with others in the same boat.

Every day you follow your moderate eating plan for good health will be another day you won't have to hide from others or yourself. You'll have more time for fun when you take less time for guilt. Imagine that!

Before you reach for that extra bite today, ask yourself:
Have I had enough of hiding and eating? Am I ready to share my guilty secret with others?

If you're nervous about anything at all, try running around the block. And while you're at it, think pleasant thoughts — about friends, parties, looking trimmer, buying new clothes in a smaller size. According to Dr. Richard Driscoll of Eastern State Psychiatric Hospital in Tennessee, the combination of exercise and pleasant thoughts helps banish anxiety.

Psychologist Driscoll worked with six groups of people who had anxieties they couldn't get rid of. He tried a number of different methods to help them overcome their fears. One group jogged in place; the second group didn't exercise at all but imagined pleasant situations; the third group jogged and imagined enjoyable scenes; the fourth group underwent systematic desensitization; the fifth group worried together and the sixth group received no help at all.

As you might guess, the group that did nothing at all, showed no change in their high-anxiety level. The other groups showed some change for the better. But the group showing the greatest decrease in anxiety and the highest relaxation level was the group that combined jogging with pleasant thoughts. Jogging alone helped as did thinking pleasant thoughts, but the combination proved to be more effective.

This simple solution to the anxieties that all dieters (indeed, all people) feel is less time-consuming and costly than psychiatric therapy.

You don't need a laboratory or a psychologist to try it — two feet and a memory are the only accessories you have to have.

Control is the key. If you don't have control over your fears, they will control you. With control, you will gain more and more freedom every day of your life. Isn't this what you've been looking for all along?

Before you reach for that extra bite today, ask yourself:
Am I willing to try anything to banish anxiety and to relax?
Have I achieved more freedom through better control?

Some overweights have a perfectionist attitude toward their diets. They say, "I'll *always* be a failure, " and simply can't cope with any errors made in following their eating plans.

This attitude can be met by the word, "Challenge!" If you are a perfectionist dieter who goes on an eating binge after every little dietary mistake, then you need to challenge your concepts.

How much reliance do you place in your new eating plan, your doctor's ability, or your own? If your eating plan is a good one, your doctor's reputation sound and your own abilities proven in other areas of your life, you may just be looking for extra support. (Some psychologists call it a need for "strokes.") You may find it necessary to wean yourself from dependence on others and learn to place more reliance on your own reliability.

Ironically, some perfectionists have far less trouble with dieting than other overweights. Bariatrician Dr. H. David Sachs says, "I point out to them that they are actually having very little difficulty since most of my patients have problems equal to, if not greater than theirs."

Another weight specialist, Dr. Joseph L. Love, finds that his perfectionist patients usually have unreasonable weight goals. "The goal is very likely to be unrealistic;" he says, "one that the patient has not had since he was twelve years of age! I always add five more pounds which seems to make the perfectionist relax a bit and accept this new goal as a possible one."

Don't be a "failure martyr." It is better to have 90 percent of something than 100 percent of nothing.

You are building a creative new life for yourself. There is always room for mistakes in the creative life. How else could you measure progress? And remember, progress is your goal, not perfection, Make some progress, today.

Before you reach for that extra bite today, ask yourself:
Am I setting myself up for failure with my perfectionist goals? Will I be satisfied with a little progress each day?

You can tell a lot about your emotions by the foods you eat. So says Dr. Harvey Einhorn, an internist specializing in nutrition and formerly vice president of the American College of Nutrition.

"The tense, anxious individual who overeats is perfectly obvious," says Einhorn. "So is the person with financial, marital or environmental problems. But the most common and least recognized is the mildly depressed individual."

Dr. Einhorn maintains that almost all overweights have latent insecurities. In fact, he says, you can tell a lot about a person's emotional history by the foods he chooses to overeat.

Here are some emotional foods:

Security foods. These are the foods of infants and include milk, eggs and butter. They give a sense of security.

Reward foods. The overweight often says, "I know I shouldn't have eaten it, but I ate it anyway." They have a subconscious desire to reward themselves with cake, cookies, ice cream or chocolate following a difficulty or a frustration.

Strength foods. A man who feels the need to show the world how manly he is may do it with beer, pretzels, steak and potatoes.

Why do most people go off diets? "For the most part," Dr. Einhorn says, "they go on a diet when they are feeling good and go off it when they become depressed."

Most overeaters and long-term dieters could add the opposite — they've gone on diets when they felt depressed, and off when they felt good. The point is that most of us respond to food at both ends of the emotional scale. Frustration, boredom, lack of planning and goal-setting, as well as elation, sudden success and over-stimulation — all of these can set us off on eating binges.

The best way to find balance in your eating is to find emotional balance as well. Conversely, nothing can level the peaks and valleys of your emotions like daily adherence to a moderate way of eating.

Is being thin the most desirable goal in your life? If your answer is yes, then you'll soon find that the taste of the most exotic dessert does not equal the satisfaction of fitting into a smaller size.

Before you reach for that extra bite today, ask yourself:
Am I using food to smooth out the peaks and valleys of my emotional life? Have I asked myself why it's not working?

Salt is one of the oldest seasonings. Most people feel that it adds zest to bland food. Overeaters are usually big salt eaters, because so many of our favorite snack foods contain generous amounts of sodium chloride, which is salt's scientific name.

But more and more nutritionists and doctors are warning that too much salt can be dangerous to your health. They say we use far more salt than our bodies require and excess salt can lead to high blood pressure and kidney disease.

Women, especially, know extra salt can result in water retention and premenstrual blues.

Science writer Marietta Whittlesey goes even further than most experts. She says salt is as harmful a health hazard as alcohol, tobacco or sugar — particularly for those with a genetic sensitivity to it. (These are people with a family health history which includes stroke, hypertension, kidney disease or premenstrual distress.)

Watch how much salt you are using during cooking or at your table. Often, you're getting more salt than you need because the manufacturer has already salted the product during processsing. Since almost all foods, even drinking water, contain some salt, you may not need to add salt during preparation or at the table.

Why should we overweights be more careful than most? Because retention of fluids is one of the consequences of eating too much salt. The body must maintain a critical balance of salt and water, but the sodium in salt absorbs water, causing us to drink more and show a weight gain.

We overeaters usually have spicy appetites. Most of us like food that is on the over-seasoned side. Nevertheless, we can train our taste buds to respond to less salty foods, which may even help us lose weight more easily. Better health and more weight loss — that's not a bad payoff for using a lighter hand on the salt shaker.

Before you reach for that extra bite today, ask yourself:
Do I add too much salt to my food and then experience that bloated-all-over feeling? Am I willing to use less salt for my health's sake?

It's more common than most people think for overweights to lose all excess weight and still think of themselves as fat.

Usually the problem begins when you are within a few pounds of your weight goal. At that time, according to bariatrician Dr. Leonard Stoll, many patients begin to have feelings of guilt for being fat in the first place, fear their ability to maintain their new normal weight or have an inability to cope with their improved physical image. Most of all they perceive that learning to live the disciplined life of a person of normal weight versus the less disciplined life of the fat person will not be as easy as they thought.

If you are approaching your weight goal, you should begin to work on a new thin image before you get there. For one thing, believe what you see. Check photos taken before you started losing weight against ones taken recently. See the difference? Next, check your tape-measure records. You can't argue with those figures.

Finally, if you are having a continuing problem "thinking thin" ask your doctor to set up a meeting with other patients who are having a similar image crisis. You'll find, first hand, how others are solving their own problems, and best of all, you'll come to understand that your feelings are quite normal.

If you find yourself unable to accept your new physical self, don't neglect the condition. Do something about it. If you don't, the whole thing will gradually assume greater proportions, until you may eventually return to the overweight state.

Remember that the compliments do stop, and adjusting to living in your new, thin body will be your job. When you think about it, it may be the happiest work you'll ever have to do.

Before you reach for that extra bite today, ask yourself:
Am I hanging on to the old fat image of me? Am I ready to go on to the happy work of living thin?

For the dieter, getting too little sleep can be an even greater handicap than getting too much. If you sleep and nap too much of your day away, you will not be using as many calories as you could, which slows your weight loss. But if you get too little sleep, you become irritable, listless and downright depressed — too depressed to stick to your eating plan.

Here are several "tonics" you can try to help you on those occasional sleepless nights:

1. *Try systematic relaxation.* Start relaxing the muscles of your feet. Let each toe become limp. Then gradually move up your feet to your ankles, then your knees and so forth until you've reached the top of your head. You will actually begin to feel relaxation following each muscle movement.

2. *Try giving yourself a massage after your bath.* Sometimes we overweights are too body-shy to ask others to massage us, but you can massage yourself with your towel. As you step out of the bath or shower, use your towel to give yourself a brisk back rub, keeping the arms as straight as possible. Don't forget the back of your neck where most tension seems to reside.

3. *Wear loose clothes.* Nothing is harder to sleep in than nightclothes that are too tight. After all you probably wear some article of clothing all day that pinches unmercifully. At night you should be able to relax.

4. *Sleep in a well-ventilated room.* We're long past the age when night air was considered unhealthy, if not unholy, so open your window and let the fresh air in.

There! It's really not so hard to get your beauty sleep, the kind of relaxation you need for the beautiful day you're going to have. You'll be alert and poised, confident and competent. You will experience a sense of awareness which will feed your creative thoughts and sensitive emotions. A good night's sleep will sustain your day, a day that will bring you closer to your weight goal.

Before you reach for that extra bite today, ask yourself:
Am I getting too little sleep? Have I exchanged eating myself to sleep for some no-calorie sleep techniques?

What do you see in your mind? Whatever you are seeing in your mind's eye today, will probably soon come into existence. That chair you're sitting on was once an image in the carpenter's eye; so that mental image you have will someday be translated into reality. That is why it is so important for us overweights to have the right kind of creative mind picture.

If you see yourself as fat, unhealthy, undesirable and unlovable, you are creating the instrument which will bring these unhappy traits to life. *Your negative thoughts coupled with your actions have created your life.*

If you can accept the above idea, then you won't have trouble with this one: *You can change your life if you change your thinking.*

How many of us overweights allow our minds to dwell day after day on the very things we hate? We see ourselves overeating, getting fatter and more unhappy. We see others rejecting us and we are consumed with self-pity.

Your creative mind can produce positive images just as easily as negative ones. You need only give it positive input. See yourself eating healthfully and getting thinner and more content each day. See your family and friends, even strangers, accepting your new image. See yourself as a self-responsible person for which pity in any form is unnecessary.

You will find that once you have established your positive goal, and begin to feed positive images to your mind, you will be able to create a new life for yourself. This is how you can make a miracle.

You have more power than you ever realized; more strength than you ever suspected; a greater ally than you ever imagined. That power, strength and ally is your own creative mind.

Program it positively, today!

Before you reach for that extra bite today, ask yourself:
Am I making positive images to replace negative ones? Do I believe that I can change my life by changing my thinking?

We overeaters, with few exceptions, have made a science of feeling guilty. We feel guilty because of the times we promised others we'd lose weight and didn't. We feel guilty for all the times we promised ourselves we were going to stop overeating, and didn't. Sometimes we feel guilty for just being alive. Sure, we feel ashamed and inferior, but we feel guilty first. For us overweights, guilt is the mother of all negative emotions.

If you are the average person with a weight problem, you are guilt-conscious. You have such a sense of your own unworthiness, you even manufacture guilt where none exists. When a person of normal weight commits a misdeed, chances are he or she accepts blame, shrugs it off and goes on. But let a fat person do something wrong and somehow weight gets into the picture. If you're fat and wrong, you're double wrong. Do you recognize the problem?

One of the greatest guilt-inducers is the simple question, "What are people thinking of me?" This is usually based upon an exaggeration of the premise that if we're fat, other people think about us a lot. This is a faulty evaluation. Most people are caught up in the problems of their own lives and don't spend much time on others at all.

When you become conscious that you are acting out guilt feelings with no basis in reality, try to concentrate, instead, on listing the good traits you have. Don't be shy. Put them all down on paper and look at them.

You should remember, too, that excess guilt is the product of a highly sensitive nature. You can turn the ability to feel deeply into an asset. Truly sensitive people when they rid themselves of guilt become creative writers, artists and actors or the kind of people others seek out for advice.

Trade your guilt for sensitivity. Recycle yourself!

Before you reach for that extra bite today, ask yourself:
Am I always finding something to feel guilty about? Have I decided to trade my fat-guilt for thin-sensitivity?

Time management expert Alan Lakein suggests people who have trouble setting priorities for their lives should ask themselves three questions about their lifetime goals. This suggestion may seem overly simple to those who haven't tried it, but it is a good way to take stock of your life — where you are and where you're going.

1. *What are your lifetime goals?* Give yourself two minutes to list these, and along with serious career and family goals don't be afraid to put down the wild ideas that come to your mind like going on an African safari or learning to sail a schooner. These two goals indicate more at second glance than at first. Perhaps you are interested in animal wild life or you have a greater need for the relaxation that sailing represents. Give yourself two additional minutes to correct your statements.

2. *How would you like to spend the next five years?* (If you're under thirty, make that three years.) You've probably listed a number of general things in your lifetime goals such as "happiness" and "success." This question will help you pinpoint your goals better. Again take only two minutes to list them and two minutes to revise.

3. *If you knew you had only six months to live, how would you live them?* This question will show you what is really important in your life. If you knew you had a short time to live, would you spend that time stuffing yourself with food? Would overeating have the same priority in your life it now holds? Ask yourself in two minutes, taking two minutes to review your answers.

Although the first two questions are important to all people, perhaps the third question is most important to fat people. We live so much in the now. Many times we think only of our need to overeat, not of consequences, not of the future.

What are your life time goals? How are you going to spend the rest of your life, whether fifty years or six months? What is your answer?

Before you reach for that extra bite today, ask yourself:
Can I learn to live beyond the next bite? Have I listed the things that are more important to me than food?

There's nothing so irritating as to be told you lack self-control. And we overweights hear that all the time. If others aren't telling us (sometimes in a nice way, sometimes not), we are telling ourselves. Even the venerable philosopher, Plato, gets into the act. "The first and best victory is to conquer self," he said. And then, like most moralists unable to stop at well-enough, he goes on to say, "to be conquered by self is of all things most shameful and vile."

The hardest thing to swallow, of course, is that old Plato is right, When we overeaters take a good look at what we have done to our lives with our forks and knives, we must admit that self-control is a desirable trait to own.

What is self-control anyway? Phillips Brooks says that it is the things we learn to do without. Can you learn to do without excess food in your life?

What else is self-control? It is sure evidence of personal courage. It tells you that you can endure. It is the only possible way you can maintain confidence in yourself. Without self-control, you can never really believe in yourself or in your abilities.

For the overeater, self-control means one thing. The ability to resist the first bite of unneeded food. Why? Benjamin Franklin said it for us even though he had his own problems with self-control. He said, "It is easier to suppress the first desire than to satisfy all that follow it."

That first extra bite is easier to stop than the binge that can follow. You know that truth well enough. Why not take the easy way to self-control today? Just don't take that first bite of food not on your eating plan. It's as simple as that.

Before you reach for that extra bite today, ask yourself:
Am I letting my desire for excess food rule my life? Do I believe, finally, that the more I give in to overeating, the less I will be able to control myself?

Unlike the alcoholic or other drug addict, it is impossible for the food addict to hide addiction. We carry our compulsion on our hips, stomach and chin for all the world to see. We think fat, are treated fat and fall into the habit of acting fat. But fat isn't who you are. Fat is a condition, not your being. Your true worth is in being, not *seeming.*

You are a dreamer. You dream of great things to do, and you dream of a body that will allow you to do them.

You live with yourself the best you can. You are not always as magnanimous and kind to yourself as you are to others.

You have strong feelings. But you do not always have a strong command over them.

You have a secret place. You try to cover it with extra food, but every now and then you look into it and see what you could be. And that look hurts worst of all.

You are sometimes confused. And you would dearly love to think without confusion.

You are a fighter. You have never given up.

You have the eagerness of hope. Your enthusiasm will one day take you to your life goal.

You have an unused freedom. You are free to live your life thin and healthy, to finally get outside your body and into the whole world of living. Break free! Use your freedom.

Before you reach for that extra bite today, ask yourself:
What is my true worth as a human being? Am I ready to declare my freedom?

When Was the Last Time You Ran Like the Wind?

If your doctor has given you a nudge (even a strong shove) toward getting more exercise, you may want to consider running.

Does that sound impossible? Do you believe fat people or women can't run? If the answer to these questions is yes — you're wrong. Not only is running for the overweight possible, but more and more women are taking it up with beautiful results for their bodies and minds.

"I run every morning with my daughter," says forty-year-old Nancy Kovach. "Within six months I lost thirty-six pounds and my mental attitude is great.

"By 8:00 a.m. I'm at my desk working rings around people half my age."

Of course, Nancy didn't start off running three miles every morning. She backed into running with a walk-jog-run program as outlined by physical fitness expert, Joe Henderson.

Henderson suggests a cautious two-month walk program, with jogging starting in the third month. Jogs can vary from one minute to five minutes, with ninety percent of them in the two-to-four-minute range.

After three months of daily preparation, you finally get wind in your face — wind *you* generate by running. Runs vary from ten to fifty minutes with the majority being twenty minutes.

Fitness expert Henderson says running is a great time to be alone with yourself and your own thoughts, create solutions to problems, and plan action. Ideas will come to you while running that you would never get any other way.

When you and your doctor agree you are at the running stage of your exercise buildup, remember to take it easy. Don't hurt yourself; don't push yourself too hard. Run at a gentle pace.

Wouldn't you like to run away from home for an hour a day?

Before you reach for that extra bite today, ask yourself:
Am I willing to try exercise as part of my new creative living plan? Wouldn't it be wonderful to have limber joints, and strong legs again?

There are any number of good diets around to help you lose weight. The real problem is changing the way you feel about yourself so that you can stick to a diet, and keep the weight off once you've lost it.

One man who has kept 100 lost pounds off for over twenty years is Dr. Peter G. Lindner, a Los Angeles bariatrician (weight specialist). "Both my parents were fat," he says, "and I was obese from childhood. According to all the statistics, I was the typical fat person who was never likely to become thin."

What did Dr. Lindner do to change his fate? He taught himself a simple form of self-hypnosis. First he identified all his bad eating habits, and then set about to remove them one at a time. Twice a day he found a quiet place and systematically relaxed every muscle in his body. During this state of calm, his subconscious became extremely susceptible to suggestion.

"I didn't try to empty my mind," he says. "That's impossible. Instead, I imagined my mind was a telescope and focused it smaller and smaller until I was seeing only one mental image. Then I began to make mental pictures of myself reaching for celery and other low-calorie foods, instead of candy. I watched myself enjoy celery, even smack my lips."

Finally, he set about to rid himself of a "fat man" self-image so he could keep the weight off. "Like most overweight people I 'saw' myself as fat in my mind. With this mental picture, I was programmed to act like a fat person, which means eating like one, too."

Each day, putting himself in a meditative state of mind, Dr. Lindner began to mentally reduce his size. "I reprogrammed my mind," he says, "imagining myself looking thinner and wearing smaller clothing every day. By the time I lost my excess weight, I not only looked thin in the mirror, but in my mind as well."

We overweights have always been told: "You are what you eat." And most of us have found this to be all too true.

Perhaps, after all, we are also what we *think*. This simple form of meditation could be a way to help you shape a thin self-image in your mind's eye — one day at a time.

Before you reach for that extra bite today, ask yourself:
Have I tried to reprogram myself to eat and think like a thin person? Do I see the kind of self-image I want to project from my mind onto my mirror?

"It's hard to develop relaxing and pleasure-producing alternatives to eating if you're under a lot of stress," says Dr. George Blackburn, director of a Harvard-affiliate weight-reduction clinic. The doctor certainly isn't trying to give overweights an excuse for postponing a more healthful way of eating, but he and other psychologists say that since food is a means of relieving tension for many overweight people, it's going to be harder to diet during stress periods such as:

1. After the death or serious illness of a family member.
2. When looking for or starting a new job.
3. During marital problems.
4. Just before or after moving.
5. While in financial difficulty.

If you find, as some of us do, that the stress periods listed above are almost always with us in some degree or other, you may *not* be able to postpone a more healthful way of eating until all these problems are resolved. At the very least, if you can't stick to a weight-losing diet during such emotional times, you can work to stay on a weight-maintenance eating plan. Serious overeating will only make any of the above problems more difficult to bear.

The point to remember is that you should try to put food in perspective. It is not a problem-solver. Overeating has never brought a loved one back to life, saved a marriage or balanced a budget. There is no emotional magic in chocolate cake.

Do your best to eat moderately while under unavoidable emotional stress. Then just as quickly as you can, get right back to your weight-losing eating plan. You'll feel better. Function better. Feel more secure.

You'll have eating under control. Won't that be a great feeling?

Before you reach for that extra bite today, ask yourself:
Do I understand that eating over a problem will not make it go away or get any better? Am I willing to use my problems as springboards to growth?

Let's eavesdrop on a diet-group meeting of former overeaters. How do they feel about themselves now that they are losing weight and turning their lives around in a productive direction?

Listen:

"I couldn't breathe very well before. Now I have lots of energy."

"I feel happy like something good is going to happen to me."

"I have peace now, where I used to feel hatred."

"I have faith that there won't be any more shadows."

"Old fears, old resentments, old guilts — all of these have been brought into the light. I've faced and accepted them."

"My feet are on solid ground instead of in the quicksand of overeating."

"I'm free now. Before I came here my life was hopeless. The emptier I felt, the more I ate; the more I ate, the emptier I felt."

"My dream has come true."

"Losing weight is one of the most beautiful sensations of joy."

"I feel good about myself and other people."

"My life seems to have some order."

Wouldn't it be wonderful to experience positive emotions like these, not just once, but every day of your life? You can. In order to find the serenity and self-acceptance these people have found, you have only to build a new creative living program as they have done. Each of them has a weight-losing eating plan and is working patiently toward increasing inner growth. Without the blinders of excess food, they see shortcomings and, from many options, choose changes.

They are healthy, vibrant, totally alive men and women. The room is so charged with high energy, it is impossible not to feel a connection with their joy. They are a diverse group. One is a teenager and another over seventy. One woman sits in a wheelchair.

If it is possible for these people to lose their excess weight and change their lives, it is possible for you to do the same. It is *very* possible.

Before you reach for that extra bite today, ask yourself:
Do I want to experience the positive feelings of weight loss? Have the blinders of excess food kept me from seeing how beautiful my life could be?

When we overweights look in the mirror and see the extra pounds on our body, it doesn't occur to us that some of those pounds have names like Envy, Disappointment, Jealousy and Hatred.

Did you ever overeat because someone had a bigger house, got your coveted promotion, married your girl or boyfriend? Of course, you did. The big troubles, the bitter disappointments, the deep wrongs — all the tragedies of our lives changed the shape of our bodies. If you are ever to lose weight and happily keep it off, you must learn to let go of even the most heartbreaking sorrow, even the greatest wrong. Let them all go. If you keep them, you risk keeping the pounds that go with them.

It's easy to see that we could harbor the big grudge. We're only human, after all. But what about the little annoyances of everyday living, the irritations and the petty vexations? "I've binged because a kitchen drawer kept sticking," said one honest dieter. "I've eaten because it was raining and I wanted sunshine," said another.

Little irritations, like these, shouldn't be nurtured, shouldn't be petted everyday, shouldn't be worried over, shouldn't be brooded about. They aren't worth the pounds they pile on our bodies. Let them go. If you sweep them out of your mind, you will be surprised at the physical and mental uplift you'll feel.

Get in the habit of letting go — whether they be petty grievances or big troubles. They embitter your life, sap your creative will and keep your attention from your top priority — to lose weight and keep it off.

Letting go is a freeing act. It frees you to see how beautiful the world, its people and, especially, you, really are.

Makes sense, doesn't it?

Before you reach for that extra bite today, ask yourself:
Am I overeating because of some real or imagined slight?
Do I really want to wear my disappointments on my body?

Some years ago Norman Cousins, the editor of *Saturday Review*, suddenly came down with an illness experts diagnosed as ankylosing spondylitis, which means that the connective tissue in his spine was disintegrating. He was given one chance in 500 to recover.

In a now famous case, Cousins (with his doctor's consent) left the drug-laden hospital atmosphere and went to a private hotel room. There he put himself through a strange but strangely logical regimen. Reasoning that since the effects of negative emotions produce negative chemical changes in the body, Cousins decided that positive emotions might produce positive chemical changes. Is it possible that love, hope, faith, laughter, confidence and the will to live have a therapeutic value, he asked?

Norman Cousins proved they did. He withdrew from pain medication and watched amusing movies. Allen Funt, of *Candid Camera*, provided some of his funniest films which a nurse ran for Cousins during periods of pain. He discovered that ten minutes of genuine belly laughter had an anesthetic effect.

Through the positive therapy of laughter and some other innovative vitamin treatments, Cousins recovered, completely.

What can we overweights learn from this experience, so much more serious than any we are ever likely to face? Just this. The process through which self-confidence can be picked up by the body and translated into physical action is immense. Never underestimate the capacity of your mind and body to regenerate themselves. You have a natural drive to live and to perfect yourself.

No one has a greater will to live, and live well, than we overweights do. So many of us have been denied the opportunities and pleasures others take for granted.

Think of it. You could have the body you've always wanted. You could have the life you've yearned to live. All you need is self-confidence and the will to live thin. That's the force of positive thinking.

Before you reach for that extra bite today, ask yourself:
Do I believe that positive emotions can produce positive chemical effects in my body? Am I willing to develop my self-confidence so that I can live the life I want to live?

Eula Weaver, at eighty-seven years, is a great-great grandmother. She has a history of severe heart disease which had her in such bad shape she couldn't walk 100 feet without being crippled with leg pain. At the Longevity Research Institute in Santa Barbara, Dr. Nathan Pritikin, put Eula Weaver on a very low-fat diet with generous daily helpings of exercise. Today she pedals a stationary bike twenty miles a day, often jogs two miles and in her spare time lifts weights.

The next time you try to convince yourself that exercise for you is out of the question, think about Eula Weaver.

But before you embark on an exercise program which will show Great-grandma Weaver a thing or two, use a few precautions.

Never start an exercise program without consulting your doctor. Depending on your general health and degree of overweight, your doctor may want you to delay a program or start a minimum program. In either event, he or she will want you to start slow and work up both speed and time, gradually.

There are special exercise programs at some YMCA's for people with health problems. These are supervised group exercising programs with paramedical people available.

The important thing is that you begin to look at your body as more than an eating machine. In simplest terms your body is a chemical furnace that burns food to produce energy. What happens to the energy once it's produced is up to you. It can be stored in fat cells or it can be expended in activity.

Overeaters produce a lot of energy, but most, because of fatigue, can barely keep going. That's the paradox of energy — if you store it, you lose it; if you spend it, you have it.

Which do *you* want to do today?

Before you reach for that extra bite today, ask yourself:
If an eighty-seven-year-old with congestive heart failure, high blood pressure, angina and arthritis can compete in the Senior Olympics, why can't I exercise a little today? Am I tired of using my body as just an eating machine?

What do you have to do today?

Sometimes we overweight people let everyday routine keep us overeating and unhappy. We can literally be overwhelmed by going to work, shopping or caring for ourselves and our families. We spend so much time on these primary activities that we have no time left for the things we want to do.

The highest priority on every overeater's schedule is time given to adequate food buying and preparation. Next, schedule time for exercise, relaxation, meditation and all the other things you are doing to prepare your body and mind for a new, growth-centered life.

Time management expert, Alan Lakein, suggests a daily schedule in which blocks of time are also set aside for the things you want to do. He maintains those people who never have enough time are apt to be wasting time because they need better organization.

There is always enough time for the things important to you.

Effective scheduling should always allow for the unexpected — the drop-in relative, the sudden job assignment. If you don't leave a bit of time in your schedule for the things you can't plan for in advance, you'll always be frustrated, defeating the purpose of a time schedule.

Proper planning will give you more freedom to accomplish and to have spare time so that you can alternate the "have to's" with the "wants." It is a boon for overeaters, who sometimes get themselves into too many activities, or give up and do nothing. With a daily plan, you won't be trapped by time frustrations — too much or too little — either of which can set you up for overeating.

Note: If you are losing or maintaining weight on a disciplined eating plan, you'll find it easier to discipline the rest of your day. And vice versa.

Before you reach for that extra bite today, ask yourself:
Have I got a good balanced time plan which allows me to take care of necessities and leaves room for fun? Am I trying to get more control over the time of my life?

Sane eating to lose weight or maintain your normal weight is the most important thing in your life without exception. You feel this more today than yesterday, and you'll feel it more tomorrow than today.

You are growing in the willingness to give in to a positive program. Old habits of using other people and other problems as an excuse to overeat are gone. You feel beautiful, intelligent and confident. You have serenity of mind and your emotions are balanced with the inner peace that makes living a joy. Nothing can happen today, that you can't handle. *Today you are good for you.*

But you can make a good day even better. Here are some ways:

Mend a quarrel.

Dismiss suspicion.

Give a soft answer.

Encourage a friend.

Find the time.

Apologize.

Laugh a little more.

Say thanks.

Forgive a wrong.

Write a letter.

Keep a promise.

Sometimes we fat people have to learn to experience joy by practicing it more. Positive feelings we thought were lost to us can be suddenly found if we look for them in our inner selves.

Believe in your positive self. Rid yourself of negative beliefs, because they are false assumptions.

Believe completely, with your total being, that you can lose the flesh that has weighed you down.

With a little effort, you can make today a weight-losing day and a happier day than you've ever known. What an opportunity!

Before you reach for that extra bite today, ask yourself:
Have I really tried to do things that will bring happiness into my day? Do I practice positive believing?

There are times when we invite our own problems. And one of the most expensive for our pocketbooks and our health is the tendency to overeat. Barring medical evidence of a glandular problem, the desire to preserve a sound body needs the *sincere, conscious and perpetual willingness to be well.*

If you have a deep desire to be well, tell yourself today that there is nothing within you which desires to overeat.

Tell yourself that you want to be well, right where you are, as you are. You don't have to be anything but what you already are to be well.

Be well now, not sometime when you feel you are more worthy, but today when you need to be well most. If you have the self-love, you will not withdraw your perpetual desire to be well from yourself.

There is a price — following a weight-losing eating plan. But that's not much of a price when you consider that you get a well body in return.

Take health, if you want it, today. The more you take, the more there will be for you.

Reaching a normal weight is the beginning of real health and a sense of well-being. Accepting anything less than a well body is like having limited vision.

Enlarge your vision. See the whole. Develop your sincere, conscious and perpetual desire to be well, to feel well and to act well.

Don't sacrifice the thrill of healthful living for the pain of overeating. Don't excuse yourself today. Tomorrow comes. You cannot elude it.

Today you have a determined willingness to be well. This is what you've been waiting for!

Before you reach for that extra bite today, ask yourself:
Do I want to be well? Do I want it so badly that I can't wait another day to start?

One day St. Francis was hoeing his garden when a man approached him, asking what he would do if he were to learn that he would die by sunset. "I would finish hoeing my garden," said St. Francis.

These words, spoken almost 700 years ago, seem to hold an answer for overeaters today. It is so easy for many of us just to give up. What's the difference, anyway, we ask? Why should we bother to strive when some disaster could overtake us? Most of us overweights are so pessimistic that we readily put off painting a picture, writing a song, starting a novel — in fact, we put off even everyday living.

Of course, we can't be sure of anything, but our lives will be what we make them, whether we have ten or one hundred years to live. The best advice still comes from St. Francis. Go on hoeing your garden.

Live today as if today were the most important day in your life. Treat your body as if what you do today makes a big difference. You will meet tomorrow with more confidence if you have done your best today, if you have finished hoeing your garden.

You have an obligation to yourself, an obligation to live your life to the fullest. Don't accept less than your best. Fulfill the present. Today is yours if you don't just let it pass unused. Follow your healthful plan of eating, and stretch your inner self in some new direction. Cultivate your own garden.

Before you reach for that extra bite today, ask yourself:
Am I fulfilling the obligation I owe myself? Who will hoe in my garden, if not me?

Whether you are looking into the world of inner growth for the first time, or you've been working in it for a while, be warned that getting to know yourself is like eating peanuts. You can't stop with just one kernel of self-knowledge.

You'll discover that growing emotionally, while decreasing your outer proportions, can be a fiercely happy experience. Without warning, an insight, like an exploding rocket, can go off inside your head. That is the "aHA!" experience. You think — aHA! — that is what that emotion/behavior meant all along.

On the other hand, growing emotionally can be difficult. You may discover things you would just as soon have left in the dark. You can't imagine how such self-knowledge can help you grow. You actually look upon some discoveries as giant steps backward. And so they may seem for a time, but you will understand as you grow along how they fit into the puzzle of your journey to self-discovery. You will see that, without occasional painful self-assessments, a real leap in growth would often be impossible. Pain is the price of admission we pay for self-growth.

Carl Sandburg said it best: "Life is like an onion; you peel off one layer at a time, and sometimes you weep."

As you touch your inner self, learn to listen and to sense your *aliveness*. Get to know the person you really are. Who do you think you are? Do you see yourself as that unhappy, overweight individual who angrily looks back at you from the mirror? Or do you see yourself as happy, confident, aware, achieving and in control of your food problem?

Get to the bottom of your inner self. See who you are and through daily action bring your inner self into harmony with your true physical image. Have no doubts. You can do it because you are a remarkable person.

Before you reach for that extra bite today, ask yourself:
Am I reaching for an "aHA" experience? Am I willing to pay the price of admission to self-growth?

A small number of overeaters have felt it necessary to seek intestinal bypass surgery. But it is a high-risk measure indeed.

The operation consists of shortening the intestinal tract from its normal eighteen-foot length to a short eighteen inches. As a result, less food (read calories) is absorbed into the body and the person loses weight.

Bypass patients just like you have to watch their diet. They can't consume too much fat, sugar or alcohol in any form because their liver just might not be able to handle these foods. Liver failure is one of the most feared aftereffects of bypass surgery. (Other aftereffects are lifelong diarrhea, vitamin deficiencies and other potential health problems.)

Not everyone is a candidate for such a drastic solution to overeating. Surgeons generally have as criteria that patients must:

1. Be more than 100 percent over their normal weight.

2. Have failed in every other diet method for at least five years.

3. Be a person whose life is endangered by obesity.

4. Be a good psychological risk — that is one who is emotionally stable enough to comply with years of follow-up care.

This surgery is very expensive and can take as long as four hours on the operating table, so that patients, despite their excess weight, have to be fairly good surgical risks.

Such surgery is not for everyone, but it was for Donna Kirkpatrick. At 350 pounds, she was afraid she would not live to see her three children grow to adulthood. Her bypass operation brought her down to 135 pounds, a happier and more healthful weight for her small frame.

Doctors estimate that only about five percent of all overweights qualify for bypass surgery. If you aren't one of this small number, however, you do qualify for another diet solution — bypassing the refrigerator. This is the "operation" that will qualify you for a thinner body without any of the risks. Why not try this inexpensive and reliable weight-reduction method today?

Before you reach for that extra bite, ask yourself:
Do I believe there is no easy way out of my weight problem? Am I willing to find a diet solution I can live with for a lifetime?

There is nothing more discouraging than to hit a weight plateau, when the diet and activities that have been working so well for you suddenly stop working. Here are some suggestions to help you jump off a plateau into steady weight loss again.

1. Sometimes a temporary 25 percent reduction in caloric increase, with a corresponding increase in physical activity will do the trick.

2. If water retention becomes a problem, Dr. Donald J. Barnes, suggests *increasing* the water intake by 15 to 20 percent which will cause diuresis and restart the weight reduction process.

3. Is your plateau a level of weight where you stayed for any length of time "on the way up?" Your body just may be reluctant to leave an old familiar location. Continued dieting and a large supplement of patience is guaranteed by most experts to eventually get you off the plateau.

4. When plateaus persist, check with your doctor to see if you are undergoing any blood chemistry or gastro-intestinal disturbances. Sometimes getting off a plateau is just the process of checking for body change.

5. Last and most important, you should check to see if you have consciously or unconsciously altered your weight-losing eating plan in any way. You may have to return to keeping a food diary to discover the culprit. Whatever is necessary, do it.

Just as a plateau in life often results in a turning point, so can a plateau in weight reduction. In any attempt to change your life by losing weight, the keynotes are perseverance and accomplishment. Take a look at how far you've come, and then take a minute to be proud of yourself. Persevere. The alternative is returning to the living hell of overeating and gorging.

Remember: A plateau is just another step along the road to your new life. You no longer dance to the tune of excess food — now you hear a different drummer.

Before you reach for that extra bite today, ask yourself:
Am I willing to work to get off this plateau, instead of giving up and returning to unhappy habits? Will I use this plateau as a turning point instead of a pitfall?

Without purpose in our lives, we would wallow in self-pity, trying desperately to find a way out of an eating problem we couldn't control. Once we had some control, but as time went on we became more and more compulsive in our eating.

We became ready to give up anything but food. We said, "I'd give my right arm if I could only be thin." We prayed, cried and were humbled by others. We saw that our lives were becoming more and more unmanageable because of our obsession. Finally, we admitted that in order to get some sanity into our eating habits, we would have to follow a new and disciplined way of eating.

When you accept a new way of eating, you have purpose in your life. You see that by bringing order into your eating, you are able to see the rest of your life more clearly. You can see where changes have to be made. You know that you can have the strength to make them.

Most of all, you discover the force of positive thinking, positive feeling and positive doing. You decide you can discover who you really are, by using this positive, creative force in your mind.

What is your purpose for living? You are beginning to see life as an adventure. You recognize your obligation to give yourself the best life you can. If you once renounced happiness for overeating, you struck a bad bargain. Any pleasure you gained from eating too much or eating certain foods, was more than erased by the pain weight gain brought to your life.

Admitting the truth can be a pleasure, a relief. Admit that food has you by the throat, that your life has no order or purpose. If you do, and then go on to a healthful, moderate way of eating, you haven't given up anything. You have acquired something. You will no longer be frustrated because you will be acting in harmony with your deepest inner self.

You can bet on that!

Before you reach for that extra bite today, ask yourself:
What is the purpose in my life? Have I discovered the force of positive thinking, feeling and doing?

Strive for insight. Get to know yourself better today. There are two ways to gain fresh insights. One is by looking at your own behavior — holding up a mirror to it. Another is by looking at the reflections of other people's behavior. Insight from these two sources will give you a self-awareness through which you can change your patterns of behavior.

Why is insight so important to us overeaters? Because it helps us make sense out of seemingly senseless acts. It is precious self-knowledge that every overeater needs.

The more insight you gain, the more signals you will begin to get. If you gain new knowledge of your negative eating behavior, you will get a "stop" signal from your mind the next time you act out that behavior. Knowledge makes it more difficult to react blindly.

Insights are positive, too. When you become aware of your positive personality traits, you will get a "go" signal from your mind the next time you start to act out positive behavior.

Insight is the key that opens the door to self. For the overeater, it is an essential part of inner growth. Many of us have used food to repress our signals, both positive and negative. Without excess food, we are opening ourselves to the uses we can make of insight to help us lose weight and keep it off.

Members of diet groups are particularly fortunate in that they are able to share insights with each other without fear of sounding stupid. In fact, your insight can turn the key to another person's hidden problem. And vice versa.

Practice sharing insights with other overeaters. The more you share the more you know yourself, the more others know you, and the less you have to hide behind pounds and pounds of extra flesh.

How can you miss?

Before you reach for that extra bite today, ask yourself:
Am I holding up a mirror to my inner self? Have I shared a personal insight with another overeater?

Sometimes when we think nothing will ever work for us again, we ask, "What's the use of trying?" This low point usually comes for us overeaters when we've fallen off yet another diet, or when we get on the scales to discover we've not only gained back all the pounds we had lost, but a few more bonus pounds besides.

Believe this. There is real hope for you. Your eating problem can be overcome, not only today, but for all the days of your life. The answer is not complicated, doesn't cost you a lot of money, doesn't require any special tools —and best of all, it never fails.

What is this magic? Simply stated, it is optimistic living. It is shifting into a positive forward gear which allows you to make steady, sure progress. Positive thinking can take hold of you and lift you up. Negative thinking can make you ask, "What's the use of trying?"

Use your creative mind, positively. What is it that keeps getting you down? Often, it's guilt that underlies depression. That's why, when you get down, you give up. And then you keep on feeling worse and worse.

DO WHAT YOU HAVE TO DO WHETHER OR NOT YOU LIKE IT.

Maybe you don't like to diet, but you sure don't like what not dieting does to you, either.

Where does it say that you have to like what you have to do? Nowhere. You'll like diet results well enough, the new body, the new positive mental attitude. Sometimes we overweights sit around waiting for inspiration to strike us. It rarely does. Inspiration comes from *doing* what we have to do, not *thinking* about it.

Sure you can justify your misery. You're fat and unhappy. That would be enough to make anyone miserable.

But you can make each new day a thrilling adventure, full of insight and the satisfaction of knowing *you are doing what you have to do.*

Make a list of things you have to do today. Get right to work doing them.

You are going to feel so wonderful!

Before you reach for that extra bite today, ask yourself:
Am I giving up when there is real hope for me? Do I think I've got to like dieting before I do it?

In the Italian children's story, the puppet Pinocchio wants desperately to be a real boy, but his habit of lying causes his nose to grow longer with each new lie. We overweights want desperately to be thin, so we can live a more normal life, but because we lie to ourselves about food, our bodies grow bigger with each new lie. Everytime we tell ourselves that we can "have just one more bite," we are falling victim to the Pinocchio Complex. Like the little puppet, we can't hide our deceptions either.

Take responsibility for yourself. Begin to modify your eating whether you feel like it or not. Don't try to kid yourself that "this piece of cake doesn't matter," or "I won't try to diet while I'm on vacation." With each new deception, you'll grow and grow.

Avoid feeling sorry for yourself, alone or with other people. Pity parties don't help!

Get a new image. (This means you'll *have* to start being honest with yourself.) Redouble your efforts to support and help yourself. Do whatever is necessary today to get where you want to go tomorrow.

Life should be an exciting, purposeful adventure. Food is only the fuel that keeps our bodies running so that we can experience life — food is not life itself. The more you gain control over your eating, the better you will live, the more you will get back out of living.

First, you have to rid yourself of your Pinocchio Complex. True, self-deception is hard to recognize. If you could see it easily, you would no longer be deceived. You'll have to work at self-honesty. It can only become a part of your life if you get to know yourself and your motives.

What's the difference? Yesterday you were weak. Today you are strong.

Today you know better.

Before you reach for that extra bite today, ask yourself:
Am I kidding myself about what I'm eating? Am I willing to work on a little more self-honesty and a little less self-deception?

Sharing deep inner feelings with others is not the easiest thing for most of us to do. We have our facade, after all, our public face, the one we show to the world which says, "Everything is really all right with me, despite the way I look." Without even thinking about it, some of us practice the big cover-up.

There comes a time, perhaps when you join a diet group, when you are bursting with new insights and feelings about yourself and you very much want to share them with one or several other overweights. Here's how you can best share feelings with others.

First, you should accept responsibility for your own feelings. Blaming others (mom, dad, wife, husband, children, boss, etc.) for the way you feel shows you have recognized a feeling but have no insight into *why* you feel that way. Beware the thought or phrase: "He/she made me feel bad."

Second, communicate your weaknesses as well as your strengths. If you only communicate what is comfortable, phoniness will establish distance between you and others.

Third, learn to listen. If you have any doubt that you don't know how to listen, tape record the next conversation you have. Play it again later. You'll discover that you were so busy thinking of what *you* were going to say next, you missed half the conversation.

Fourth, don't try to overwhelm with your feelings. Choose simple words. Don't try heavily analyzing your feelings unless you are a psychologist. Sometimes when we think we're sharing, we're really just showing off which usually means we won't get much positive response from others.

Remember some of the best insights come from other people. This means we can't always be filling the air with our own words. We have to let silence work for us. We also have to allow others time to respond to our feelings.

Wouldn't it be awful if you missed some particularly helpful response just because you couldn't keep your mouth shut? (And haven't we all done it?) Practice listening and learning today. You have so much to learn and so much to give.

Before you reach for that extra bite today, ask yourself:
Have I shared my true feelings with others? Am I learning from other overweights as well as teaching them what I know?

Have you looked at life from both sides of the scale? Of course you know what it's like to be fat. But if you have ever been thin, you also know what it's like to be on the winning side of the scale.

"It is wonderful to be able to wear last year's winter clothes this winter," said one dieter. "Yes," agreed another going a little further, "and to have all your clothes just one size instead of every size from thin to fat."

There is a physical freedom in losing weight that is more than just carrying fewer pounds. This physical freedom is partially in your head; it makes you walk proud. Because the psychological effects are disastrous, it can be far worse to regain lost weight than never to lose it in the first place.

Don't take that chance. Can you take the uncertainty of being fat again? Can you take the traumatic conflicts every overweight must face? The sneers on the faces of adults? The little child who asks in a loud voice, "Mommy, why is that person so *fat*?"

Once you reach your natural weight, hang on to it with all your strength. The order moderate eating brings into your life, the new healthy body you own are both too precious to give up lightly. Everyday *reaffirm* on which side of the scale you want to live.

It is so easy to rationalize. It is easy to say, "Oh, now that I'm thin, I'll never get fat again," as if some magic wand guards you from harm. *You* are the only magic you have — you and your positive, creative mind. Your self-image is the first positive thing on your list every morning. The real test of how you look at life is how you look at yourself. What do you see? You see a thin, vibrant body full of health and hope. You see two eyes undulled by excess food, looking out at the challenge of life, with confidence.

Make a choice today. When you step on the scales, choose the winning side and the way of eating which will get you there and keep you there. Don't settle for anything less!

Before you reach for that first bite today, ask yourself:
Wouldn't it be wonderful to be one size the whole year 'round? Have I *reaffirmed* on which side of the scale I want to live?

Harvard nutritionist, Dr. Jean Mayer, once observed that overweight teenagers playing games used much less energy than their teammates of normal weight. The same is true for adults. We overweights are remarkably adept at accomplishing physical tasks with the least amount of effort. While it may pay off in dollars to conserve electric and gas energy, it will *not* pay off to conserve your own energy.

Exercise is an obvious way to use up energy stored in the form of extra pounds. The difference between walking and driving three miles to work is approximately an eighteen-pounds-per-year weight loss. And that without changing the amount you eat!

If you tend to be one of those who resists a formal exercise program, you can sneak in a great deal of exercise without feeling it — except in weight loss.

1. When you go shopping, park as far back in the parking lot as possible and walk to the store.

2. Don't take elevators when you can climb stairs.

3. Instead of hiring yard or housework done, do it yourself, and put muscle into it.

4. Bicycle short distances for shopping or visiting.

These are only a few of the ways you can change your habits to use food energy. You can probably think of others.

There's a story about an old woman who tore up her house trying to find her glasses, only to find them sitting securely on her forehead. Supporting your diet with "sneak" exercises is a lot like this woman — what you need is really right near your nose, if you look for it.

Today, tell yourself that you are going forward the best you can — perhaps only in little ways, but in time they will add up to a big weight loss.

Get the best of yourself.

Before you reach for that extra bite today, ask yourself:
Have I looked for little ways to increase my energy expenditure? Am I satisfied with a little progress each day?

John Stuart Mill said that we should "learn to seek our happiness by limiting our desires, rather than attempting to satisfy them." He could have been speaking directly to those of us who try to satisfy every desire with food.

How many times have you overeaten because you were disappointed? You didn't get the boy/girl. You didn't get the job. You didn't get the recognition you deserved. How many times?

Not giving in to desires can become as much of a habit as satisfying them. Saying "no" can weaken the desire to eat, and strengthen your new desire to live without excess food. It is not as hard to say "no" to extra food as it is to say "yes." Why? Because one bite is too much and the entire contents of your refrigerator are not enough. Such is the nature of the overeating compulsion. It is *never* satisfied, only temporarily sated.

Justice Oliver Wendell Holmes said that "life is action and passion..." Sometimes we overeaters put passion first and action later. We *are* passionate people. We have strong drives, diverse appetites and deep feelings. As for the action side of our nature, it is often not fully developed.

Develop your ability to act. Words, alone, may express feelings, but *action* will alter your life.

Practice saying "no" to your desire for excess food, and "yes" to your desire for a healthy, slender body. The more you practice, the easier it will be.

Tell yourself today that you are worthy of a new life. You must believe this, or you will not allow it to happen. Then swing into action. Follow your weight-losing eating plan, and be receptive to self-insight. If you limit your desire to eat, you'll be able to put into action those other passionate desires you've been denied so long.

Before you reach for that extra bite today, ask yourself:
Can I say "no" to my desire to overeat? Is my desire for a healthy, slim body the number one priority in my life?

One of the behavior modification techniques that works best with overweights is to remove the convenience of eating. We like the kinds of food that take little preparation and are easily available for popping right into the mouth.

Dr. Richard Stuart suggests making every "food experience" a meal. Even when you eat a "junk food" snack, he says, sit down at the dining table, use a table cloth and silverware and go through the same routine you would for seven courses. Make it as tough on your habit as you can.

One dieter achieved complete control over his snacking habit by making this contract with himself: He would only eat by candlelight, dressed in a jacket and tie. It wasn't long before he had lost his appetite for snacks.

One of the hardest habits to break is the bread eater's. One method to discourage bread eating is to take out only one slice at a time — and toast it before eating. For each slice you must then get up from the table, go to the bread, take out a slice, put it in the toaster, wait for it to toast and return to the table. This whole boring routine has been proven to reduce bread consumption. The important thing here though is that the overeater keep the contract with him or herself: only eating bread at the table, toasted.

But man or woman does not diet by eliminating bread alone. This technique can help control other snacking habits. You'll find that you have more than one food-related problem and you'll have to eliminate each one, starting with the worst.

Get to work on your eating problems today. Leo Tolstoy once said that a person's happiness in living is involved in work. You may be an engineer, a teacher, a typist, a homemaker, but whatever your job, if you are overweight, you have other work to do.

Plan for your future. Plan to eliminate, one at a time, all the snacking problems you have. Make a contract with yourself, and then keep it. Even if you are an important executive, making contracts worth millions every day, this small contract with yourself could be worth more — your health and happiness.

Before you reach for that extra bite today, ask yourself:
Have I made a contract to eliminate my snacking foods one at a time? Am I getting on with the "work" of my life?

You select the thoughts that you store up in your brain cells out of millions of thoughts that pass through your head. The most beneficial kind of thought for an overeater is a decision. A decision to do something about your weight brings relief. Doing nothing saps your confidence in yourself.

What are some decisions you can make today?

1. Decide that there is no way you can "have your cake and eat it too."

2. Decide that today is a better day to start the rest of your life than tomorrow.

3. Decide that your best investment is in yourself.

4. Decide that with a positive mental attitude you can't help but win.

5. Decide that a new pattern of positive action can only be the result of a new pattern of thinking .

6. Decide to let your mind grow in its capacity to absorb more and more positive thoughts.

7. Decide that there are no more excuses for overeating.

8. Decide that nothing free is worth having and that you will not be able to get by with a minimum of effort.

9. Decide that you must keep busy. Boredom is one of your worst enemies.

10. Decide that since life is largely a matter of choice, you choose to live it healthy and slender.

You are capable of making good decisions, good choices for your life. If you believe that today is the first day of the rest of your life, act like it!

Before you reach for that extra bite today, ask yourself:
Have I made positive decisions which will affect my life? Am I willing to act on the decisions I make?

August 24　Let's Take a Look at Your "Big" Frame

Ask any overweight about his or her body build and chances are the answer will be, "Why, I have a large frame, of course."

Although there is usually some self-deception involved, the truth is that most of us see ourselves as big, too. It is also difficult to look under the flesh and determine what kind of bone structure we really have.

Here's a guide which doctors use to determine whether your body build is small, medium or large.

Small frame means a slight, delicate build with narrow feet, thin chest, small ankles and wrists. Don't think this frame only applies to women; it applies to men as well.

Medium frame indicates a muscular, athletic build with V-shaped chest, sturdy ankles and wrists.

Large frame means a person who is built stockily, with heavy muscles, big hands, husky-looking ankles and wrists.

Now take a good look in the mirror. Try to look under the extra pounds and you'll probably find that you have a medium or small frame. Of course, this means the next time you look on a weight chart you'll have to revise your goal weight — downward.

Why is it important to know your real frame size? For one reason, you play a deadly game when you try to deceive yourself about anything to do with your body or diet. We overweights are such good self-deceivers that one little deception can lead to another and another. The truth, the absolute truth, is our only friend.

Today you will see your body size as it really is. The truth won't hurt because you are working to bring your outside image into line with your inner image. And you have hope, glorious hope, which is the antidote to the pain of truth.

You're going to have a sensational day!

Before you reach for that extra bite today, ask yourself:
Do I really have a big frame? Have I rid myself of all my little, deceivers?

August 25   The Strength of Positive Affirmation

For years, you have repeated negative statements to yourself, such as: "I can't eat less," or "I can't diet because I always fail," or "I am unable to think positively." You have been used to affirming negative feelings.

What would happen if you used this powerful technique to affirm positive feelings? Might you not then be as successful with the positive things you want to do, as you have been successful with the negative ones?

To change your subconscious pattern from negative to positive you must mold new ideas and new concepts into your mental processes. You can do this with affirmation, by combining words and mind pictures.

Decide what you want. Let's say, if you are a woman, that you want to have a body that will fit into a size twelve dress. If you always criticized yourself and lamented over your lack of ability, then you have only to reverse your affirmation.

Get a mental image of yourself in a size twelve dress — not just a weak image, but a strong, intense image you can feel with all the cells of your body. Then repeat, quietly, or better yet, out loud, "I can. I will. I am able to reduce my body to a size twelve dress."

Now comes the work. You must repeat this positive affirmation at least fifty or, even better, a hundred times every day, while holding your vivid mental image.

You must repeat your own affirmation many times over a period of days and weeks until you have created a new, positive subconscious structure which will take the place of the old negative one.

Old habits of negative thinking are firmly embedded in your mind. It will take time and effort to root them out and replace them with the positive thoughts you can use to change your life.

Start today!

Before you reach for that extra bite today, ask yourself:
Do I believe that what I think I can do, I *can* do? Have I set about replacing old negative mental structures with new, positive ones?

Sometimes you cry (wallowing in yet another diet failure) that there are no more doors for you to open. But always there is one more door.

Sometimes you think that quitting is everything — the end of the line. But it is only one end. At the other end is a beginning.

Always you feel regret and more inadequacy when you overeat again, when you could celebrate the days you controlled your eating force. Even for a little time.

Sometimes you have to believe that today is an opportunity for correction.

When you look in your mirror and see your flesh, notice also the resilience which underlies each pound. Even while you cry, "There are no more doors," your hand reaches out to open the next one.

Try to help yourself. Did you know that a moderate way of eating is a statement of self-love?

You have a mind that allows you to offer shallow self-deceptions, and at the same time you have a deep understanding of who you are. In a way, it helps.

Ask yourself once in a while: What is a day worth to me?

Sometimes it is difficult to trust a body whose appetites betray you time and again. But distrust is a cage for overeaters. To be free you must always trust again. When will you?

You know your mind by heart. It is the safest place of all, because you can make new imprints there, whenever you choose. When do you choose?

Remember this: You are only between seekings. You are only between doors.

Before you reach for that extra bite today, ask yourself:
Will I never give up? Am I reaching my hand toward the next door?

To take or not to take vitamin pills is a question all dieters ask sooner or later. But do you really need them, to begin with? If you eat a varied diet and are in good health, probably not. Sometimes when we overweights are on weight-losing diets, our doctors will suggest a multi-vitamin just to be on the safe side. There's nothing dangerous about a moderate supplement approved by your doctor.

But be careful when it comes to falling for the megavitamin-popping craze — going on vitamin pill binges which are supposed to help you lose weight faster, improve your sex life, protect you from cancer, or help you grow a thick head of hair.

You hear these claims all the time, but not one of them has been substantiated, and excesses can be toxic, expecially of Vitamins A and D.

Vitamin C is another vitamin which has claims made for it — from curing the common cold to protecting against cancers caused by chemical pollution. Although there does seem to be some evidence that C is a help with colds, the other claims are speculative at best, and harmful at worst. Too much C can destroy Vitamin B12, with anemia the possible consequence. When it comes to vitamins, we dieters hear a familiar refrain: everything in moderation. It turns out that most of us can get all the vitamins we need right in the food we eat, which, for us, is a happier possibility than swallowing pills.

But overeaters constantly look for an easier, softer way to lose weight and keep it off. Wouldn't it be nice, we think, if our only problem was a vitamin deficiency — pop a pill, and off come the pounds?

It's a good thing to remember that different people have different nutritional needs. Check with your doctor or nutritionist about yours. (Don't take the vitamin advice of friends or neighbors.)

Eating is only one of your human needs. It might be pleasant today to dwell on another need you have. Which one will it be?

Before you reach for that extra bite today, ask yourself:
Am I taking the wrong advice about vitamins? Do I remember that moderation is the dieter's number one rule?

One of the best things dieting homemakers can do for themselves is to keep food out of sight. Does that sound impossible? After all, part of the definition for homemaking means handling food — and lots of it.

Do it this way. If you must work in the kitchen, removing temptation is not easy but it is possible. One method is to take a single ingredient from the cupboard or refrigerator at a time, and return it before you take out another.

Dr. Richard Stuart, the behaviorist, also suggests that you choose dishes that require *elaborate* preparation rather than easily prepared (convenience) foods which lend themselves to snacking.

Above all, banish from your home all those containers, such as candy dishes or cookie jars, that serve to remind you of your appetite for sweets.

If you're alone for a meal, such as lunch, don't eat standing up. Sit down at your table, use a small plate and serve yourself just as if you were having a fancy luncheon.

There's a reason for the small plate. We overeaters were taught to finish — and we delight in finishing — everything on our plates. Studies show that, even though we're full, we don't stop eating until our plate is empty. It's the same principle as the bowl of salted peanuts: We gobble up the entire bowl long after we have tired of their taste.

Set a goal for yourself today. Plan to give the rest of your life as much of your power of concentration as you give food. If you have not been in the habit of setting goals for your life, you will be amazed at how much satisfaction you'll derive from the simple process of goal-setting.

Try to make them attainable, and don't make too many at one time. That's the secret of reaching goals.

Before you reach for that extra bite today, ask yourself:
Do I think I can't lose weight because I'm the family cook?
Am I willing to set a small goal and attain it?

August 29   How to Slow Down Automatic Eating

Studies have shown (and we know it ourselves) that overeaters are compulsive not only about quantity and frequency of meals, but about fast eating. We wolf down meals, completing them long before others do. It may take us half an hour to prepare a meal, but only two minutes flat to eat it.

Two psychiatrists, Walter H. Fanburg, M.D., and Bernard M. Snyder, M.D., have come up with several ways we can eat more slowly. Their tips give our stomachs time to send signals to our brain that we're not hungry anymore.

Here are six slow-down techniques which have proved helpful to others.

1. Do not pick up another bite of food until you have chewed and swallowed the one in your mouth.

2. Take a rest period after a certain (say five) number of mouthfuls.

3. Put your fork down frequently.

4. Pay more attention to the taste, smell and texture of food.

5. Try to be the last person to finish each course of a meal.

6. Never finish a meal in less than twenty minutes.

There, that takes care of meals. But how do you slow down when you open the refrigerator looking "for a little something?" The trick here is to make the tempting snack foods as inaccessible as possible. Put them in the back of the refrigerator — way back. And put your low-calorie beverages, skim milk and vegetable sticks up front, *where you'll see them first.*

What's that you say? You've heard all this before. That may be true, but if you're not *doing* it, hearing it obviously hasn't helped you lose weight.

Get into action. Slow down your eating. If eating has become an automatic process, stop and savor and taste. Enjoy.

Before you reach for that extra bite today, ask yourself:
Have I tried to slow my fast, automated eating? Am I making meals more pleasant by taking time to really enjoy what I eat?

Self-actualization is a term used by the human potential movement to indicate the continuing struggle to become what you *know* you are.

Actualizing yourself is like declaring your own independence — proclaiming your own life, liberty and pursuit of happiness. It is an attempt to find the *whole* you.

You may think you see the whole you, especially when you look in the mirror. But you do not *see*, unless you are what you want to be. Are you?

You are absolutely unique in this world. Without you the world would be diminished. Do you believe that? You must. It is part of your pursuit of wholeness.

What do you want to be? Are you moving steadily, daily, toward your goal? If you are, you are pursuing happiness. If you are not, you are probably unhappy.

For overeaters self-actualization usually takes the form of losing weight first. Somehow the extra pounds cover more than just our real shape. They obliterate our human potential; they hide our abilities and skills. We must begin the struggle out from underneath our flesh before we can begin to fully realize who we can be.

Getting to know yourself is like getting a second chance. You no longer have to flounder around blindly. You can move forward to meet your goals with confidence.

Living is a challenge. Don't just let it happen to you. Use your creative mental force to meet the challenge of living today. Sure you have some emotional scars. But they don't add up to future failure, unless you allow failure to engulf you.

You will find that as you actualize yourself, you will give birth to a new, free image of your capabilities.

You can be thin. You can become a "whole" person. Absolutely.

Before you reach for that extra bite today, ask yourself:
Have I declared my independence of food? Am I allowing my weight to cover up my human potential?

A famous eastern philosopher has an aphorism which should be a daily standby for us overweights. He suggests we say to ourselves: "I will be what I will to be. I will do what I will to do."

Here is the most positive affirmation of personal, mental power. There is complete positive energy in the statement. There is no hesitation, no limited phrase, no "maybe."

We overeaters fill our lives with "maybe's," "but's" and "sometimeses." We approach life so tentatively.

There is boldness in, "I will be what I will to be; I will do what I will to do." There is control there.

Say it aloud to yourself, morning, night and noon. If you believe you have positive power, there is no need for you to live in misery. You can change your condition. It all has to do with changing the patterns of your mind. It is not even too difficult.

Instead of applying the tentative word "maybe" to our goals, try using the positive word "will." You will find that the force of this word will stabilize your thinking and give you new hope.

The power of a positive thought is very strong. It can awaken strong feelings, especially when you repeat it over again and again. Each word will become a new imprint on your conscious mind, giving you the power you need when you need it.

Strong, creative thoughts will help open a new channel which you can use to get to know the inner person you are.

You will be what you will to be; you will do what you will to do. There's no doubt about it.

Before you reach for that extra bite today, ask yourself:
Have I got rid of all the "maybe's" in my mind? Do I believe that a positive thought is so powerful it can help me live as I want to live?

Diet Workshops, with hundreds of groups throughout North America, uses many behavior modification techniques with its members. During a six-weeks program, members take the following steps:

1. The first week practice sitting down while eating, plus using the proper utensils. (If you work, clear your desk, and set a place as you would your dining table.)

2. During the second week, practice eating with no distractions — no reading, radio listening, TV viewing. This will help you concentrate *only* on your eating.

3. In the third week, adopt a slow eating style.

4. In the fourth week, write your daily menu (including any snacks allowed) in advance. This halts spontaneous eating.

5. During the fifth week, put some time between your desire to eat and the act of eating itself. In other words, give yourself a mental "O.K."

6. The sixth week calls for a discipline overeaters rarely practice. Leave some food on your plate. This shows that you have control over food; food doesn't have control over you.

What's all this talk about behavior modification? You know, it's not really new. A Columbia University professor, John B. Watson, first described it in theory back in 1913. But it has only been used successfully with overweights during the past ten years.

It seems fair to say that becoming aware of the way you *act* when food is around and the unconscious *cues* you get which make you want to eat help you to know yourself better.

But even sound psychological techniques can't help unless *you* make them help. You are what you think you are and can do what you think you can do.

Diet Workshopper Betty R. has one behavior modification technique she uses when everything else fails: "I just remember when my five-year-old son came home bruised and bloody because he fought some other boy who called me 'Fatty.' "

Before you reach for that extra bite today, ask yourself:
Am I planning my eating so that I have control over food?
Have I become aware of what I do with food?

September 2   Do You Know Where You're Going?

The philosopher Sam Jones said with some humor: "How do I know what I'm thinking until I see what I've said?"

A lot of us probably think we won't know where we're going until we get there, but that's not necessarily true. There are tests you can apply to your life which will indicate in which direction you're going. More important, these tests will let you know how much you are growing as you are going.

Of course, you've set goals for yourself. If you're overweight, you already know how much weight you want to lose.

Test your growth these three ways.

Ask yourself:

1. What am *I* doing to accomplish the results I want? Too often we rely on others, a doctor, for example; or on things, a pill, for example.

2. In the light of continuing self-knowledge, is the goal I set for myself realistically attainable? Sometimes in the first flush of determination, we set a goal that is impossible. We may want to give up altogether when we realize what we have done. Why not revise our goal before we get to the give-up state?

3. What has my present accomplishment taught me about what I can expect of myself for the future? Our accomplishments can teach us what we need to know for future goal-setting if we really learn to assess them honestly.

These questions are a checklist to point you in the direction you want to continue moving. You are on a journey, and you'll make better time and progress with a periodic check of your road map.

You may want to set some goal every day you live. That's your way of saying, "I will never give up on life." Lovely.

Before you reach for that extra bite today, ask yourself:
Will eating excess food help me move in the direction of my primary goal? Have I checked my road map to see that I'm still on course?

September 3 What If You Can't Control Your Temper?

We overeaters sometimes have a great deal of anger bottled up inside. Most of us don't have the self-assurance to direct anger toward our problems, especially since we try to put on such a good face for the world. What happens to our legitimate anger is that we hold it in until it explodes. We direct it against ourselves in one big angry eating binge.

Has this ever happened to you? You are in the midst of a big explosion. Everybody within hearing distance is getting a taste of your anger, when the doorbell suddenly rings. "Oh, hello, Mrs. Neighbor," you say sweetly, "it's so nice to see you."

You have easily controlled your anger because you needed to. You control your anger in situations where you think you cannot get away with it.

What if you no longer allowed yourself to take your anger out on you? You would only need give yourself the same sweet recognition you would give a friend or neighbor, treat yourself with the same consideration and kindness.

The trouble with taking out your anger on your own body is that you don't solve the problem you're angry about, you create a new and far worse problem.

Why not use anger in a creative way? Anger is really just undirected energy. If you learn to direct it outward at your problem (instead of internalizing it), you can use this energy to find solutions.

First of all, get your anger under control by treating yourself the same way you'd treat someone who rang your doorbell in the midst of an angry explosion. Next, direct your anger toward your real problem — fat. Get angry enough to do something about it. Try a diet. That's a marvelous form of directed energy. When you lose weight, you'll really have something to shout about!

Before you reach for that extra bite today, ask yourself:
Is my anger directed at me instead of my problem? Do I know that my real anger is directed at my fat?

Remember when obstetricians used to tell expectant mothers to eat for two? Those happy days are gone forever. Now doctors know that big mothers have big babies, and big babies can become big (read "fat") adults. Overweight mothers also run a greater risk of complications during pregnancy and at delivery time.

Dr. Kenneth Travers says that pregnant American women average a weight gain of twenty-seven pounds. This certainly means that they *should not* eat for two. If you're pregnant, you need about 10 extra calories a day in the first trimester, 85 extra calories per day in the second trimester and 220 extra calories daily in the third trimester. That means that your intake at time of delivery will only be about 2,300 calories per day — not enough to lose weight on, but not enough to gain excessively on either.

"When I got pregnant," says one dieter, "I thought it would make my fat legitimate. I gained sixty-one pounds during my pregnancy and spent two days in false labor before my baby was born."

Another overweight mother reported: "I gained thirty pounds while I was waiting for my baby — and she was adopted."

Pregnancy and motherhood can be protective shields for overeaters to hide behind. Sooner or later, however, the pounds must be faced.

At this often heard phrase, many of us sigh. Impossible, we say. The problem is too big.

"Not so," comes the answer from deep in our inner selves, "the only impossible thing in the world is quitting."

What is your conception of things that *are* possible? In our society we have been taught that everything should be easy and, moreover, instant. We demand instant solutions to problems when there is only steady progress toward solutions.

Within the limits of your life so far, you have seen many miracles. Why not believe that one will happen to you if you help it to happen? You haven't even begun to discover what is possible for you. Before you're through, the word "impossible" will no longer be in your dictionary.

That's the spirit!

Before you reach for that extra bite today, ask yourself:
Why do I continue to think of myself as a victim, someone things happen to? Have I tried to start a miracle in my life today?

We overeaters have lived in two very different worlds that were separated only by one act, one moment of decision.

One day we lived in a world filled with unloving, hostile people; a world devoid of empathy and compassion; a world of suffering and despair.

There seemed no way we could escape. When we struggled against our place in that world, we were laughed at or scorned.

We walked down streets, avoiding the eyes of oncoming people, because sometimes we could see disgust mirrored there — their own and ours.

On occasion, because of a pressing inner need, we would reach out our hand, only to draw it back, empty.

Then we made a decision. We would control our eating and not be controlled by it from this day forward. We would grow mentally and emotionally and take our rightful place with mature people.

By this act of decision a new world was created. Where before we saw and felt only pain, we now felt that the world was a challenge for our creative mind. Where before we saw disgust, now we saw admiration. Where before we saw only eating as a solution, now we saw endless options. Where before we came out empty-handed, now we had another hand in ours.

Had the world really changed that much or had we changed?

If you would change the world, first change yourself. How? Make a decision. Which world do you want to live in? It's your choice.

Before you reach for that extra bite today, ask yourself:
Which world do I live in? Is today the day I make a decision about how I plan to spend the rest of my life?

Many of us overweights tend to worry a great deal, mostly about things we can do nothing about. Here's a good lesson in accepting the things you can't change: *If you have lemons, make lemonade!* In other words, learn to make the best of what talents you have.

That doesn't mean you can't create or learn to innovate. Just the opposite. If you don't spend time flailing around against the inevitable, you'll have more time and strength to pursue what you can do something about — or better yet, what you want to do.

What is the one (or more than one) thing you've been postponing all your life? Perhaps, you've been telling yourself, "I'll do it when I've lost weight." Do it today. Or at least begin today.

Study, write, dance, think, run, act, play, paint, draw, design, learn, fly, sing, do,

You are the biggest obstacle in your path. *You are!* Why? You are always telling yourself, "I can't," "I'm too old," "I'm too fat," or "I'm not good enough." Don't fill your head with limiting phrases.

You don't have to be good at something to try it, to enjoy it. We're not talking about a new career, although one could come out of trying something you've always wanted to try.

There you have it — acceptance and action. Two ways to live a dynamic life. Without these two friends in your life, you can easily convince yourself that life is dull, painful and empty. Don't you believe it. Go get 'em!

Before you reach for that extra bite today, ask yourself:
Am I wasting energy fighting again what I cannot change?
Have I done something today that I always wanted to do?

There is one desire all people, thin or fat, have in common, and that is the desire to control their own lives. It is a comfort to know that living need not be a matter of fate or luck, that we as individuals can have a deciding hand in it.

The operative principle for controlling your own life is that the creative process can conceive an image which can become real. This principle works for health, self-fulfillment, success, freedom from anxiety or building better relationships. In fact, what you can do with your mind in building a thinner image of yourself, you can do for many other areas of your life as well.

Get acquainted with your own mind. You can do this by meditation, or if you prefer, quiet times with yourself. These are your listening times. So often, we are so busy talking that we forget to listen — to ourselves.

Listening to yourself during quiet moments is a little like turning up the volume on your television set. The more you turn , the more you get, the more power you get, the more you accomplish and come to believe in the strength of your own mind.

Tune in to your creative, positive mind. Learn to give yourself some time each day to let your creative mind power work for you with whatever problem you want to tackle. Trust this power, and it will become increasingly effective.

Today is the day to start unblocking your mind, to get rid of all the false information — the "I can't" information — you've been feeding it all these years. If you do this, your image will grow stronger every day. This is the most basic mental work there is. Next to your healthful, moderate way of eating, creative mental work will do the most to clear away the roadblocks of your life.

There — now you've got it!

Before you reach for that extra bite today, ask yourself:
Am I tuned in to my creative mind? Have I turned up the volume to get more mental power?

September 8   It's Time to Recognize Change

Quite often people have a mind set that is hard, if not impossible, to change. For example, if you develop a reputation for being the family spendthrift, no matter how you may mature into fiscal responsibility, some people will always assign the spendthrift role to you.

It's bad enough when others label us and try to keep us confined to our labels long after we've outgrown them; it's even worse when we do that to ourselves.

To affirm that a change has taken place in ourselves requires a lot of assurance. This is especially true when we have lost weight and our attitudes about ourselves are in sad need of revision.

One way to recognize change is repetition. If you are, repeatedly, day after day, eating differently and not acting out your old "fat role," then you can use this repetition as a sign of inner change.

Another way to recognize change is insight. Your experiences cannot be denied. Say you have gone shopping twice now and each time returned with a size smaller clothing, these experiences confirm that you are in the process of changing your body.

Sometimes we hang onto old labels because they are comfortable, or because we get a sympathetic reaction from others. We say, "Oh, I'm really not very nice," or "I'm just ugly and fat." Two ways to diminish the stranglehold of old labels and grow in our new identification are by recognizing the repetition and experiences which affirm change.

Stop limiting yourself to old roles. Encourage yourself in new, more positive ones. Psychologist James Kilgore says: "If you don't live it, you don't believe it." He suggests that *belief* is a powerful affirmation, *confirmed* by action.

Therefore, believe only what you want to live.

Before you reach for that extra bite today, ask yourself:
Have I been confining myself to narrow old labels that have nothing to do with the new me? Do I recognize that my acts confirm my beliefs?

During the premenstrual period, many women have a craving for sweets. This craving doesn't last long, according to doctors, usually one day, but it can play havoc with a diet.

Here are some suggestions from weight experts for satisfying this craving without consuming too many empty sugar calories:

1. Practice relaxation techniques, says Dr. Carl L. Ebnother, who equates this craving with premenstrual tension. Self-hypnosis, meditation or exercise can relieve the tension and along with it, the sweet craving.

2. "I have observed this craving happens just prior to the menstrual period," says Dr. Francisco Gnecco-Mozo. "Eating artichokes or dill pickles frequently calms the need for sweets." (Who would think artichokes would substitute for candy? Apparently two foods scientists, whose recent research indicates that one-fourth an artichoke heart has the sweetness of two teaspoons of sugar.)

3. Low-calorie sodas and increased protein consumption is the prescription of Dr. Halford R. Price. The protein can be taken in the form of extra beef or eggs, or protein powder added to low-calorie soft drinks.

4. "Cravings indicate need," says Dr. T. C. McDaniel, who checks his patients for hypoglycemia and also for vitamin and mineral deficiencies.

If you have a premenstrual craving for sweets or an abnormal craving at any other time, you should check with your doctor, especially if you discover you can't handle it by yourself. When you ignore the problem, it can set you up for unnecessary weight gain, plus reinforcing old eating habits you're trying to change.

You've come too far to quit now. You have too far to go not to keep a steady forward pace. There may be trouble spots along the road, but you are laying the groundwork for a new, dynamic life. And what's more, you're getting the hang of it — beautifully!

Before you reach for that extra bite today, ask yourself:
Am I dealing with temporary cravings? Do I believe that there is help for any problem I may encounter on the road to a slimmer body?

What an exciting time this is! We live in a world of movement, action and achievement. Medical problems are being solved right and left; perhaps in our time there will be a cure, or several cures, for obesity. But the point is, we can't wait for a "maybe" miracle to happen to us; we'll have to go out and make our own miracle.

Our ancestors thought miracles were supernatural, that is, "beyond the natural." A modern definition is "supremely natural," the result of our working with natural laws. For us overweights, this means we must work within the confines of the laws of energy, if we wish to lose weight and maintain our "natural" weight. And then, truly, we will be making our own miracles.

Tune in today to the natural power of your mind. Negatives are minuses. Discard them. Positive thoughts are pluses. Now, put the positive together with your right to make choices. You live in a democracy; you have an inalienable right to choose your own course. Positive power and choice — now that is the stuff of which miracles are made everyday.

Did you ever stop to think that overeating is an act out of harmony with the natural? It dulls your senses, limits your free choice and creates a negative aura around your body. It is an act against Reality.

Reality is health, a body that pulses with life and a mind that illuminates the truth. A moderate way of eating for vigorous health *feels* like the Truth.

Miracles are not things that happened to other people a long time ago. Miracles happen today, to people like you, who make them happen.

Work on your miracle. (There! Don't you have real respect for yourself?)

Before you reach for that extra bite today, ask yourself:
Have I been waiting for a miracle to happen, a cure to be found, when I could be making my own miracle? Am I using my positive power and choice today?

"Nothing succeeds like success!" goes the old saying and there's a lot to that. Research shows that the more weight you are able to lose, the more you think you can lose — and the more you can help others with a weight problem.

What are the elements of success in weight-losing? Dr. Peter G. Lindner who has treated thousands of patients over a twenty-year period has ten year follow-ups on many of his patients. He says the ones who have successfully kept their weight off have three things in common. They are:

1. Knowledge.
2. Attitude.
3. Behavior.

These successful people had developed the knowledge that overeating was harmful to their health and self-esteem. Second, they believed that quitting overeating was the most paramount experience in their lives. Third, they had taken their knowledge and attitude and translated them into behavior changes which together insured their continuing success.

When does your preparation for lifelong diet success start? It starts *right now*. Whether you are sixteen or forty or sixty-five, it starts right now. Where does it start? It starts with your own powerful, positive image. This is basic to success because such an image gives overweights *permission* to learn and to change.

Losing all your weight won't mean that there will be no more problems to face. What it will mean is that you can face life's disappointments with all that weight *off your back.*

Wouldn't that be a blessing?

Before you reach for that extra bite today, ask yourself:
When will I give myself permission to lose weight? Have I developed the habits of success?

One of the most startling and thought-provoking studies on overweight was recently completed by the Gerontology Center of the National Institute of Health. In comparing the mental and physical health picture of excessively overweight people in their thirties, it was found that they approximated the statistics for thin seventy-one year olds. In other words they had the mental and physical profile of people *twice* their age. Add to this, that life expectancy is lowered as much as fifteen years for the very obese. From the standpoint of these "lost years," *overweight can be regarded as a form of premature aging.*

Now that's bad enough, but what about the years we *do* live? There are problems there, too. Many of us have breathing problems because of the excess weight on the chest wall, adult-onset diabetes, joint problems from carrying extra pounds, childbirth complications, blood pressure and kidney troubles and, of course, heart complications. On top of all these potential disasters, many of us just plain feel mentally rotten about ourselves.

The fact that overweight is bad for us is not exactly a news flash. You'd think all this information would make us a nation of thins. But it hasn't. Why not?

"When I was in my twenties," says one dieter," a doctor tried to scare me thin by saying I wouldn't live to reach forty.

"He scared me all right, but when I'm scared, I overeat."

Despite this dieter's reaction to the doctor's dire warning, she became a successful weight-loser. She found the loss of a healthy life more frightening than the fear of death. "I hated to waste all those years being only half alive," she said.

Sure it's important to prolong life, but it's even more important to be fully alive no matter what your age. If overweight can be regarded as a form of premature aging, then losing weight can be looked on as a kind of fountain of youth.

Wouldn't it be nice to be really young again — in body and mind? You know how you can strip the pounds and the years off. Simply follow one of the dozens of healthful weight-losing diets around. If you do, you'll find the fabled fountain of youth. Drink deep.

Before you reach for that extra bite today, ask yourself:
What is my real age? Am I willing to reverse the aging process by following a weight-losing diet?

"You look so haggard and drawn," your friends say, after you've lost a lot of weight, "Don't you think you'd better stop that diet?"

How do you handle friends and family who are honestly worried about your appearance? Here are some ways:

1. The first sight of a much smaller you is bound to be a shock. Let them get used to your new face.

2. Tell them most people losing large amounts of weight look haggard until they have been down for a time — then their skin tone improves. The little wrinkles and loose skin will firm up, usually after an initial flabby period.

3. Ask them to remind you to drink more water. Most overweights do not drink enough to keep good firm skin.

4. Tell them that you are under medical supervision and will check with your doctor for his opinion.

Honestly, sometimes all the chatter about "haggard and drawn" appearance is nothing less than a little jealousy. First, take a look at where the remark originates. Is this person overweight? Or does he or she have a stake in keeping you fat and dependent?

It is indeed surprising how our friends and relatives can be enthusiastic up to a point. But when we get to a place close to true thinness, some people manifest an extreme desire to tempt us off our diet.

It's your life — and your face. If you do look a bit gaunt at the end of a diet, you can be assured that your face will fill out somewhat during a few months of weight maintenance. If you are not looking gaunt (to yourself or your doctor), then you can forget the remark since it's obviously a manifestation of conscious or unconscious jealousy.

The important thing is you are changing your life. Other people will just have to get used to it.

Before you reach for that extra bite today, ask yourself:
Am I using a chance remark about my appearance to go off my weight-losing diet? Have I given myself the opportunity to live with my new face long enough to get used to a thin one?

If you have found a properly moderate and healthful way of eating, you are certainly losing weight. As you lose weight, chances are good that you are also searching for personal inner growth. If this is so, then you have developed that especially mature discipline, consistency. It is the mark of growth, the capstone of thoughtful change.

Don't mistake disciplined consistency with perfectionism. They haven't anything to do with each other. Whenever you say, "Nothing I do is ever good enough; I always fall short of my expectations," then you are talking about compulsiveness, not consistency.

The very word *consistency*, when used in a mature sense, means the freedom to make choices and commitments. The really mature person advances in self-growth based on his or her ability to make commitments, accept their responsibilities and act on them.

The consistent person has a real contentment. Gaining in happiness is as much a journey as a goal. When you are consistent, you can count on yourself to get you where you should go.

Consistency where diet is concerned usually means the ability to advance in small but steady increments until the proper amount of weight is lost. There is nothing so frustrating, nor anything which can fill you with such anger and depression, than to lack consistency in weight loss. It is far better to lose steadily one pound a week, than to lose five pounds one week in a burst of dietary showmanship and then lose nothing for weeks.

See yourself as a consistent person, as a person who, week after week, makes the proper commitments. See yourself as the kind of person you can count on to get you to your goal — on good days and bad. See yourself making wise choices, carrying out your program intelligently and achieving your goal.

This is the image of yourself as you really can be. Yes, you can.

Before you reach for that extra bite today, ask yourself:
Is the pattern of my thinking hopeful? Am I consistent enough so that I can count on myself today?

Guilt is often the subject of Overeaters Anonymous meetings since that group deals with the feelings that lie behind their overeating. "We are people who can't let go of guilt over anything," explains one member, "without first punishing ourselves for the transgression, and our punishment finds its expression in overeating."

Another member told of guiltily sneaking out of bed in the middle of the night while the rest of her family slept: "Food was comforting, but it didn't last," she said. "I always had to get up and go back to feel good again."

A third member said that another word for guilt is resentment. "Anything you feel guilty about," he explained, "you are bound to resent."

Many of us overweight people carry a load of unnecessary guilt around with us. But we learn to travel light as we lose weight because we lose the need to punish ourselves for being fat in the first place.

Some of us even feel guilty for losing weight because others — family, friends or co-workers — have trouble adjusting to our change. Remember: *Change is your right.*

As you lose weight, you will learn to feel without reacting. Your emotions (even guilt) won't always drive you to the refrigerator.

Finally, many of us overweights absorb so much of society's teaching that overweight is "bad," we feel guilty about things other people wouldn't consider guilt-worthy. *Don't pay debts you don't owe.*

Let go of any false feelings of guilt. Let go and *feel* what's happening to you right now. Endorse your own feelings. They're yours. You have a right to them. You do *not* need to pay for them.

More and more these days you are bringing a welcome measure of self-control into your life. And every measure of self-control brings a measure of self-esteem.

Now, how do you like that?

Before you reach for that extra bite today, ask yourself:
Am I sabotaging my best efforts, acting out guilt feelings? Do I pay debts of guilt that I never owed with my overeating?

The role that regular physical exercise plays in the prevention and management of overweight is something that most of us talk about, but all too few of us ever do anything about. And yet the reality is that in any program of *fat* control, exercise (which is simply the expenditure of stored fat energy) is more important than you could possibly imagine.

Do you need more proof? Think of it this way. What do farmers do when they want to fatten cattle? They restrict their activity by confining them in small areas, *where the animals can get no exercise.*

If you wanted to deliberately fatten yourself, the best prescription would be to confine yourself to as little exercise as possible. If you wanted to un-fatten yourself, you would do the opposite.

But losing fat isn't the only thing your total body has to gain from exercise. Here's what happens: Living cells constantly metabolize. Oxygen and nutrients move in and waste moves out. There is an increase in the number of red blood cells, clotting time is slowed and your blood is more capable of delivering more oxygen to all the body cells. The vitality of every single cell depends upon nutrition and *activity.*

Dr. Albert F. Robbins, a bariatric physician, counsels anyone over thirty years old embarking on a physical exercise program to have a thorough examination. And, if you're over forty years old, you should be checked for heart disease; over fifty years old, you should start your exercise program by walking, bicycling or swimming before you undertake anything more strenuous.

"Never exercise less than two hours after eating," says Dr. Robbins, "and certainly not in very hot, humid weather since severe fluid and electrolyte depletion and body temperature elevation can occur."

The sedentary nature of your way of living has upset the energy equation of your life. You will have to set it aright again. Couple a sensible diet with regular exercise and you will have your body functioning the way it was meant to .

Why wait to feel better? What's wrong with starting today?

Before you reach for that extra bite today, ask yourself:
What role does regular physical exercise play in my life?
Am I fattening myself just the way a farmer fattens cattle?

September 17   Are You the Master of Your Body?

Eastern philosophies and religions teach self-mastery. Through the use of diet, meditation and ritual, their members are urged to gain control over body, mind and emotions. Self-mastery is a very positive course, whether it's your religion or your need — as it is with overweight people.

Master Subramuniya advises: "Repeat the phrase 'I am the master of my body.' Sit and feel that you are the master of your body. Say it to yourself over and over again.

"Now quietly, without thinking, feel and visualize that you are the master of your body. Really know that you are the director of your physical vehicle, all the while visualizing and feeling exactly what you eventually want to be like. Because what you cause now, you cause in your future."

Think of that. *What you cause now, you cause in your future.* Every little bit of positive affirmation you can awaken today adds up to a more promising future for you. Don't just try to master your body. Also say and feel to yourself that you are the master of your mind and emotions. Repeat over and over, "I am the master of my body, my mind and my emotions."

Does this sound silly to you? Childish? If so, is what you are doing now working in your life? If the answer is "no," give yourself as much positive input as you can. Use these phrases or others, but *do* begin to program your negative mind with positive thoughts.

For too long you have been defeated; perhaps telling yourself you deserve to be defeated. That's not true. Learn to distinguish carefully between what is negative and what is positive. Just because you have always told yourself something, you may accept it as truth. Get it out and take a good look at it. Reject it, if, after careful examination, you determine it is false.

For example, if you have always told yourself, "I'm fat, and there's nothing much I can do about it," reexamine that assumption. It is untrue. You *can* do something, because you are the master of your body, your mind and your emotions.

Before you reach for that extra bite today, ask yourself:
Am I willing to do anything to help myself think more positively? Do I believe that I can master the cravings of my body?

Are you a night eater? You are not alone. Many overweight people consume the bulk of their calories after six o'clock in the evening. Some are unable to sleep without a stomach full of food, and still others awaken in the night and remain insomniac until they have satisfied their night craving for food, usually carbohydrates.

If you have this problem (or if you have periodic cravings of any kind), you may want to take some of the following suggestions of weight-control experts. Here they are:

1. Keep a bottle of a noncaloric drink *at the bedside.*

2. Have your physician check you for hypoglycemia, a lowering of blood sugar levels during the night.

3. Eat a protein snack or a piece of fruit before retiring. Fruit contains fructose and insulin isn't necessary in its metabolism, so a hypoglycemic reaction is less likely.

4. Ask yourself if night eating compensates for the lack of sexual activity.

5. "Substitute something for food," says Dr. William A. Bailey, "whatever is moral, legal and available."

6. Discuss the use of a temporary sedative with your doctor.

7. Try a hot shower or mild exercise before going to bed.

8. Occasionally, a bulking agent such as psyllium seed can be used in the evening meal. Ask your doctor.

Deep-seated habits require you to be ingenious; to try anything that sounds reasonable. The important thing is that you really want to change your night-eating behavior. After all, no one, (and that includes your doctor, a fellow dieter, or your mate) can help you night after night. Eventually, you'll have to take care of this job yourself.

And you can, if you believe you can. You've got the power. Use it.

And sleep well.

Before you reach for that extra bite today, ask yourself:
Have I been honest with myself about my night eating? Am I willing to try to overcome craving whenever it occurs, day or night?

You may not consider yourself an isolated person. You work with people, have a family, friends and certainly deal with service people in stores every day. But if you have the feeling of being "cut off" then you, too, may consider yourself isolated — really alone.

"I had a lot of friends," says one dieter, "and a loving family, but no one seemed to share what I felt. I found myself being less and less active. Sometimes I spent the whole week staying in the house seeing nobody."

It's not that you are really isolated from others, but that you feel isolated within yourself — lonely in a crowd.

One of the best ways to break out of a shell is to make contact with another person *who can understand your feelings.* For overeaters, nothing can fill this bill better than a group of people wrestling with the problem of overweight.

Overeaters Anonymous goes one step further and urges each member to get a "sponsor," a more experienced member who can help resolve the feelings of fat isolation. OA members telephone their sponsors to talk over current emotions and have face-to-face sessions to discuss long-term living problems. The sponsor is non-judgmental, and helps the newer member come to grips with and work out solutions for feelings of isolation. Usually, the advice is to get out of self, to reach through loneliness to another person struggling with an overeating compulsion.

Being alone inside yourself is a form of hiding from truth. Of course, it's good to stay in touch with yourself, but when it takes the place of interaction with others, it can be a way of avoiding the insights other people can bring into your life.

Isolation is one of the agonies of living. You've been alone long enough. You've suffered alone long enough.

Reach out.

Before you reach for that extra bite today, ask yourself:
Do I feel "cut off" from other people? Am I willing to reach through my loneliness to another suffering overeater?

At a diet therapy group, several of the members had reached their natural weight and, with a farewell speech, were "graduated." Listen to what they had to say, and what you have to expect from your own weight loss.

"When I was fat," said Irene speaking happily in the past tense, "I was always suspicious and sullen. After losing 180 pounds, I take things at face value instead of reading things into them."

A college student named Sharon was ecstatic about a twenty-four-pound weight loss. "I have become an almost entirely different person," she reported. "I am able to function better in every area of my life."

Ted, a man of few words, said simply, "I like myself."

"I'm more active," said Roberta, who lost fifty pounds, "and I can do almost anything without the physical strain I used to feel. Also, I'm sexier."

Said Jerry: "I got rid of the 'crazies' as I got rid of the pounds."

This is what you can expect from losing weight — and more: clear thinking, more pep, the ability to cope with everyday living and good feelings about yourself. These seem to be the universal results of getting to a natural weight and rearranging your thinking patterns.

Say to yourself: *I believe that I can live a day at a time without overeating.* Every one of these successful dieters had to have such a belief. They had to have real faith that they could survive without excess food.

You can have that kind of faith by feeding your mind on positive "I can" thoughts. Others have. Irene used them to lose 180 pounds. That's more than the person she is today!

"What's the use?" you ask. Just this. You *owe* it to yourself. Pay up!

Not tomorrow.

Today.

Before you reach for that extra bite today, ask yourself:
Would I like to have the good feelings only weight loss can bring me? Do I believe I can live without excess food like Irene, Sharon, Ted, Roberta and Jerry?

The first day of the fall season has particular meaning for fat people. If you were overweight last Christmas, you promised yourself earnestly that you would not be fat another holiday season. If most of the year has passed and you haven't lost weight, the first day of fall is panic time. "How can I lose all this weight in three months?" you ask yourself with that "what's the use" tone.

The answer is, of course, that you may not be able to lose *all* your weight by any certain date. An *eating-to-live plan* is not something you do until you get to a certain date; it's a way of living with food every day for the rest of your life.

Too often we try to sidestep our eating problem, or tunnel under it, or jump over it or even run away from it. You'd be surprised at how small a trouble is when you turn around and take it on — even losing weight.

If you take care of today and all your todays, Christmas this year or any year will be just another day. You will be able to enjoy it for what it is rather than fear it for what it isn't — just another Christmas you didn't get thin for.

Enjoy the first day of fall and all the days of this beautiful season. Just like spring, fall is a time of year which shows the most change. Fall is a little like you, moving inexorably toward the goal nature planned for it.

You are moving toward your natural body and your natural state of inner growth. You will find that there are lots of things you can do if you try. You can even quit overeating.

Believe it!

Before you reach for that extra bite today, ask yourself:
Am I in a panic because I haven't been working toward my goal? Am I in a season of change?

It is not possible to help anyone who stands in his own way. Sometimes we overweights say we could quit overeating if we could get a promotion, but we can't get a promotion because we're too busy overeating. We say we could quit if the one we loved really loved us back, but we can't get the girl/boy because we are overeating, and feeling miserable about ourselves most of the time. Over and over again we complain that if things were only better, we could stop overeating when if we *stopped* overeating, things *would* get better. Our problems seems to be that we stand squarely in our own way.

Get yourself out of the way. You sure can't fix up the world, but you can fix yourself.

Putting preconditions on a new way of life never seems to work for us overweights. We can't bargain our way to thinnesss.

What does work? Getting busy works. Following a weight-losing eating plan and getting our thinking straightened out works.

Don't spend time crying over what you don't have. Today is here, now. Maybe yesterday wasn't so good, and who knows about tomorrow. But today works. Why not try making today work for you?

Sometimes we overeaters wait for life to happen to us. Sometimes we feel "special" and think that eventually we'll get the breaks that will make taking off weight easy. It doesn't happen that way. We make our own breaks when we get out of the way.

Pursue happiness. It follows that if you are miserably unhappy today, you can change tomorrow by changing the things you are doing. You have duties to perform for your job, your family and, above all, for yourself. If you divide your time among these responsibilities, you will have little time for worry, fear, self-pity or envy. Without these destructive emotions confusing your life, happiness will flow in to fill the gap.

Concentrate on your assets. Move toward life.

Before you reach for that extra bite today, ask yourself:
What am I doing to help myself? Am I the one standing in the way of my own happiness?

Because overweight people have often been characterized as "jolly," it will probably surprise you to know that psychologists consider anger to be one of the outstanding traits of overweights. However, much of our anger isn't acted out against others, but against ourselves.

Have you ever been so angry at someone you binged just to "show" them? Have you ever gotten so angry about something that you overate out of spite? Of course, you have. But far worse yet, you have overeaten because of anger without even knowing it. Fat people have cravings, headaches, neck pains and ulcers — all because of unresolved or hidden anger.

Perhaps you don't see yourself as an angry person. You may think you are more often hurt. According to Psychologist James Kilgore, hurt and anger are two sides of the same coin. He says that often when people feel hurt, they get angry and retaliate. (We retaliate by overeating. "I'll show them," we say.)

Sometimes anger can be passive and remain unexpressed. Then it becomes like a giant sponge, soaking up vital energy and eventually causing depression.

Don't be trapped into overeating by anger. Expressing it in a nonviolent way is the best way of treating this problem. It will give you relief so that you won't have to *do* something about it.

Anger, at best, is an emotional luxury that overeaters cannot afford. No matter how justified, the price we pay is too high.

Each day is related to our life as a brick is related to a house. Each day is a whole day and stands alone, and yet each one supports the other days that go to make up the years of our lives.

Don't add any angry bricks to your house-of-life. They won't hold up. Instead, build each day with the bricks of strength, determination, self-control and health.

You'll have quite a house when you finish.

Before you reach for that extra bite today, ask yourself:
Am I being trapped into overeating out of anger? Do I realize that the only thing eating will "show" people is a bigger body?

It might be well for us overeaters to watch our eating pattern in public restaurants — because some researcher might be watching us. That's exactly what happened when a group of psychologists set out to watch the differences between thin and overweight eaters in a cafeteria-style restaurant.

Using a standardized checklist based on prior research, the observers unobstrusively recorded various aspects of eating such as speed, the occurrence of extraneous behavior between bites (that is, toying with food or taking sips of water), and ratings of mood and tension.

A clear pattern of the *thin eaters* emerged. They took fewer bites per time period, took smaller bites, had more frequent non-food responses (such as playing with food, hesitating, putting utensil down, drinking between bites), stayed at the table for a shorter period of time after eating, were rated less tense and left more food on their plates.

In a second study the same patterns were observed in a school cafeteria with fat and thin children from seven to twelve years of age.

The study's results are obvious, but they bear repeating for emphasis.

Thin people do eat differently, and they start eating differently at an early age.

What does this study mean to you? Simply this. If you begin to imitate the way thin people eat, you will have a better chance of weighing what they weigh.

Recognize that your behavior contributes to your weight problem. Don't stick your head in the sand, refusing to have anything to do with new-fangled theories.

Today, try to imitate the eating habits of thin people. Eat nutritious food in a calm and courteous manner. Allow your meals to become a part of your day, but not its whole focus. You'll find that you have more time for fun. You'll be thinner. And best of all you'll *feel* thinner.

Think how great you'll look!

Before you reach for that extra bite today, ask yourself:
Am I trying to eat more like thin people? Wouldn't it be wonderful to feel thin again?

One of the most negative things we do to ourselves is to expect a rapid and large weight loss. While that does happen to a fortunate few, most of us plod along at our two pounds a week or even less. What should we do when our great expectations don't materialize?

Remember if you don't set up hurdles in your path you won't have to jump them later. To say to yourself, "Oh, I'll probably lose at least one pound a day," is asking for disappointment — and disappointment begs for discouragement.

Most dieters find it easier not to look at short-range weight loss. There are always those weeks when there is no loss, or a much smaller one than you'd planned. Instead, take a look at your overall weight loss. Sometimes it helps to visualize what the pounds mean by finding their equivalent in everyday objects. For example:

Four pounds equals a telephone.

Eight pounds equals a gallon of household bleach.

Twelve pounds equals a bowling ball.

Twenty pounds equals a good sized Thanksgiving turkey.

Forty pounds equals a well fed four-year-old child.

When you visualize the weight you've lost in this way, it does seem like an accomplishment, doesn't it?

One other suggestion to help you stave off diet disappointment: Consider carefully before you compare your weight loss performance with others'. Somebody has always done better than you. This kind of competition sets up a winner and a failure. In reality, both of you have won.

You are getting that winning habit. Hooray for you!

Before you reach for that extra bite today, ask yourself:
Are my weight expectations unreasonable? Have I visualized my total weight loss so that I can lick temporary disappointment?

Have you been intrigued by all the new vegetarian diets? Such diets are not really new. One of the earliest has been around since 750 A.D.

The Chinese emperor Yung-Tse Tang chose a beautiful young woman named Jade Ring to be one of his concubines. Because of her great beauty, the emperor singled her out to enjoy fabulous dinners with him. These feasts were designed to avoid monotony and to pique the appetite — a rich dish offset by a delicate one, a cold dish with a hot, a highly seasoned one followed by a bland, a sweet one followed by a salty one, and so forth until both emperor and his mistress were exhausted.

However, it wasn't long before Jade Ring began to grow fatter and could no longer wear her pretty clothes. Shedding many tears, she begged the emperor for his help. The emperor saddened by her unhappiness ordered the imperial doctors to devise a weight-losing diet on pain of death.

The emperor's chief physician began a search across China to find a cure for Jade Ring. During his travels he discovered that the thinnest people in the country were Taoist nuns and monks who were vegetarians because of religious preference. The doctor secreted himself in a monastery kitchen and learned the secrets of Taoist thinness. On returning to the palace, the doctor made these recommendations to the emperor:

1. Jade Ring should get more exercise by dancing and participating in some sport.

2. She should abstain from wine and her favorite food — hot sweet bean cakes, and instead choose her diet from fruit, vegetables and nuts.

Of course, Jade Ring soon lost a great deal of weight, returning to her former beauty, and the doctor was appropriately rewarded by the emperor. Although the doctor didn't write a best-selling book called *The Taoist Fruit and Vegetable Diet*, his secrets were incorporated into a poem which is still read today.

Does the 1,200-year-old diet sound familiar? It should. Exercise coupled with a fruit, vegetable and protein diet is the basis for most responsible diets today, whether they're vegetarian or include meat.

Before you reach for that extra bite today, ask yourself:
Am I waiting for the perfect diet before I start to lose weight? Have I decided that I am willing to give up my own brand of "hot, sweet bean cakes?"

It's a bit disquieting to learn that psychologists consider overweights to lack a well-developed sense of reality. Alcoholics call it the ability to "look through the bottom of the bottle," which means being able to see the consequences of the act of drinking. Similarly, we overweights do not deal with the consequences (read weight gain) of overeating, while we are in the act. In order to successfully bring our eating under control, we must learn to think of the consequences *before* we eat, not after.

This is a tall order. It means that we overweights must reverse thinking patterns completely. We must get a "new religion." Eating right for weight loss and eventual weight maintenance must become so important to us that we would do anything to keep it. There must be a deep shift in emotional tone. Old negative feelings must disappear. New positive feelings must emerge.

A heightened sense of reality means that we must lose our feeling of defiant individuality so that we can live in peace and harmony with our environment. When we no longer defy, we are open to help and guidance from others. At the same time, we must relinquish negative and aggressive feelings toward ourselves and toward life.

When you accomplish this transformation, you will find yourself almost overwhelmed by feelings of affection, friendliness and a pervading contentment within.

No overeater ever starts out to *eat the whole thing*. We fool ourselves with little bites, and a slice here and there. What if you can take just one bite and stop? It's still the same kind of curiosity that's killed many a cat. What we need is a warning bell that goes off in our heads *before* we start the dreary process. Developing a good strong sense of reality could be what you need to plug into your warning bell to set it off when you need it.

Wouldn't that be clever?

Before you reach for that extra bite today, ask yourself:
Why not stop right now before I overeat, so I won't have to shed all those tears later? Have I plugged my warning bell into my reality circuit?

Famous cover girl model Cheryl Tiegs once found herself weighing an unmodel-like 150 pounds. How does she stay so thin today? "I have to work at it," Cheryl says. "Every day it's a challenge. I have to be conscious of what I eat and how much."

Did Cheryl find it easy to lose her excess weight? "It's never easy," she adds. "You must put yourself in the right state of mind and be determined to make yourself the best you can be."

Nobody just wakes up one morning to find they are fifty pounds overweight. To get there, you must literally make yourself "unconscious." We overweights can use food to block out what we don't want to recognize — especially the part of us that yells, "You're gaining too much weight!"

There's an old saying, "Where there's life, there's hope." Nobody hangs on to that more tightly than fat people. But before we can *really* believe, we have to put ourselves in the right frame of mind, like Cheryl Tiegs, by improving our concept of ourselves.

Do you support the idea that you deserve your happiness? If you don't, happiness will not be yours. Your mind must, in effect, give you permission to be happy, before you can truly become so.

Let a positive image of yourself give you the permission you need to hope — to go forward toward happiness — toward thinness. Like Cheryl Tiegs, make yourself the best you can be by imagining, in the first place, that your best can be very good.

There is hope in your life. *You* are your hope, because you can become whatever you want to be, whatever you think you can be. And you will achieve it, too — all of it.

Before you reach for that extra bite today, ask yourself:
Am I fully conscious of what I'm doing? Have I made myself the best I can be?

Today is the day you are going to do a great deal for yourself. Whether you are losing weight, maintaining your natural weight or sitting on the fence, there are good things you could do to improve your outlook on life.

Are you tired? If you have been working hard, why not take some time off today and rest. Give your body a holiday. But that doesn't mean you should overeat. Excess eating would only make your body work that much harder.

Do you feel guilty about something you said or did? Acknowledge it and make amends as best you can. Cleansing your conscience can be a great relaxer.

Are you angry about something? Admit it. Express your feelings in the open. Oftentimes you'll find that angry feelings exposed aren't nearly as awesome as they were hidden deep inside you.

Take a chance today. Do something, even if it means you'll risk failing. It's better to try than to just sit there and moan.

Talk to somebody else about your fears. A funny thing happens when you share anxieties. You find that other people look at things differently, sometimes they even have solutions. Reach out to others. If your need is honest, they will rarely disappoint you.

Life is not as complicated as we overweights tend to make it.

Let your instinct for survival take over today in a positive way. Rest. Make amends. Admit anger. Risk. Reach out. With a prescription like this, you are bound to feel better — much better — by this evening.

Happy days are here again!

Before you reach for that extra bite today, ask yourself:
What have I done today to improve my outlook on life? Are my survival instincts alive and well?

The Institute of Human Nutrition recently estimated that overweight people eat as much as fifty percent of their food *away* from the table. It's apparent that a considerable change of habit will have to be made before weight loss will be achieved. Here's what bariatricians (doctors who specialize in treating overweight) advise their snacking patients:

"I tell my patients to sit down for a moment and ask themselves, 'Am I hungry?' not 'Do I want to eat it?'" says Dr. Barbara Felland. "The answer is usually, 'No, I'm not hungry.'"

"Eat all the three percent carbohydrate, raw, chewy vegetables you want," advises Dr. Clara Younger. If she has a patient whose stomach objects to raw vegetables, she adds, "Then eat them cooked."

"I tell my patients that the sneaking cycle can reexplode into their former stuffing syndrome," says Dr. Thomas R. Gleeson.

You're not busy enough if you're doing a lot of snack sneaking, say a number of doctors. Snacking, they agree, is quite often done to relieve boredom or tension. Try some new activities, such as hiking, skating, or square dancing.

Constant snacking all day is even harder on the discipline you're trying to build into your life than it is on your figure. If you can't say no to your small food demands, how can you say *no* to the big binges when you're tempted. The answer is, you probably won't. A disciplined way of eating for health and thinness is built in little steps every day, in quietly saying no to your mental demands for a return to old habits.

Set up an image of yourself as one who eats at a lovely dining table, with beautiful service and healthful foods. See yourself eating only in this place in your mind. If you do, you couldn't possibly eat in the bathroom, hanging over the kitchen sink, behind a door or in the garage. You don't have to sneak. You can walk right up to life and grab it. Remember life is a feast, not a snack.

Before you reach for that extra bite today, ask yourself:
What do I need with a snack when I have my whole world to conquer? Am I going to spend my life grabbing a bite here and there, or am I going to sit down to a beautiful feast?

A private California weight-loss clinic called Lifestyle has been working with overweights on concepts of self-control. First, the patients are taught that self-control is a trait that can be developed, not some mysterious power from outer space. Second, self-control, they are told, is nothing more or less than an ongoing, never-ending series of choices.

To increase self-control you must increase conscious awareness of choices and learn the skills necessary to implement them. For example, if you eat too much at the theater you might work out choices that include:

1. Saving calories to allow for theater eating on a given evening.

2. Eat a meal before you go to the theater.

3. Bring along a low-calorie snack.

4. Refuse to eat at the theater at all.

The important thing, says the Lifestyle program, is to praise yourself for eating in a controlled way, or limit your self-criticism if you overeat. When overeating occurs, it only means you have to plan a better strategy for the next time.

At Lifestyle, much attention is paid to building controls into your eating life: *start controls*, which are responses preceding eating, and *stop controls*, responses involved in limiting eating once it begins.

One of the best stop controls is a vivid mental image of yourself, looking the way you want to look. If you have programmed your mind with relaxation and positive self-imagery, you can call up these images when you need them most.

There can be no liberty for any overweight as long as he or she is a slave to overeating. That is why it is so important to build thoughtful control into our lives.

You will not be a slave to your food desires today. You will work out choices which will give you real freedom to live as you want.

Today, you have another chance. Take it.

Before you reach for that extra bite today, ask yourself:
Am I developing self-control as part of my lifestyle? Am I sick and tired of being a slave to overeating?

Your heart, according to the ancients, is the seat of all emotion and, especially, of love. Even so, the heart needs a little love, too, and the best way we can show how much we think of it is to exercise. According to studies, few people today, not even longshoremen, get enough exercise to *protect* their hearts.

After a twenty-two-year-long study to reduce fatal heart attacks, Dr. Ralph S. Paffenbarger, Jr., at the University of California, says that vigorous exercise is beneficial for almost everyone. "Everyone should have a medical examination and start off slowly," he says. "Don't go slamming out in true American fashion, trying to run a mile the first day."

Start out walking, until you get to the point where you can walk 3½ to 4 miles in an hour — that's a pretty fast clip. It will take a few weeks to build up to this rate, so have patience.

Next, walk for five minutes, then jog for five minutes, until you can build up to a thirty-minute jog at least three times a week. "But watch for any signs of chest pain or discomfort," warns Dr. Paffenbarger, "and stop immediately if they appear."

Of course jogging isn't the only way to get *vigorous* exercise. Swimming (if you keep moving the entire thirty minutes), running in place, dancing, bicycling, rowing and jumping rope are also rhythmic and provide the entire body with exercise.

The point is, exercise, if it's going to be good to your heart, can't be sporadic. In exercise, as in dieting, consistency is everything.

Here's another good exercise for your heart. Eat for the thin person you are inside. Be good to yourself today, and give yourself some honest affection. Why not go farther — love yourself!

Your life is a looking-glass, returning to you what you give it. Give it love — for your heart, and for all the rest that goes to make up the wonderful, unique person you are.

Before you reach for that extra bite today, ask yourself:
Have I given my heart some love? What have I done that is good for me today?

October 3   Idle Hands are the Devil's Refrigerator

Perhaps the title above takes a few liberties with the old Puritan saying which encouraged some of our ancestors to work harder, but you get the point. It is very difficult to remain true to a weight-losing regimen and a growing self-awareness when idleness is the order of your day. This lesson has been hard-learned by too many of us overweights who tried it.

Keep busy. There is so much for you to do, so much for you to learn. How many things have you left undone in your life because you thought you were too fat to accomplish them? Do them today, or at least make a good beginning.

Of course, it's also possible to overwork, to become a compulsive worker. Since we overweights are people who tend toward over-everything, we have to be especially careful that we don't use work to make up for our physical shortcomings. Then too, it is possible to overwork until we convince ourselves that we need *extra* food just to keep going.

Moderation in activity seems to be as important to us overweights as moderating our food intake. Too much or too little — both can contribute to our eating problem.

But don't confuse resting with idling. Rest is necessary. It's the pause that refreshes our bodies and our spirits.

Food, work, rest — all in their proper proportion — are part of the constructive program of living you are building every day. They will bring a marvelous new experience into your life. It's called Harmony.

Before you reach for that extra bite today, ask yourself:
Do I know the difference between rest and idleness? Am I willing to get to work for my new life?

There are times when a real anxiety overtakes us and we wonder why we are what we are. Our lives seem to be floating in a sea of meaninglessness. Sometimes our response to this depressive feeling is frantic activity; at other times it is withdrawal. We overweights are particularly good at withdrawing, because we never withdraw alone. Food goes with us.

When anxiety drags you down, and you feel a sense of detachment from the world and from others, the best antidote is to try to develop new relationships. It's not a simple task. Sometimes you have to push yourself for your self's sake.

First of all, try to express in your verbal and physical actions understanding and concern for other people. You can readily see what would happen. You would be unable to continue any preoccupation with yourself and your own feelings. And that's exactly what you want to happen.

Next try to share with others. Share experiences. Feelings of fellowship will grow out of honest sharing.

Finally, try to return what is given to you. If someone shows you warmth, acknowledge it, and respond to it in kind. Be sensitive to the overtures of others and they will be sensitive to yours. Anxiety breeds on supposed rejection, when it could be only a lack of appreciation.

Don't brood when you feel a lack of purpose in your life. Brooding only makes these negative feelings take on immense significance. Open yourself to others, to their feelings and ideas.

If you do, you will find it difficult, if not impossible, to continue a morbid fascination with your own "down" feelings.

You have years of creative living left. You will experience it hour after hour, day after day.

Your greatest achievements await you.

Before you reach for that extra bite today, ask yourself:
Am I dwelling on my own "down" feelings? Have I tried to express, share and return human warmth to others?

A Yoga master has this to say about creation: Begin to know that creation is merely recognizing what is already there — that there is nothing new; everything is within you and is portrayed on the outside as you become aware that it is already created, finished, within you.

Everything is within you. Think about it. All the things you want to be, you already are. All the things you want to have, you already have.

Why don't you know this? Because you have not expanded your awareness. When your sense of awareness is limited you are unable to focus.

Focus on the way you create. Concentrate your awareness on what you are inside so that you can project it outside yourself.

A Sanskrit proverb begins: *Look to this day, For it is life, The very life of life.* Become aware, today, of all that you are, for only then will you know what you can create out of this day.

You can begin the creation of a new life during the next twenty-four hours. In order to match your outside to your inside, you must begin to bring order to your eating and to your thinking. When you do, you will quiet the conflict within you. The reason so many of us overweights have self-image problems is that what we see in the mirror and what we feel inside do not match. When that happens a continous battle begins which can wear us down in short order.

Everything is within you. Think about it. Think about it. Think about it. Think about it.

Before you reach for that extra bite today, ask yourself:
Do I know that creation is merely recognizing what I already have? Am I spending today as if it were *The very life of life?*

What kind of labels do you put on yourself? Do you say, "I'm a fat person without much hope," or "I'm a bad person and I deserve what I get," or "Since I'm fat, I must have done something wrong"? Of course, you may have some positive labels too, but chances are all too good that most of them will be negative.

Some psychologists call this kind of labeling "negative self-hypnosis." It makes us dwell on defeats instead of wins; we spend a great deal of time convincing ourselves that what we want to do is impossible.

Today, why not try the reverse — positive self-hypnosis. Encourage yourself. Don't make sweeping statements which seem to prove in advance that you are incapable of performing whatever it is you want to do. Even if you have failed in the past, who knows (certainly not you) what you will do in the future?

Today you are different than you were yesterday. Tomorrow you will be different than you are today. You are growing each day, therefore how do you know what you will be capable of tomorrow?

Look at yourself. You think differently. You respond to many life situations differently. How can you think that you can't accomplish tomorrow just because you didn't accomplish yesterday? That negative thought denies the reality of your own growth.

And you are growing in your inner self, while your outer body is shrinking to its natural size. When a food temptation comes, you don't say, "I have to give in because I used to give in." You say instead, "I'm growing every day, so I no longer have to succumb to certain foods."

Your new life depends on staying "food sober" and putting positive labels on yourself. Repeat over and over again, "I can do it; I will do it."

There, take a bow!

Before you reach for that extra bite today, ask yourself:
Am I putting negative labels on myself and then making them come true? Have I decided to look at myself in a new, positive way?

Psychologist Virginia Satir developed a list of personality styles which tells us a great deal about how different types of people view themselves in terms of self-esteem. Which one of these are you?

1. The *placater* says, "I'm worthless, you're worthy." This is a feeling we overweights often find ourselves expressing. We assume that if other people are thin, they are automatically more worthy than we are, since fat is "bad."

2. The *blamer* says, "I'm worthy, you're worthless." This person is an attacker, always accusing others of being at fault. He or she is a finger-pointer. The fat *blamer* says, "My mother made me fat," even after being responsible for his or her own eating for twenty years.

3. The *calculator* says, "I'm not worthy, but you're not worthy either." This person believes that all people should sacrifice themselves to a cause or circumstance.

4. The *distracter* says, "Nothing is worth anything." Such a personality type never shares him or herself, because basically, he or she feels unworthy. When the distracter is fat he or she will often say, "What's the use!"

5. The *actualizer* says, "Everything has worth." Most of us overweights aren't there yet, but we're working toward becoming actualizers. We share feelings. We take ourselves and others seriously. We are honest. We take risks because that is the way we grow.

If you believe in your own worth, it means you have more to offer to yourself, others and the world. A feeling of self-worth says that you *value* yourself. You are important.

And you are.

Before you reach for that extra bite today, ask yourself:
What personality type am I? Am I working to become an *actualizer*?

Carlos Castaneda has written: When a man (or woman) decides to do something he (or she) must go all the way.

The most successful maintainers of lost weight seem to be people who do just that — go all the way. "My whole life depends on not overeating," said one maintainer in a special meeting for people at their natural weight. "Nothing in the world can make me overeat.

"I have promised myself I won't do it. And I won't break my promise to myself. I feel that I have given up my right to overeat, and that decision, once made, is final."

This ex-overweight has gone all the way. Her commitment is absolute.

There is a joy in this maintainer's words, a joy of attainment, a joy in powerful positive movement. This is the inevitable payoff for commitment.

You cannot rely on anyone else's image of you. Your concept of self-worth is the only one that counts when you need it to get between you and the refrigerator. Sure you want others to think well of you, but you should concentrate first on *your* image of you. It's got to be a healthy one if you are going to enjoy life in a thin body and a mind uncluttered by self-hatred and confusion.

Prepare to go all the way. Eat moderately today — as if your whole life depended on it. It does.

Don't let the child in you say, "I probably won't be able to do it." You don't need a cushion against failure so that later you can say, knowingly, "There, I knew I couldn't do it."

Sometimes we go a bit further and say, "O.K., I'll try." Even that response is motivated by fear of failure.

Go all the way today. Say, like the successful maintainer, "Nothing in the world can make me overeat."

Now, that's a real commitment!

Before you reach for that extra bite today, ask yourself:
Am I ready to go all the way to commitment? Do I have a well-developed sense of my own self-worth standing between me and the refrigerator?

Do you think of yourself as being beautiful? Most fat people do not. Fat in our society is the equivalent of "ugly." But even though we tend to think of beauty in terms of perfect features coupled with a perfect body, beauty is more than this. We have a great deal of beauty in our lives, and we can easily have more.

Beauty is good adjustment, anything that has unity. Your healthful way of eating is a good adjustment. And that is beautiful.

Faith is beauty. And you have an instinctive faith in your future which springs from within.

You have an *idea* of beauty. Sometimes it hurts because you don't think you can live up to it.

A quality which is most beautiful, is sensitivity. And you are certainly sensitive.

There is but one essence of beauty, and that is truth. Whether you like it or not, you are face to face with truth whenever you step on your scales. It is difficult to believe without the experience, but even weighing your body *can* be beautiful.

Make today a beautiful experience. Do beautiful things for yourself. Put away what is ugly in your life — the binges, the awful depressions, the helpless feelings. Bring some beautiful symmetry to your day, today. Eat moderately, exercise for health, grow mentally and emotionally — for us overeaters *that* is perfect symmetry.

Have a beautiful day!

Before you reach for that extra bite today, ask yourself:
Am I looking for the beautiful in my life? Can I do more to make today a beautiful day?

The whole process of self-realization is a lifetime of getting to know your own internal truths.

What you really seek is not perfection, but daily fulfillment.

To learn *what you are not* is as important as learning what you are.

Self-truth is a realization brought into the light.

When you master yourself, you master self-knowledge.

Self-realization is knowing your own way without depending on others.

Before you can rise above your own limitations, you must know what they meant to teach you. Every time you withdraw from stress before you learn, you fail a little.

There is no such thing as self-knowledge without difficulty. It is the *direction* you travel that is important, not how much trouble you have along the road.

The longer we overweights search for self-knowledge the more natural this new way of living seems, and the more we realize that our old overeating lives were unnatural, physically and mentally.

At first we wondered how we could possibly live without our food crutch. But as we learned more and more about our own capabilities we discovered that we could rely on ourselves.

Start building your new life today. Reeducate your mind to think positively. Learn to look for the pluses in your life instead of the negatives.

The process of self-realization is not a speedy one. It will take you longer than a day. But it will be worth your trouble. The hour will come when you will have forged a new power in the center of your "self," and that power will help you reshape your whole life.

With such a foundation, you can't help but win.

Before you reach for that extra bite today, ask yourself:
Am I working to know who I really am? Is self-knowledge my goal for today?

In a sense, overeating is a search for the end of loneliness. And it's true that for a moment overeating can block out a sense of loneliness. But all too frequently the feeling returns when the eating binge ends. Isn't there some more mature way of dealing with lonelinesss?

Maturity is the ability to function in the world independently — that means without being dependent on others and without the crutch of an addiction.

Death is the ultimate loneliness, but we experience everyday losses that are difficult for us to cope with, too. Take for example the loss of a job, moving from one home to another, divorce, or a minor loss, such as misplacing your billfold. For overeaters, each loss, small or large, can throw us into an overeating binge in an immature effort to cope with the loneliness we feel over the loss.

What is the antidote for loneliness? Self-love and love for others. Love is a feeling of being included in the mainstream of life. It is knowing you are not different or set apart from others. Love, unlike loneliness, knows the world is not indifferent to our pain. If you can replace loneliness with love, you will have no need to fill your empty spaces with extra food.

You used to depend on overeating for a lot of things. It picked you up when you were down. It made you feel less lonely and unloved for a brief moment. But then it dropped you very low. Are you finished with your false dependence on food? Have you begun to develop the concept of your own independent abilities which will safely bring you through any problem?

A famous writer once said: What makes life lonely is the want of motive.

What is your motive for living? Part of your responsibility to yourself is to give yourself a motive. What could be a better motive for an overeater than to live the rest of life without overeating? Self-love is almost impossible while overeating, because food builds a barrier between you and your motive for living.

Today you will not overeat. You will be motivated to move farther down the road to health and slimness. You can make it work. Yes, you can.

Before you reach for that extra bite today, ask yourself:
Am I overeating out of loneliness? Have I taken the love antidote for loneliness?

As every school child knows, this is the day we celebrate Columbus' discovery of America. Poor Columbus! He didn't know where he was going; he didn't know where he was when he got there, and he didn't know where he had been when he got back.

Poor overeaters! We have the same troubles that Columbus had. We need a surer sense of direction. We must lead ourselves with clear purpose, a vision of our own and a willingness to determine the path for ourselves. This is accepting responsibility and developing judgment.

You must have a goal. A new world — the world of thinness — can be your goal. How can you steer a course for your new world? With determination and enthusiasm and a deep desire, you can turn your life around.

There's a whole new life for you to experience when you stop growing physically and begin growing mentally and emotionally. But first you must cease to overeat. Try it today, and make a list of the experiences you now have that you would formerly have blocked out with food. For example, list the hopeful experiences, the helpful ones (where you were able to help others because you had become able to help yourself) and the honest ones. By honesty you can mean not pretending to be someone or something you are not.

There, that's about it. This can be a good day in your voyage to self-discovery. Remember, there's a whole new world waiting for you to find your way to it. And you will with your goal of a healthier, happier life.

A goal is not an ideal which becomes part of your life. A goal is an ideal which *becomes* your life.

Have a happy voyage.

Sail on, and on, and on.

Before you reach for that extra bite today, ask yourself:
Do I have a sure sense of where I'm heading today? Am I making a list of the positive experiences I'm having on my voyage to self-discovery?

There are many formulas for success in business, in social life and in family living — all of them having about the same ingredients. Can you use a formula for success to lose weight? Try these:

1. *Openmindedness.* Most really successful people, including many millionaires and heads of corporations, are flexible in their thinking. They never make a decision which isn't open-ended; in other words, one that they can't amend later given better information.

2. *The ability to turn a problem into an asset.* W. Clement Stone, the multimillionaire insurance executive, says, "In every adversity there are the seeds of a possible equal or greater benefit." Search for the advantage in your problem. It may be difficult to find, and not immediately apparent, but it is usually there.

3. *Willingness to take a risk.* Successful people do not place blame on others or second-guess themselves. They have the ability to get up one more time than they are knocked down.

4. *Ability to see more than one way to do things.* One thing may be right today, another tomorrow. One way may be right for you, another way for somebody else. Successful people have the ability to be tolerant and flexible.

5. *A talent for accepting help.* Nobody can do everything all the time. The willingness to accept appropriate help from others is a sign of self-confidence.

One other trait seems to motivate successful people. They have the ability to search out other successful people and allow their example to guide them.

There it is — the formula for success. Whether you want to be a business success or lose pounds, these ideas can help you chart the right course. Who knows? Maybe you'll be both, successful and thin.

Now wouldn't that be exciting?

Before you reach for that extra bite today, ask yourself:
Have I a personal success formula? Will my behavior today advance my goals of a thin body and a clear mind?

The "art" of living is not an action determined by a set of rules, but an individual exploration of harmony. We overeaters are good at finding devices that separate us from others — we clown, we withdraw or we reject. If we are to successfully lose weight, keep it off and experience inner growth, we will have to seek harmony and balance in our lives.

Eating moderately and growing mentally and emotionally is a way of living so vital, fresh, original, spontaneous and dynamic that life becomes a joy which no problem can take away.

To find harmony in your life, you will need to live naturally, which for overeaters means to eat naturally. Giving up frantic binges and huge sweet offerings is the first step toward inner harmony, toward inner peace.

To live is not merely to experience, but also to act. But there is no right action without understanding. Understand today what you must do, and why you must do it.

Expand your thinking, while keeping it open and sensitive. What do you want to give yourself most, today? Now, act, with the full force of your being. Don't bother at all, if you can only give a little part of yourself. A small effort won't do. Let's say you want to begin a weight-losing eating plan, or to make the one you have now even better. You can do it. Just live every moment today as though you were building a perfect body, cell by cell.

Philosophers call today the *Eternal Now.* So think of today as an eternity. You will follow every positive thought with a positive act. You will recreate yourself minute by minute, molding each part nearer to your goal.

Live!

Before you reach for that extra bite today, ask yourself:
Am I practicing the "art" of living? Am I living in the *Eternal Now?*

One thing you must have is a balanced supply of crucial minerals. You only need them in minute amounts, says Dr. Henry A. Schroeder, an authority in this field, but they are "the basic spark plugs in the chemistry of life." The list of trace minerals you need for biochemical and physiological health reads like a geology student's final exam: fluorine, chromium, manganese, iron, cobalt, copper, zinc, molybdenum and iodine. There are dozens of other elements that occur in concentrations too small to measure, which work in thousands of intricate ways. Deficiencies can cause serious health problems. For example, lack of iodine causes goiter. Lack of fluorine causes weak bones and poor teeth. If you don't get enough iron, you become anemic.

The right proportion between minerals seems to be one *key* to good health for dieters. Take for example, the three elements cadmium, zinc and copper. Too much copper in proportion to zinc may be a signficant cause of high blood cholesterol. Too much cadmium may result from eating highly refined foods. Too much zinc can result from eating a diet too high in fats.

Most experts in the field agree that except during certain times (such as pregnancy) mineral supplements are probably not necessary *if you eat a healthful, balanced diet.*

But, of course, that is the whole problem with overweights. We have often been called "overfed but malnourished," because we tend to concentrate on high-sugar, high-fat foods.

Health is a precious asset. Ill health is a liability. Aren't you tired of living a half-healthy life? If you suspect you may have a mineral deficiency, see your doctor, who may prescribe a mineral supplement. But can you guess what his long-range prescription will be? That's right. A properly balanced diet. Don't let that worry you. While you are getting your body's minerals straightened out, you'll also be losing weight. That's a natural result of moderate, balanced eating.

You don't have to wait for your body to threaten you with a breakdown before you begin your new eating plan for optimum health. You're too smart for that !

Before you reach for that extra bite today, ask yourself:
Am I eating a healthy, vitamin and mineral rich balanced diet? Do I want a healthy body?

Have you made it your business to learn more about nutrition? Oh sure, you know generally that certain foods containing a high carbohydrate or fat content are not good for your diet. But have you ever taken the trouble to learn what foods in combination make more complete proteins, what vegetables contain high concentrations of essential vitamins and minerals, and what foods supply necessary roughage to compensate for today's bland, processed foods?

This information is not a secret. Most state health departments, the federal government and a number of good books (with more being published every year) contain enough information to help you choose the most nutritious foods.

"Man is what he eats," says an old German proverb, and the increased obesity and other ills of the twentieth century have seen this speculation come true in a negative sense. Most food consumed by Americans has rapidly increased in hard fats, sugar and super-refined ingredients from which all fiber has been removed. The most obvious example, say nutritionists, is the cotton-like white bread on most American tables.

You owe it to yourself to discover what the food you take into your body will do for your weight loss or maintenance, and your future health. This is one of the concerns of a responsible person, whose diet is engineered to provide optimum good living.

Start today, making a study of the food you eat to determine what it's really doing for you. If you discover that some of it is just sweetened fluff, you may decide to remove it from your diet completely.

One of the responses many people, especially over-weights, give to the suggestion they study something, is, "Oh, I haven't got the time to spend on that!" Think of it this way. With an increased emphasis on good nutrition in your life you are certainly going to have fewer "sick" days, spend fewer afternoons in bed because you don't have the vitality you need and in the end, you'll probably add years to your life.

You're not *spending* time, you're *buying* time.

Before you reach for that extra bite today, ask yourself:
Does my body need this food? Have I obtained the nutrition understanding I owe myself?

When we overeaters think about eating, we tend to dwell on the kick we got out of certain favorite foods, the pleasure, the escape from boredom, the release from fear or anger and the companionship of eating with others — especially when they, too, were overeating.

What we don't think about is the physical unpleasantness — bloat, gas, nausea — and the emotional unpleasantness, the remorse, the waste of precious time and the facing of another day fatter than we were before.

We think about the assets of eating, rather than its liabilities, when we think about the "pleasures" of overeating.

What has excess food ever done for you? Think about that for a moment. Is there any tangible advantage to being fat? Are you better loved, happier, more pleasant, handsomer, more successful? Of course some actors who claim to have made a career playing fat people might have some justification for finding fat to be a career advantage. The rest of us haven't been nearly so lucky.

Fat has held us back from becoming the people we want to be in every part of our lives.

To be losing weight or to be maintaining a natural weight is to find the real "kick" in living. Overeating may have given us a temporary sense of exhilaration, but it didn't last. It was too soon followed by incredible guilt, anguish and utter desolation. Sometimes on "the morning after" we were inconsolable in our grief — grief for our bodies, grief for our shredded feelings and a special grief over what might be if we could only get control over our lives.

In truth, self-control is the *real kick* for people like us. Losing weight is the *real kick*. Living without constant self-recrimination is the *real kick*.

Why don't you think some positive thoughts today? Think what it would be like to look in the mirror and see someone you respected. Think what it would be like to wake up tomorrow with a real feeling of "self" satisfaction.

These are not illusions. You *can* have them. Why don't you? It would be heavenly!

Before you reach for that extra bite today, ask yourself:
Am I thinking of the way it really is when I overeat? Do I know where the *real kicks* in life come from?

You may not realize it, but you are prejudiced. You have picked up one of American society's most prevailing biases. You don't like fat people. And guess who's at the top of your fat hate list? You!

If you're overweight, it is impossible to live in a thin, chauvinist world without picking up negative attitudes about fat people in general and about yourself in particular. You read that a worker is discharged because of obesity, which tends to confirm the idea that fat people are lazy and can't keep up. You turn on your television set and, in between food commercials, thin models tell you that you really shouldn't "let yourself go."

Open your newspaper. When people are described as "pudgy," "hefty," or "large," the tone is more apt to be critical. It's not often you find people described as "too thin."

Go to your doctor. Chances are he or she isn't over-fond of overweights. Not only does he or she reflect society's bias, but many regard us as their professional failures. Attend church. What is one of the seven cardinal sins? Gluttony!

Apply for admittance to a top college. If you're fat, according to a study by Dr. Jean Mayer, you are more likely to be turned down, regardless of your grades or IQ.

With such relentless indoctrination, is it any wonder that you are prejudiced against overweights? Is it any wonder that you don't even like yourself?

Gradually, other voices are being raised. NAAFA, the National Association to Aid Fat Americans, attacks fat-prejudice wherever it occurs. They picket a store that refuses to show their large-size clothing or large-size mannequins; they chastise a television performer for making derogatory remarks about overweights on a national program.

Overeaters Anonymous, along with some doctors and psychologists, declares that overeating is a disease, and those afflicted are no more to be publicly derided than the cerebral palsied.

Protesting poor treatment for and the bad image of overweights doesn't mean you won't continue following your lifelong goal of losing weight and maintaining weight for your health and happiness. It only means you'll demand simple justice for others and for yourself.

Before you reach for that extra bite today, ask yourself:
Do I care about other overweights? Do I care about myself?

When we overeaters look at the shambles of our lives, we understand that we must find a new structure to build on. The first element in our new master plan is a change from living-to-eat to eating-to-live. Next we have to reprogram the way we see ourselves in our mind's eye so that we can reflect a positive image when we look at ourselves.

There are five qualities you'll need to develop to help make this new master plan a reality. Don't worry about having to become someone you're not. All these character traits are already part of your resources. You just have to tap into them.

1. *Take a risk.* One of the reasons we overweights tend to *give up in advance* is because we dare not risk failure. Failure to stick to our diet has always devastated us. As we grow older, we tend to protect ourselves from hurt, and sacrifice the desire for emotional growth (and even thinness) for "security." Once you discover that security for overeaters is not possible where there is no control over food, then you may stop playing it so safe.

2. *Get ready to go it alone.* You may not always be able to rely on others. "I have a sponsor, many friends and a supportive family," said one diet club member, "and still I am alone when I have to withstand my urge to overeat." There are many times others can help, but when they can't, be prepared to stand alone.

3. *Make a commitment.* Don't allow any diversion to deter you from your commitment to a new healthier, happier life.

4. *Believe you can do it.* If you believe in yourself, you can accept your "downs" as easily as your "ups." False pride will not stand in your way, because you will have *real* pride in your ability to change your life.

When you truly believe you can lose weight, maintain a normal weight and restructure your life for happiness, you won't ever have to put up the "false front" of overeating again.

5. *Accept change.* You have mature, consistent values so that change, when it comes, does not threaten you or drive you to food.

All these resources are yours — part of you already — just waiting to be developed. Start structuring your new life today.

Before you reach for that extra bite today, ask yourself:
Am I willing to tap into my own resources to structure my new life? Do I believe in my abilities so that I don't need to put up the "false front" of overeating?

In order for you to free yourself from the prison built by compulsive eating, you must first know what true freedom is. How much freedom do you really have?

Freedom is obedience to our inner law, the one which seeks expression through us. We abuse the law of nature if we overeat. Conflict results.

Freedom must first seem desirable before it is possible. Think of freedom simultaneously with security, stability, progress and creativity. Theses are not the attributes of slaves to food.

True freedom consists in knowing ourselves — our thoughts, motives, desires, and behavior. Without freedom there can be no creation.

There is no freedom where there is no self-mastery. If we are driven by habit, we are not free.

Without freedom there can be no happiness because there is no room for change and all growth is stifled.

Freedom is order. Order is freedom.

When freedom is your compulsion, there is no room for another.

Freedom is the absolute discovery of *your own way.*

It is a wonderful thing to live free from the overwhelming desire to eat compulsively. It is even more wonderful to be, once again, a creating, successful individual, rather than an out-of-control eating machine. To have a master living plan, to live in harmony with self and others, that is happiness and freedom.

Isn't it about time you were free?

Before you reach for that extra bite today, ask yourself:
Do I want to free myself from the prison of overeating? Am I willing to fight against the compulsion which has enslaved me?

If you think you're a failure, listen to the story of a real failure: He lost his job and was defeated for the state legislature, both in 1832; failed in business in 1833; his sweetheart died in 1835, and the next year he had a nervous breakdown; he was defeated for Speaker in 1838 and for Congress in 1843, he was finally elected to Congress in 1846 but lost his race for renomination in 1848; he was turned down for land officer in 1849, defeated for the Senate in 1854, for Vice President in 1856 and again for the Senate in 1858. For a politician who finally became President of the United States in 1860, he was quite a loser. If you think you're a failure, you're not even in the same league with Abraham Lincoln.

He was plagued with depression all his life. Some of his aides feared he might be suicidal. Of all the presidents, he was the most hated; his character and that of his family were assassinated long before he was. And yet he never quit, but seemed to grow ever stronger with each new challenge.

Nobody's suggesting you have to duplicate Lincoln's life. Far less. One act on your part would turn your life from negative to positive. You have only to eat moderately.

When you do you will be living each moment more fully; every feeling, every emotion will be heightened. Even little things will be exciting to you because you will be more alive than you ever have been.

Think how relieved Lincoln would have been if moderate eating would have cured all his problems. Think how fortunate a cancer victim would feel if moderate eating would effect a total cure.

And yet, try as hard as we do, some of us overeaters fail time and again to lose weight and then keep it off. What is the answer? It has to be persistence. If Lincoln had given up after his first defeat, saying, "Oh, well, who wants to be in politics anyway," he certainly would never have been one of the world's great men. But he endured, defeat after defeat, until he triumphed.

And so you can.

Before you reach for that extra bite today, ask yourself:
Will I never give up in my search for a life free from compulsive overeating? Do I believe that in the end I will win?

Violence on television has been the concern of parents since the medium first started airing programs in the late 1940s. But there's an even greater violence that television does to children and adults alike, and that is the violence of the sugar and sweetness come-on. Candies, cookies, snacks, soft drinks are TV's regularly touted products. The result? At least eighteen rotted, filled or missing teeth out of our natural thirty-two, and millions of bodies exploding with sugar-produced flesh. Now, that's real violence!

It is impossible to determine how much television commercials have cued viewers to overeat. We have to discover that individually. But if you are spending any amount of time sitting in front of the TV set eating, then you can bet you're being turned on when you tune in.

When you have knowledge, you have a way to correct negative eating behavior. The more you are able to amend your eating ways, the more you begin to see that your new life, where eating is under control, is a more enjoyable life. *You learn that you are much happier without excess food.*

Some of us overeaters go even further. We believe that certain types of food — primarily refined sugar and starch — are poison to our bodies, that one bite will trigger an obsessive physical and mental desire to eat more. Much like the alcoholic, we can stay "sober" without it, but once we succumb, we are helpless to stop.

You know whether or not you can handle certain foods, the ones most often advertised on television. If you decide you can't, perhaps you can find ways to tune out commercials that trigger your craving. Try keeping something positive to read beside your television viewing chair, so that you can block out the negative "sweet nothings" you are hearing.

Train your mind so that the crucial moment will pass without your taking that first extra bite.

Go ahead and relax with your favorite program today. But stay on your toes!

Before you reach for that extra bite today, ask yourself:
Do I have a real problem with sugar? Have I learned that I'll be much happier without excess food?

"Last year I celebrated my twenty-seventh birthday by buying my own cake and ice cream," the pretty woman told her fellow diet therapy group members. "While I was in the market, I stepped on the scales, and they jammed. I ran to my car and cried.

"But to ease my grief, I went to another store, bought a dozen pastries and ate them all.

"Eating was the way I coped with my problems. And although it sounds preposterous, it was the *only* way I coped with my weight problem."

One man, self-described as a successful engineer, reported humorously: "I would reel into my office, reeking of chocolate. I was so fat that one day I broke through my chair, and my secretary couldn't help me off the floor."

Pauline, at fifty, told about getting up night after night and eating herself sick, so that she couldn't get out of bed in the morning.

All these people have one thing in common. They are no longer fat. What was their answer? They turned their lives in a new direction when it became *more painful to overeat than not to overeat.* They made a conscious decision to live without excess food, and by taking all the help they could get, they restructured their lives

It's not easy to turn away from a food-centered lifestyle, especially when you've made food your highest Reality. But it is possible. For you, it is very possible.

Your life is the only Reality. It needs a consciousness that is not blocked by overeating, but is free and open.

Hasn't overeating hurt you enough? Doesn't it make your every day just plain miserable? Aren't you ready to surrender to the joy of a fresh, new Reality?

Today you will discover that your life is the only Reality, that you can begin to build a master plan of living in which food will play a very small part.

Most people make resolutions at the beginning of the New Year and then call it quits. As an overeater, you have to make the same resolution every day of your life — to refrain from overeating.

That's your answer.

Before you reach for that extra bite today, ask yourself:
Have I found that it's more painful to overeat than not to overeat? Do I believe that it is possible to exchange the reality of food for the reality of truly living?

The German philosopher Goethe said: "Give me the benefit of your convictions."

The positive thinker does not feed doubts, but fights the whole process of doubting which weakens the will to positive action and feeling.

Take a look at your own language for example. Examine all the doubting phrases. Sometimes we overeaters think it's noble to say, "Well, all right, I'll try again." But that is a statement that reeks of doubt.

One of the most destructive things that doubting does to us is sap our motivation — and without motivation, we overeaters are in trouble.

Strike out at doubt wherever you find it in your life. Whenever you hear yourself saying, "I guess," or "I can't," change to affirmative language.

Shakespeare summed it up: "Our doubts are traitors, and make us lose the good we oft might win by fearing to attempt."

How often have you sabotaged a diet effort with doubt? Doubting language or thoughts can actually set a trap which you unknowingly spring on yourself.

Today when you have a doubting thought or say a doubting sentence, write it down on a piece of paper with a line drawn vertically down the middle. On the right hand side of the paper opposite the doubting statement, write down an affirmative or positive statement. For instance, if you say, "I guess I won't make my weight goal," counter that doubt with the phrase, "Yes, I *will* make my weight goal." If you do this often enough, you will begin to rid yourself of your doubting habit. Practice affirming the positive.

It won't be long before you will begin to see signs of positive growth.

There's no doubt about it!

Before you reach for that extra bite today, ask yourself:
Am I getting rid of all doubt? Am I convinced that I can be what I want to be, do what I want to do?

So many overweights tend to think of themselves as "different." One of the best rewards of joining with a group of others in our shoes is that we quickly discover that our problems are only *average* ones. We are not alone, so we no longer need hold ourselves apart from others.

It's hard to change habits, responses and beliefs about yourself. It takes a lot of effort. One way is to change the language you use about yourself to yourself and others. For instance, many dieters tend to overuse biblical words such as "sinner" and "devil" in describing unsuccessful diet efforts. Some psychologists think it's just as negative to use terms such as "saint" and "angel" in describing successful dieting. In effect, the use of biblical language leaves the overweight with a sense of *moral stigma,* an unnecessary burden for people already overburdened with society-induced guilt.

Be careful how you talk about yourself. Don't use "loaded labels" which have a real tendency to drag down your self-esteem.

Use success words when you think and talk about yourself. Here are a few: confident, courageous, understanding, accepting, goal-oriented, creative, loving, thorough, hard-working, attractive, honest, strong, willing, open-minded, persistent, determined and faithful.

There, that ought to be enough to get you started. You'll think of more when you begin to see yourself in a more positive way. And one of the most positive ways you can see yourself is as a member of the mainstream of life. You are not "different." You have a health problem. And you're working on it.

Besides that, you're a very nice person. Believe it!

Before you reach for that extra bite today, ask yourself:
Am I using success words to describe myself? Do I no longer believe that I am "different" from other people?

We overeaters are great worriers. Deep inside we may carry the seeds of self-doubt from which all worry sprouts. A sense of insecurity creates such fantastic emotional tensions that worry actually becomes a safety valve. How can you get rid of this lack of inner security? Here are some ways.

First, you have to admit to yourself that you worry because, deep inside yourself, you feel lost.

Why do you feel so insecure? Psychologists agree that the insecurity complex results from thinking too much without *putting thoughts into action*. When you do this, you live in a state of perpetual frustration. You come to doubt your goals, and lose confidence entirely in your own abilities.

"Too much energy churning the higher brain centers in vicious circles," says Dr. Henry Link, explaining consistent worry, "and not enough energy driving the body in action."

Your second step, obviously, is to form an adequate inner sense of security.

For once, the cure is apparent. You must put those innermost thoughts, wishes and desires into action or you will be doomed to feelings of insecurity and worry.

What you know and feel must find full expression in what you do, if you are ever to live at peace with yourself. That means to achieve a real sense of security, you must express your inner mental energies instead of constantly frustrating them.

ACT!

Before you reach for that extra bite today, ask yourself:
Am I worrying because I have failed to take action on my thoughts, wishes and desires? Am I ready to act on my desire to lose weight today?

We overweights wrote the book on guilt feelings. We blame ourselves for everything, accepting public guilt for being too fat and nourishing private guilt for everything from disappointments to secret hates. *Not only are we guilty about our fat, but we get fatter because of our guilt.* Some of us even recognize the double bind we're in. When told she was just wallowing in false guilt, one group member said, "I might as well. I don't have anything else to feel guilty about today." We can all smile at that, but dealing with deep-seated guilt day after day is no laughing matter for most of us

Here are some things psychologists suggest we do to overcome paralyzing guilt:

1. Analyze your reasons for feeling guilty. Then forgive yourself for past wrongs and proceed to new things.

2. Don't brood over failures or assume an excessive burden of guilt for them. The sensible thing is to see where mistakes were made, resolve them, don't repeat them, and then forget them.

3. Look at your guilt for what it is — an act of self-indulgence. *Are you using guilt as an excuse for standing still in your life?*

4. Ask yourself if you enjoy guilt. Does guilt make you feel more important? Does your guilty feeling take the place of something more positive in your life?

Adults with healthy emotional attitudes do not enjoy guilt. They recognize guilt and they get rid of it. One way this can be done is to write down on a piece of paper what it is you feel guilty about. Then tear it up in little pieces or burn it in the fireplace. This helps to dramatize the idea of ridding your mind of guilty feelings.

Of course, one of the best ways to be guilt-free is to prevent guilt in the first place. When you have done or said something that bothers your conscience, admit it to yourself, then to the other person and then *make it right.* You will feel better instantly and this action will kill any gathering guilt feelings.

You've got too much life to live to waste even a minute on feeling guilty. Don't you agree?

Before you reach for that extra bite today, ask yourself:
Am I *enjoying* the self-importance of heavy guilt? Have I taken steps to remove guilt feelings over which I might eat?

Your mental health is just as important as your physical health. Research tends to show that if you have emotional problems, you'll have a more difficult time losing weight than you need to. How do you feel mentally? Do minor problems throw you into a dither? Do you have trouble getting along with other people? Do the small pleasures of life fail to satisfy you? Before you get caught in the mental depression trap, here are some things you can do.

1. *Talk it out.* Don't bottle it up. Confide in someone you admire.

2. *Escape for a while.* Lose yourself in a movie, a book or a game, so that you can prepare yourself to deal with problems.

3. *Work it off.* Do something constructive with your pent-up energy.

4. *Give in sometimes.* You're not always right, but when you are, stand your ground calmly.

5. *Take one thing at a time.* You don't have to change your life in one day.

6. *Go easy with criticism.* Are you expecting too much of yourself and others?

7. *Make yourself available.* If you're feeling "left out," it may be that you are always waiting to be asked.

8. *Leave time for recreation.* If you drive yourself so hard that you never have time for fun, you'll be a candidate for real emotional problems.

Take care of your head just as you are taking care of your body — for health and for a better life.

Remember, you must have faith in yourself, in others and in every human being's ability to grow. That is the basic philosophy of good emotional health.

It's obvious you've been looking for peace of mind — that quest is universal. But you have been looking for it in the wrong place — the refrigerator. Try these eight *new* "places" first. There's not a calorie in the whole bunch!

Before you reach for that extra bite today, ask yourself:
Am I following a moderate "emotional diet" as well as a diet for my physical self? Do I practice the philosophy of faith?

October 29
                           Relax and Take a Trip
                          (Without Going Anywhere)

At the Institute for Behavioral Awareness, psychologist Frances Stern is teaching overweights how to relax, and take a little "mind trip," which helps them lose weight more readily.

Prepare to go on your mind trip by relaxing completely. Start with your hands. Make a fist and tighten it. Then tighten your wrists, then your forearms. Hold them that way while you count to twenty. (You'll be trembling.) Relax and let your arms go loose. Breathe deeply for another twenty seconds.

Now relax your face. Frown and tense up all the muscles around your mouth and eyes. Wrinkle your nose, clamp your jaw, tighten your chin and forehead. Hold it for a slow count of seven. Relax, again.

Arch your back and raise your chest. Push your shoulders back as hard as you can until your shoulder blades pinch like a West Point cadet's. Count seven and relax.

Tighten your stomach until it's hard as a rock. Count seven and relax.

Tighten all the muscles in your feet and legs, starting with your toes and working up to your thighs. Count slowly to twenty and relax.

You should be physically relaxed by this time, even though you have only been at it for a few minutes at most. Now, it's time to relax your brain. Try taking a trip to your favorite place. It can be a place you remember or a place you've seen only in pictures. But go there anyway, really go there. See it in color, smell it, feel it. Experience your favorite place as vividly as you can. Then slowly count backward from ten and return to the real world.

Now that you're relaxed and have taken a pleasant trip, you'll be ready to get down to the business of this day. What is the most important thing in your life? To lose weight and structure a lifestyle that will help you maintain your weight loss.

That goal should keep you busy achieving and having fun all day. But don't take someone else's word for it. Try it out for yourself.

Before you reach for that extra bite today, ask yourself:
Am I relaxed today? Am I willing to try anything to turn my life in a positive direction?

A wise philosopher once said: "Success consists of a series of little daily victories." Make a list of your daily victories today, no matter how small they are. Is your list anything like this one?

"I was patient with my neighbor who asked me too many questions about my weight."

"I congratulated myself on a two-pound loss."

"I used all my five senses today, instead of concentrating on just the sense of taste."

"I laughed."

"I fed my hope, by eating moderately."

"I did not waste time."

"I took advantage of an opportunity."

"Waiting took up very little of my day."

"I was content, today, with my progress."

"I did not eat compulsively."

Are you beginning to know what it means to feel alive and to face each day without the fear of an overeating binge? This contentment comes to all of us as we begin to achieve important goals, the ones that satisfy our deepest desires.

One of the easiest ways to achieve, according to experts in the success field, is to state your goal without an alternative. Research shows that when a person wants to do one thing *or* another, he or she seldom gets beyond the "or."

Don't give yourself an "or." Freedom from overeating and all the misery it brings to your life is your goal. And more. You have another positive goal of changing your life through inner growth.

Take a close look at all the little victories and achievements of your day. You'll find there are more of them than you first thought. That's the way of positive thinking — there's more that is positive in your life than you ever realized.

Today, you'll know this is true.

Before you reach for that extra bite today, ask yourself:
Have I counted my little victories today? Am I getting rid of all the alternatives so that I can concentrate on achieving my goals?

No matter what prompted you to turn to exercise — whether it was to lose weight, firm up a body that had just gone through the weight-losing process, or for that good-all-over feeling — total fitness should be your goal.

Your ideal exercise plan should consist of the following:

1. A daily "diet" of balanced exercise to tone up your body and speed up your circulation.

2. Supplemental physical recreation, such as dancing, bicycling or sports.

3. Stepped-up physical activity to make your body exert itself, such as walking, climbing stairs, stretching, bending and squatting.

Of course, no amount of exercise will help much without unbalancing calories and energy expenditure. In other words, use *more* than you take in.

Remember to build in safeguards so that you will be able to stick to your exercise plan. Don't make the mistake of setting up one that will take too much of your time. It's better to exercise ten or twenty minutes a day every day than in sporadic spurts of heavy exercise. The physical benefits of occasional exercise reverse themselves within a matter of days.

Next, remember to enjoy what you are doing. To get the most out of exercise and to stay with it, you should be enjoying yourself. If it's a bore or a chore, you might as well forget it, because you probably will later on.

But don't give up too soon. As with many new experiences, the first few days are the most difficult. After that, pride and just plain feeling better will help make exercising easier than you ever thought it would be.

If you are a social type, perhaps you'd rather exercise with other people. Think about joining a class when you set up your ideal exercise plan.

You have been spared all the daily drudgery that your grandparents performed as a matter of course. But then they didn't have as much trouble with their weight, either. It looks like you'll have to put back in the form of an exercise program some of that time modern technology has saved for you.

That's not such a bad deal!

Before you reach for that extra bite today, ask yourself:
Have I worked out an exercise plan ideal for my lifestyle and health needs? Have I stopped kidding myself that I don't have the time to exercise?

What would make you happy today?

You won't have to think hard or long to come up with an answer. The one happy idea uppermost in your mind every minute is the thought that you can lose weight and look and feel like a healthy person again.

And you can. Each day, as you grow in self-knowledge you are a comfort to yourself, you are bringing happiness within reach. You are less turned inward and think more about other people. Like the character in *"No, No, Nanette"* you are singing, "I want to be happy, but I won't be happy, 'til I make you happy, too."

You are less impulsive. The old "grab and snatch" life of living-to-eat is gone, and you feel calmer and more content.

It is easier for you to feel satisfaction as you moderate your eating and restructure your life. No matter what your achievements, it was awfully hard to admire yourself when you were overeating.

Feeling a sense of happiness is a wonderful change in your life and you appreciate it, but there is still one question. How do you *stay* happy?

Many philosophers believe that continued happiness is based on a life which has a sense of purpose, and striving.

The poet Robert Browning said it best: "A man's reach should exceed his grasp; or what's a heaven for?"

Often, we overweights don't think much of our "reach." We downgrade our abilities to achieve, and sometimes even adopt a "what's the use" attitude and give up. But that negative attitude is not for the person who is seeking a way to maintain a happy life.

Strive. Push yourself. Never let yourself give up on You. Today is another happy day you can give yourself, another day of food control for health. Happy, positive, achieving days are learning days. Sometimes we over-eaters think we only learn from our mistakes, but we learn from our achievements as well.

Yes, you can stay happy. That's your job — for life.

Before you reach for that extra bite today, ask yourself:
Do I really want to give up misery for happiness? Am I willing to strive and persevere?

The first commandment of every overweight should be, "I am kind to myself."

Selfish? No. Take a look at your life and you'll discover that when you have been unkind to yourself, you haven't been kind to anyone else. You can't give love, attention, gentleness, and kindness to others when you can't give them to yourself.

You must be kind to you. The world you live in isn't always kind. Think about the black rings on your shirt front or dress because your stomach is too close to the car's steering wheel. Remember the terrors of summer when it's time to come out from behind a suit jacket or winter coat. Don't forget the embarrassment of getting into a friend's car and struggling to extend the seat belt so it will buckle. And remember how tight and uncomfortable the buckle was because it wouldn't extend far enough. Think about the plane trip you took where you had to sit sideways all the way. And don't forget pulling with all your might on a zipper with the perspiration running down your face.

When you remember the hundreds of humiliations overweight has caused you, don't be ashamed to follow the first commandment. *Be kind to yourself.*

But just what is the ultimate kindness you can do for yourself? That's the easiest question in the world to answer. Free yourself from the fat that has made your life miserable.

Are you being kind to yourself today? Have you chosen a moderate amount of healthful food to eat at regular mealtimes? Have you planned to spend some time exercising, relaxing and getting to know the positive you?

You are on your way to a whole new, thin life. It's not just the healthiest thing you can do for yourself, nor the happiest — it's the kindest.

Did you know, you're a very kind person?

Before you reach for that extra bite today, ask yourself:
Am I practicing the first commandment of overweight?
Have I had enough of the humiliations of being fat?

You may never have thought so before, but you have a real friend in your tape measure. Don't cringe. All that embarrassment you felt in the past when sales clerks and dressmakers (even your mother) brought out a tape-measure to take your body measurements — well, all that embarrassment is over. *From now on, measuring will be a pleasuring.*

When you're losing weight, as you are, you're not just losing pounds, but inches — lots and lots of inches. "I couldn't believe it," said one dieter, now at her normal weight, "but when I added all my lost inches together, they totaled 137, more than *twice* my own height."

You'll be cheating yourself out of some real fun and fullfillment if you don't buy yourself a fabric or plastic tape measure. Be sure and get the kind with large, clear numbers for easy reading. After all, you want to be accurate.

Now once a week — let's say on Monday morning — measure your waistline, rib cage or bust, abdomen, hips, upper thigh, calf, ankle, upper and lower arms.

Make a chart and keep a record. Although the scale sometimes gets stuck for a discouraging week, your measurements will continue to go down.

One caution: Every overweight seems to lose first what he or she needs to lose least, and last what she or he needs to lose first. Your face, bust and waist may be normal in size long before your hips catch up. Don't despair — they will pare down eventually, if you stick with your diet and exercise regimen.

Are you getting satisfaction out of living a life where you are not scared to death of a tape measure? Isn't it just about worth anything to you to live without such a silly, but nonetheless real, fear?

Isn't it fun to "measure up" to your best expectations?

Before you reach for that extra bite today, ask yourself:
Have I turned my long, thin enemy into a friend? How many inches have I lost?

Reading food labels is not an easy habit to form. But then what good habit is? Like other positive things you're doing for yourself, learning to read labels on the food you eat will give you help where you need it most.

You won't believe how many foods (some you wouldn't expect) have a high sugar content. Just to name a few, there are hot dogs, canned vegetables, peanut butter and catsup.

If you're trying to limit your sugar intake, you should certainly read the labels on processed foods *before* you toss them into your shopping cart.

Why is sugar used in so many foods that don't need to be sweet? "Two reasons," says Dr. Ira L. Shannon, a biochemistry professor at the University of Texas. "The American people like the taste, and it's the cheapest filler food processors can find to take up space in food."

Dr. Shannon says that *most* of our sugar intake comes from processed foods so that many people don't know how much they're really getting.

When we overweights diet to lose weight or to maintain a natural weight, we cut back drastically on our refined sugar intake. We certainly don't expect to be sabotaged by a can of tomatoes!

Read labels for sugar content. Federal regulations require ingredients be listed in order of quantity. If the product you're buying has sugar as the second or third ingredient, it's probably got too much sugar for your diet.

One of the problems we overeaters have had in the past is that we ate without looking, without really *knowing* what we were eating.

Pay attention today. Be aware.

Before you reach for that extra bite today, ask yourself:
Have I checked my purchases to see that I'm not getting too much hidden sugar? Am I really paying attention to the quality of my food?

Psychologists have an expression when they talk about the people who are meaningful in our lives. They call these people "significant others." Perhaps no other single group of people need each other more than do we overeaters. Other people are absolutely essential to our continued growth and self-acceptance. That is perhaps the best reason for the growth of diet groups, whose members now number in the hundreds of thousands.

Why is this true? Here are a few reasons you should consider before you dismiss the possibility that such a group could help you.

1. Other people, even though they may have an overeating problem greater than yours, have strengths from which you can benefit.

2. You need others to share your enthusiasm — to practice on. And when you're down, you need the enthusiasm of others to help lift you up again.

3. Other overweights will often refuse to verify your negative self-image, helping you to fresh insights.

4. Success is attractive. The success of others will spur you on, and your own success will help others do what you're doing. Both are great affirmations of your new way of food-controlled living.

5. It is a simple truth, whether you're five or fifty-five, that people learn better from their peers than from anyone else.

6. Other people help motivate. When you tell yourself and others what you intend to do, you are more apt to do it.

7. Other people help to expand your value system.

In the Broadway show *Funny Girl*, the lead character, Fanny Brice, sings a song which says: "People who need people are the luckiest people in the world."

What do you think?

Before you reach for that extra bite today, ask yourself:
Have I discovered how important other overweights are to my recovery from compulsive overeating? Do I really care today about other people?

It is said that everything we do has its side effects. What are the side effects of losing weight after existing for any length of time in a fat body? Here are a few.

You'll never again have to cross the street to hide from an old friend who's not seen you since you gained so much weight.

You'll not have to make up a lame excuse to step out of the picture just before it's snapped.

You'll never have to dread family holiday get-togethers because your mother will look at you with concern in her eyes and your brother-in-law will make hurtful jokes about your weight.

You'll never have to hear a little child ask you point blank, "Why are you so *fat?*"and not know the answer.

You'll never have to stand in the middle of the gym on weigh-day while your teacher calls out your weight in a loud voice and all your classmates snicker and poke each other.

You'll never have to hear some friend say, "But my dear, you have such a pretty *face*," and *know* what she means.

You'll never have to watch the exasperated look on your doctor's face when he tells you: "If you insist on carrying around this much weight, you won't live past forty," and wonder later if death is worse than living fat.

You'll never have to be the *only* one left at the table during a dance.

You'll never have to starve at dinner parties to prove you're on a rigid diet.

You'll never have to spend another social evening talking about diets when you'd rather discuss literature or the theater.

What are the side effects of losing weight? You will be who you really are, and you will be thin.

Before you reach for that extra bite today, ask yourself:
Am I ready to enjoy the happy side effects of losing weight? Will I do whatever is necessary to become the person I really am?

It's one thing to need people in a beneficial way, a way which is a two-way street of getting and giving. It's quite another thing to be dependent on others.

Quite often when a need for other people is an unhealthy one, people can become *substitutes*. The obvious examples are a parent who lives through her child or a wife who lives through her husband. When we hand over our self-responsibility to others, we place an extra burden on them and open the door to resentment on our part. It's not often that others can *always* measure up to our desires.

Overweights can use other people to *substitute* for their inability to take control of their own food problem. Take the do-gooder. This person is constantly helping others and being concerned for their welfare, but he or she may lack the ability to make a simple decision to do something for him/herself. Psychologists call this kind of dependence "other centeredness."

Another unhealthy way overweights need other people is as scapegoats. They have to find someone to blame because they can't take the blame for their unhappiness on themselves. This attitude can result in such classic excuses as: "My mother made me fat," or "I'd get thin if only *they* didn't make it so hard for me."

People need people. But they need interdependence, not dependence.

Are you too dependent? Psychologists say if you need to consult others before you make every decision, you may be too dependent on people.

Striking a balance between too much dependence and isolation from others seems to be the happy solution. Moderation (there's that word again) is the key.

There's one decision only you can make for yourself. How do you want to live? Fat or thin?

You decide.

Before you reach for that extra bite today, ask yourself:
Do I use other people as my excuse to overeat? Have I decided to make the most important decision of my life?

There are certain things we need from other people, from doctors and from family. That is all part of the healthy interdependence of restructuring a positive new life. But what do you need from yourself to make the equation work? Here are some gifts you must make to yourself if success is to be part of your future.

1. *Affection.* How do you feel toward yourself? Do you really care? Do you love yourself? Are you good to yourself? You can date the second you begin to make progress from the moment you know that *you count.*

2. *Respect.* How do you respond to yourself? Are you constantly downgrading your abilities, or do you recognize that you have real capacity as a human being?

3. *Skills.* Do you see that you have special talents and try to do your best to develop them?

4. *Knowledge.* If you do not know enough about nutrition and health to accomplish the thin life you want to live, have you given yourself the opportunity to acquire this learning?

5. *Power.* Have you taken control of your own life? You may be able to make powerful decisions in the business world, but if you can't manage your own food problem, you are not using the power you have to benefit you.

6. *Self-realization.* The greatest gift you can give yourself is to realize your dreams. It is on this level of self-realization that you will find new meaning and satisfaction in life. You will be the very best you can be. How many people reach self-realization? Will you?

These gifts you can give yourself have the most value of any you will ever receive. And the great thing about them is that they are gifts you have it within your power to give.

When you look at your life and especially your weight problem, you can't help but realize that you can have your dream starting today if you just give yourself the six gifts of success.

Nothing is stopping you!

Before you reach for that extra bite today, ask yourself:
Do I treat myself with affection and respect? Do I fully use my skills, knowledge and power?

You have decided where you want to go. You have a good idea of how to get there, and you have been developing goals to achieve success. Of all the insights you've had, the most powerful is: An affirmative feeling about yourself is absolutely necessary for success. This is one of the most important truths of your life.

To believe in your *right* to fulfillment and happiness opens the door to the knowledge of truth. But just what is it? Truth is:

A progressive attachment to quality living.

Absolute love, including yourself.

The action of a positive mind.

All the dream-inspired visions of life lived thin.

The language of creative living.

But truth is much more to overweights than truth in philosophical terms. We face practical truth every day. Such as:

Telling your real weight to the driver's license clerk.

Not starting a fight with your family so they'll leave you alone to eat.

Being honest with a friend about your weight problem, instead of putting on a big front.

Facing daily problems instead of escaping to the refrigerator.

Truth is within you. It is part of your positive, creative mind. Now, you can *see* your own progress.

Isn't that what you've been waiting for?

Before you reach for that extra bite today, ask yourself:
Am I full of truth? Has the truth helped me to see where I am going?

Meetings of diet groups, whether they are psychologist-led or just fat people sharing their experiences with each other, can be extremely inspirational. Here are some comments overheard in such a meeting which any overweight will recognize as coming from positive feelings generated by losing weight.

"When you're eating properly, all your time and emotions aren't going into food."

"I don't think 'food' all the time."

"I never knew what peace of mind an extended diet can bring day-by-day."

"I won't kid you. It takes courage, and lots of it."

"The cravings don't make you fat. It's what you do about them."

"I'm worth something today."

"I feel really alive."

"One thing I've learned: *When all else fails, follow directions.*"

"I can get close to people now."

"I used to be sluggish and tired. Now I hold my head up whenever I walk into a store."

"Just being able to cope with living is a big relief."

"As my weight goes down, so does my sensitivity. I'm aware that not everyone is out to get me."

"We're not bad people trying to get good. We're sick people trying to get well."

"There's always somebody to help me."

"Just taking weight off isn't enough. I have to rearrange my life."

"I no longer live in the world of 'should haves.' "

Who said you shouldn't eavesdrop? Sometimes when you listen in, you hear things you never forget.

Before you reach for that extra bite today, ask yourself:
Do I identify with other overweights? Can I learn from them?

Traditionally, America honors its military veterans on this day. Perhaps someday we'll set aside a special day to honor veterans of the War Against Fat and award medals to the survivors of the "battle of the bulge."

That analogy is only half-facetious. You know well enough that this fight is the most important fight in which you are ever likely to be. It is literally a matter of life and death, win or lose. But in your case you will *win*. You will *live* your life healthfully and happily.

Sometimes our problem looms so large on the scale, we become overwhelmed. Those pounds appear to be insurmountable. Our future seems dim indeed, if it means more of the same depressing way of life. But remember, no problem needs to be solved all at once. And try to believe that you have something to say about what happens in your life. *You have control.*

The philosopher Kahlil Gibran has said: "Your daily life is your temple and your religion. Whenever you enter into it, take with you your all."

Have you entered today with all your resolve, all your will, or are you floundering with only half your mental resources? Are you willing to let each day be your "religion" or are you devoid of any faith in yourself?

Just below your conscious mind are old, negative attitudes etched in stone. They tell you that you "don't stand a chance," that you "always fail so go ahead and give up." Get rid of these concrete memorials to failure. *Blast them out!* Abandon the old way of negative thinking, if you are to have room for the positive.

Today is not a day for drifting, it is a day for acting. Like a good soldier you will continue putting one foot in front of the other until you get to your target. And you will.

Happy Diet Veterans Day!

Before you reach for that extra bite today, ask yourself:
Have I decided to take control of my life? Am I going to shoot down negative thinking?

Television and movie star Lorne Greene realized one day on the set that he could no longer bend over and tie his shoes. "I knew I had to do something," said the actor, "and I began by giving up mid-morning pastries and starchy commissary lunches."

Next, Greene checked into a hospital and was placed on a diet and exercise regimen which he has followed since, keeping off sixty-three excess pounds for more than ten years.

Greene walks for exercise. "It may seem like an insignificant thing to a lot of people," he says, "but it's great exercise for stimulating the bloodstream and heart.

"I also eat sensible food. I'm not a vegetarian but I've cut down on my meat intake and eat more fish and poultry. And I've almost given up using salt, sugar and caffeine.

"I've found I just don't need a lot of the foods I used to put into my body."

The star of the long-running television hit *Bonanza* has done something every overweight can do. From an obvious beginning (cutting out "goodies"), he has refined and improved his diet and exercise program over the years until he has a plan he can live with comfortably.

A good master plan for living is not a static thing. You can change it as you grow willing to change. Sometimes you have favorite foods you think you'd die without. Sooner or later, you discover you'll not only live, but you'll live far better without them. As Lorne Greene did, you'll find you don't need a lot of the foods you put in your body.

Have you worked out a diet/exercise plan you can live with to get thin and stay thin? Have you become willing to refine your master plan as you grow in confidence?

When you do, you will have found what Lorne Greene has found — a real "bonanza."

Before you reach for that extra bite today, ask yourself:
Is my master plan for living a "living program," one that grows as I grow? Am I looking for my "bonanza" in the right place?

Eating can become almost rhythmical for some over-weights — a constant beat which has them reaching for excess food over and over again through the day.

When overeaters make a decision to follow a new master plan of living, there can be anxiety because this old rhythm is being circumvented.

When this happens, when anxiety (even hyperventilation) occurs, try a different rhythm. Breathing is one of your body's fundamental rhythms, not the pseudo-rhythm of overeating you've imposed on your body.

Sit in a relaxed manner and try practicing what Indian yogis and Chinese Taoists call "watching the breath," with the idea of *letting* yourself breathe in a more natural fashion than you ever have before. Don't force. Let it become as slow and silent as possible.

Don't grasp at air anxiously. Don't hold onto it in fear.

Breathe freely and fully release it. Ease the breath out of your body. Zen author Alan Watts says to ease your breath out "as if the body were being emptied of air by a great leaden ball sinking through the chest and abdomen and settling down into the ground."

The next in-breath should just be allowed to follow as a natural reflex action. It is allowed to come, then is allowed to go, the leaden ball, as Watts says, giving it the sense of "falling" out, as distinct from being pushed out of your body.

This technique of *watching and letting* the body's natural breathing rhythm can be one of the best anxiety-releasers of all. And as your anxiety goes, so does your desire to return to that old destructive rhythm of pushing one bite after another into your body.

Today you will respond to a different rhythm.

Before you reach for that extra bite today, ask yourself:
Have I replaced a negative body rhythm with a calming one? Am I trying to overcome anxiety without overeating?

William James once gave this advice for uncovering the positive treasure of your mind: "Seek out that particular mental attitude which makes you feel most deeply and vitally alive, along with which comes the inner voice which says 'this is the real me,' and when you have found that attitude, follow it."

Look inside yourself, deep inside, and see what attitude makes you come alive. Could it be this one? "I am able to moderate my eating, lose weight, and restructure my life."

Say these words aloud to yourself. Does an inner voice respond: "This is the real me"?

Even though you may have listened to every false and limiting belief that your negative mind ever entertained, you are unable to bury positive attitudes forever. The power of that one positive thought, "I am able to change," is stronger than all the negative thoughts you have ever had. Truth always struggles to be free.

Listen to your deep inner voice. It is a growing, vital awareness. You can't stop it. Overeating only quiets your inner voice for a moment, and then it reappears stronger than ever.

Allow the positive voice inside you to become a conscious action. Listen to the "real you," and act on what you hear.

You are like a block of marble waiting for the sculptor's hand to free the real you by chipping away the excess stone. Only you are both marble and artist. You will free yourself by your own positive attitudes.

When you have established your true identity, when you have listened to your inner voice, your life will move in a new direction. Doors that were closed will open. Possibilities will become realities.

Best of all you will have control over a rather minor physical function called eating — a very small part of living that *nearly ruined your life.*

Listen to the inner voice that tells you who you really are. Seek out the attitude that makes you feel alive.

Then follow it!

Before you reach for that extra bite today, ask yourself:
Am I seeking and listening? Do I long for the day I can look in the mirror and say, "This is the real me?"

November 15   You Don't Have to Be an Einstein

You don't have to be an Albert Einstein to apply the law of inertia, one of the primary laws of physics, to your weight problem. This law states: *A body remains at rest until a force is applied to it.* Inertia is the quality in matter that resists change. A good example is your automobile which doesn't move until you start the engine. Likewise, your weight won't change until you apply the force of positive thinking, feeling and acting.

As in matter, there is a quality of inertia that sometimes grips overweights and holds them motionless. We become weighed down with the emotions of fatness, until we cannot move. It is a truly destructive state. It is a time when we sigh and tell ourselves, "Well, I guess I'll just have to learn to live with it." But this hopeless state of inertia doesn't last forever, and soon we are right back in the same old conflict of being fat and not liking it one bit.

Only one force can cause us to begin again to move toward a thinner, healthier way of life — the force of a positive mind. As long as you tell yourself you can't lose weight, you won't. As long as you convince yourself that you're helpless, the law of inertia will have you by the throat.

Apply the force of your positive mind to your own diet inertia today. You *don't* have to learn to live with fat. You *can* change thought patterns and behavior. Like the physicist's law, change will occur in direct proportion to the amount of force you apply. Doesn't your car go faster when you step down harder on the gas?

If you want your life to change, you'll have to do the job yourself. It's your responsibility. And that's the way you really want it. You certainly wouldn't want to hand your life over to someone else.

Today's the day you are going to get off dead center and start applying positive force to your life.

There's no stopping you now!

Before you reach for that extra bite today, ask yourself:
Am I really satisfied with the way things are? Am I willing to apply positive force to get my life moving again?

A great thinker once said: "Thought attracts what is like itself and repels what is unlike." In other words, our thoughts can act like a magnet to other like thoughts.

When you think negatively, other negative thoughts are attracted to your mind while positive thoughts are not attracted. Take this chain of negative thinking, for instance. "I'm just a big, fat slob. I've failed to lose weight so many times, I don't deserve to be thin. I might as well go ahead and eat." One negative thought is attracted by another, and so on, until there's not much opportunity this overweight will be a successful loser.

On the other hand, when you think positively, other positive thoughts are attracted to your mind while negative thoughts are not attracted. For instance: "I'm a worthwhile human being. I'm going to lose weight now. I deserve to be thin and happy. I'm going to start a new eating plan today." One positive thought has been attracted by another and another until a bright new opportunity opens for this dieter.

It's just plain smart to fill your mind with the positive thoughts you need to have to get where you wish to go. When you do this, you not only attract other like thoughts, but you actually *exclude* negative thoughts. There is no room in a positive, creative mind for negativity.

Make your mind into a positive magnet, one that attracts the kind of thinking you'll need to lose weight and keep it off. If you do, you'll be a great thinker, too.

Open your mind and let the light shine in.

Before you reach for that extra bite today, ask yourself:
Is my mind attracting positive thoughts? Am I a magnet for the good life?

As a group, we overweights typify the thinking problems of many minorities. Often we feel powerless to choose for ourselves. Our future seems to be dominated by the hopelessness of the present. We are on a negative carrousel going nowhere.

You have the right to choose what kind of life you want to live and how you want to live it. Choice is not a privilege, it is a right. But choice is also an inherent responsiblity of life. If you abdicate that responsibility, you will drift hopelessly, aimlessly, waiting for something or someone to make your choices for you.

Positive attitudes toward choice-making can help you make right decisions about your life.

Think to yourself today: I am endowed with the ability to make positive choices. I have the *power* to make wise choices. Nothing in the world can make me choose gloom, despair, or unhappiness in my present or in my future.

Making creative, positive choices is a happy way to fill your mind with the raw material you'll need to lose weight and maintain your natural weight.

You are not helpless. When you think so, it is only negativity telling you that you cannot have the body and health you desire so deeply. Feeling helpless is an old habit with overweights, but we can choose to let go of this negative feeling and replace it with positive choices. If we crowd our mind with right thinking, we'll naturally exclude any negative choices from our choosing process.

Begin working on your positive blueprint for tomorrow, today. Do you want to lose weight and turn your life around? Make it happen, by making positive choices.

Today you will choose to gain control of your desire for excess food. You will choose to think "health." You will choose some area of inner growth on which to concentrate.

You have the *power* to choose. Once you start, you won't be able to stop.

Before you reach for that extra bite today, ask yourself:
Am I tired of feeling helpless about my own life? Am I ready to exercise my right of choice?

When you're losing weight your bathroom scale can be one of the greatest motivators to keep you going. There's a great thrill when you step on the scale and find you've broken another "Pound Barrier." Since we overweights have an emotional response to our body weight, dropping below the weight we were last year at this time, or when the baby was born or when we were married — all these can give us a special motivation to continue dieting.

But there comes a day when your scale turns on you. Like most things, this apparent treason is not all bad. It simply means you've reached your weight goal. It's a happy day, but you have lost your motivator.

The best way to integrate your scale into your new, thin life is to switch it to the role of friendly monitor. This will be its lifelong job.

We are all yo-yos to a certain extent. Our weight fluctuates up and down. Accept the fact that your weight monitor will show a fluctuation but keep the string on your yo-yo short — only two or three pounds long.

When your scale shows a weight gain, your new behavior should be to immediately start a weight-loss program until the extra weight is gone. Remember what you used to say? "It's probably just that time of the month," *or* "I'll cut back next Monday"? That old system of postponement didn't work, and before we knew it, we were ten or twenty pounds overweight again and feeling hopeless and helpless.

When it comes time to say goodbye to your old motivator, just turn around and say hello to your friendly monitor — the best watchdog your new body will ever know.

Before you reach for that extra bite today, ask yourself:
Is my old motivator now my everyday monitor? Have I decided to keep the string on my yo-yo very short?

It can't have escaped your notice that some people lose their excess weight while others lose their way, and sink into a pit of hopelessness. Have you attributed weight-loss success to luck, superior intelligence, education or money? Actually, these factors seem to make little difference in success of any kind. Rags-to-riches stories of poor people with deprived backgrounds are almost cliches. What then makes the difference?

The first difference we see in successful people is that they believe their *dreams can come true* for them. They consider nothing impossible, and have a reservoir of faith in themselves.

Second, these people are capable of quick adaptation. They intuitively understand that *they can't stand still*, that life moves on every day.

Third, successful people, while they may have fear, don't let fear stop them. They *work through problems* in spite of every difficulty. They act as if they have courage whether they do or not.

Fourth, they *give each goal along their way enough time* to happen. We compulsive eaters are impatient people. We want to take off weight right now. Successful people realize that every day is important to the learning, growing process, and that they'll need all these days to be ready to live the thin life.

Think how you fit into this picture of success. Do you believe your dream can come true for you? Are you willing to move forward a little each day? Can you work through problems without giving up? Are you able to give each goal enough time? If you don't fit this picture now, you can learn easily enough. Don't you recognize the outline? This is the very image of a positive, creative thinker, the person whose dreams become visions of what can be.

Tell yourself today that you are going to practice for success. That your dream of living in a healthy body and mind will come true.

Say this: *It can happen to me.*

Before you reach for that extra bite today, ask yourself:
Am I willing to work for success? Can I put myself in the success picture?

Emotional support is a two-way street. You have to learn to give it and take it. Both supply essential nourishment that helps us grow. And inner growth gives us the added support we need to withstand the demands our bodies make for excess food. Here are some ways to develop support habits — for yourself and for others.

1. Train yourself to seek out positive qualities in yourself and others.

2. Transcend negative feelings about other people by *deliberately putting yourself out* to help them.

3. Don't attach strings to the helpful things you do.

4. Make a list of the areas in which you feel negative about yourself. These are the areas where you need the most emotional support from yourself and others.

5. Realize that you usually recognize the faults of other people because you hate them in yourself.

6. Find something to praise — in yourself and in others.

7. Learn to tell when someone needs your support but can't ask for it. Learn to ask for support when *you* need it.

8. You can support others without subordinating your own values or needs.

The most important thing in your life is to reach your natural weight and develop the kind of emotional stability which will insure that you'll never again get fat. This insurance can be bought very cheaply. You must simply give yourself the benefit of every emotional doubt, and you must allow others to contribute to your well-being, while contributing to theirs.

It's simple. You have a high degree of responsibility for your own behavior and you are aware of its consequences for others. That makes you a strong person indeed. And, ultimately, a thin person.

Before you reach for that extra bite today, ask yourself:
Do I give myself the emotional support I can give? Do I take the emotional support others offer, and look for ways to support them, too?

November 21   What Are You Doing Thanksgiving?

The United States has a special holiday to celebrate the bountiful first harvest of the Pilgrims at Plymouth Colony in 1621. We celebrate by gathering together with family members and eating traditional foods. Some of us celebrate by overeating these traditional foods and everything else in sight. Thanksgiving has been one holiday when eating, even for overweights, has been sanctioned by everyone. "Oh, you can't diet on Thanksgiving," we're told every year. And hardly needing more encouragement, we've sometimes joined the general feasting.

This Thanksgiving give thanks for the food you *don't* eat. That's the only way an overeater can truly celebrate Thanksgiving.

"I can't take a holiday from my compulsion to overeat," says a dieter who should know. "One Thanksgiving I casually decided I could handle some sweet desserts I hadn't eaten for over a year. It was five months and forty-two pounds later before I came off that binge."

Not everyone has "binge foods," but if you do, don't think that you're immune to them due to some holiday magic. Thanksgiving can be just as festive when you're eating properly. Just because you've decided that moderate eating is the way you are going to live your life, don't think parties, holidays or family gatherings won't be any fun. That's like the alcoholic who doesn't see how he can enjoy himself without a drink.

Here's the real fun of holidays: getting on the scales the next day and seeing that you've held your weight; feeling no overeating guilt; keeping your hard-won self-esteem.

The truth is that we overweights don't really like holidays very much as long as we're practicing overeaters. "The year I followed my eating plan despite the holiday atmosphere," says a dieter, "was the first year I truly enjoyed Thanksgiving."

Isn't it about time you truly enjoyed yourself on every holiday? You can, when you learn that holidays aren't just for eating. They're for living happily ever after.

Happy Thanksgiving!

Before you reach for that extra bite today, ask yourself:
Will I enjoy Thanksgiving as much the day after? Do holidays have more meaning for me than just what I'm going to be eating?

It's one thing to tell overweights to love themselves. This sounds good. But how can it be put into action? Sometimes we feel so unlovable. After all, aren't we the physical opposite of what lovable is supposed to be in this country?

Trying to fall in love with yourself might sound a little silly if it weren't so important. *Everything* in your life will evolve from the way you *see* yourself. Without self-love there can be no positive living, no weight loss or weight maintenance and no inner growth.

How can you learn to love yourself?

First, try not to be impatient at your own rate of growth.

Next, treat yourself with the same kindness you show other people. Ease your hurt feelings, whenever possible.

Give yourself the attention you need. Don't forget others, but don't ignore yourself in the process.

Then, recognize how *teachable* you are, how willing to learn and how capable of new learning.

After that, you must give up the *right* to be mad at yourself for every misstep. This is the only way you can be "unselfish" with your own life.

Finally, act with sincerity and integrity toward yourself. If you make a promise to change your life, then begin to do so in good faith. If you can't count on you, then who?

These are the vital elements that express love. When you act on them, each action will strengthen your ability to show love to yourself.

Don't think this is all a gigantic piece of selfishness. Haven't you already given self-hate a chance? Did it make you into the sort of person you wanted to be? Were you more loving, kind, selfless, sincere toward others? Of course not.

It's pretty standard psychological and religious fare that you can't give away what you don't have. If you don't have love, then love, like charity, is better started at home.

Go ahead and give loving yourself a try. You know, you're really a very lovable person!

Before you reach for that extra bite today, ask yourself:
Am I practicing self-love with every action? Do I know that by loving myself, I'll be able to give more love to others?

Potentially our minds have limitless power for change, but in actual practice we overweights can apply brakes in the form of "limiting" thought behavior to our power for growth.

There are four ways you can limit your limitless mind, four ways you can hamper your own progress.

First, you can spend a lot of vital energy wallowing in guilt for past mistakes. It takes an enormous amount of psychic mind power for self-condemnation and self-pity. It applies an absolute brake to your creative thinking processes.

Second, and on the other side of the same coin, you can spend far too much time dwelling on yesterday's successes. An overemphasis on past glories is really an unrecognized fear of the future. It's far easier, you think, to rest on your laurels than to risk an uncertain tomorrow. This mind-limitation effectively halts any forward movement.

Third, you can use your age as a limiting excuse. When you are young, you are always too young; when you are older, you suddenly become too old. Age has nothing to do with capability, unless you make it a limitation.

Fourth, you can fail to believe in your own personal growth. Many people project today's problems into the future, and then, based on present knowledge, think tomorrow will be no different. Have faith in your ability to change. What seems unsolvable today may have a ready answer in the future.

What is the state of your mind? That's not an idle question but a vital one. If you think in a limiting way, your mind will have reduced scope and fewer options with which to work. But if you let go of limiting thoughts and behavior, your mind's potential is infinite. It knows no bounds if you leave it unbound.

You can lose weight and live a fulfilling, growing life because you have let go of self-pity and are responsible for today; you dwell in today and plan for tomorrow; you are just the right age, whatever your age; and you believe in your own ability to grow and solve future problems.

This is where you are today. And this is a very good place to be.

Before you reach for that extra bite today, ask yourself:
Have I thrown off all mind-limiting thoughts? Have I released the brakes of limiting behavior so that I can use my full potential mind power?

"I was old when I was fifteen," says one dieter, "dragging around with never enough energy to get me through a teenager's day."

You don't have to be old to feel old. You just have to be fat.

Most diet doctors get as many complaints from their overweight patients about the way they feel as about the fat on their bodies.

Dragging around all that extra weight is enough to make anybody tired. But even worse, most of us, when we are overeating, concentrate on high-carbohydrate foods that sap our energy.

It isn't normal to be tired all the time, to sleep too much, and feel so enervated it's torture to try to accomplish even simple everyday tasks.

This illness (let's call it "Fat-igue") is one of the few that can be cured almost instantly. No, you don't have to take a pill or go into therapy; you simply have to follow a plan of eating that starts the weight-loss process and reduces carbohydrates to a reasonable level.

When you are following a master plan for health which includes healthy eating and generous portions of daily exercise, you'll just plain feel good. It will be like living inside a new body, one you never knew before.

O.K., this is not exactly new information. You've heard it a thousand times. If you're already following such a plan, you know how much better you feel. If you're not, you weren't listening all those other times.

This time *you will.* You're listening.

Before you reach for that extra bite today, ask yourself:
Am I eating for new energy as well as a new body? Am I tired of feeling too old for my age?

Most of the accidents — on highways, in homes, or on the job — are a result of hurry. People impatiently rush ahead, throwing themselves out of balance, and before they know it, they have an accident.

Haste is the enemy of every diet. Sure, you're impatient to get the weight off. It's killing you to be fat — physically, as well as emotionally. But speed in dieting, like speed on the highway, may not get you to your goal faster.

Pushing toward your goal at an unsafe rate of speed is inconsistent with the positive reordering of the structure of your life. It's bound to lead to faulty judgment. "I'll skip breakfast today," you say; or "I'll fast for a week," hoping to step up the weight-loss process. Most likely, you won't. You'll get too hungry. Maybe your entire master plan will be thrown out of balance.

The answer to the hurry-up syndrome is to commit yourself to the *way* you plan to lose your weight. You're correct to select a goal first. That's important. But almost as important should be selecting the *method* you plan to use to lose your excess weight. If you are committed to a method which regulates your diet and weight loss, then you won't fall victim to the hurry-up syndrome. What's more, you'll probably enjoy the "trip" that much more. Each day will bring fresh insights. You'll be learning about yourself, so that when you reach your natural weight you'll have a lot of new confidence. But it takes time to build confidence. You won't get it if you hurry up. You won't have time.

If you haven't committed yourself to a goal and a *way* to reach that goal, do it today. It will bring you mind-patience and inject good balance into your life.

It's your life. It's an exciting journey. Why hurry?

Before you reach for that extra bite today, ask yourself:
Why am I in such a hurry? Have I committed myself to a *way* to reach my weight goal?

November 26   Are You Confused About Exercises?

There are four basic categories of exercise — isometrics, isotonics, anaerobics and aerobics. Each one answers a specific physical need. If you are confused about the differences between the variety of exercise methods (each with their own passionate adherents), read this before you make a choice.

Isometrics. The object of isometric exercise is to promote muscular strength and bulk through contractions. This is accomplished by pushing or pulling against an immovable object, such as a door frame, or by pitting one group of muscles against another which will give you the same effect.

Isotonics. These exercises are a newfangled name for old-fashioned toe touches, push-ups and sit-ups which your high school gym teacher called calisthenics. They serve mainly to limber up or to condition the body. Weight lifting and not-too-active sports such as shuffleboard and pitching horseshoes are also isotonic exercises.

Anaerobics. A fifty-yard dash is a good example of this exercise, which is used to build endurance and stamina.

Aerobics. This physical activity increases heart and respiratory action for a sustained period of time. Running, jumping rope, cycling, swimming and paddle ball all fall into this category of exercise.

There, you have the four main divisions of exercise. Which one is for you? First you have to determine if you are physically ready. If you are much overweight or have a history of heart or other health problems, a physical examination is not just necessary — it's essential.

But after your doctor has given you the green light, he or she may be able to help you work out a balanced program which uses some parts of several of these exercise disciplines.

Fitness, like Rome, can't be built in a day. But, on the other hand, it can't be built without a day. Today.

Before you reach for that extra bite today, ask yourself:
Have I chosen the proper exercise program for my body's fitness? Have I chosen the right day to begin?

It amazes most doctors and families, but we overweights rarely lose our appetites when we're ill. "It doesn't matter how sick I am," says one overeater, "I can still eat." Another added: "I can remember staggering with a raging fever to the kitchen for extra food to hide under my bed." Even a broken leg didn't stop him, one dieter remembers: "I crawled from the back bedroom to the refrigerator."

Even illnesses like influenza or stomach aches which ordinarily cause most people to completely lose their appetites don't seem to halt the run-away compulsiveness of overeaters. Our need to eat goes beyond hunger or the need to sustain health.

There is also a definite tendency toward pampering yourself when you're sick. A continuous flow of snacks — wet, cold, sweet treats — should make it all better, we think, like a mommy's kiss. "I couldn't remember," said an overweight, "whether I was supposed to feed a cold or a fever — so I fed both just to make sure."

The truth is you shouldn't overfeed any sickness. Your body will get well faster if it doesn't have to handle all that food. And you won't get on the scales after a dire illness and complain, "See, I even gain weight when I'm sick!"

We play sad little tricks on ourselves sometimes, even when we are ill.

Have you finally learned that extra food and sweet treats won't "make it better?" Whether you're sick in body or emotion, what you overeat will only make you fatter, not better.

When you're sick in bed, you may have to switch your eating plan to lighter foods, substituting a blander protein for the vegetables more difficult to digest.

Or your doctor will suggest what your diet should be. He certainly won't prescribe huge doses of your favorite binge dessert.

But in your positive mind you really know this. You just have to put it into positive action. And you will. You've gotten much too smart to kid yourself any longer.

Before you reach for that extra bite today, ask yourself:
Do I overindulge when I'm sick? Have I decided not to play any more "sick tricks"?

Changing careers in mid-life has become an accepted fact of modern life. And a career change is really what you are doing. You are leaving your worn-out, old fat career for a healthy, new thin one because you are highly motivated to live differently.

You have asked yourself: What do I want to do with my life? And the answer is, coming back loud and clear: lose this miserable burden of overweight!

Changing your eating career requires you to change your behavior — not just a slight change, but a considerable change.

First, you need to acquire a positive feeling about yourself, not just by sitting around and thinking about it, but by putting your desires into action.

Second, you have to establish the pattern of action that will allow you to change to your desirable new career choice.

The career you have chosen is self-motivating in many ways. You are readily able to see the outcome of your new choice. You see yourself thinner, more attractive and happier.

You are motivated to change your career because you believe you can do it; other people are losing weight, so you know it is possible. Even more, you know you have the skills to accomplish the change.

You are motivated, too, because you have not given yourself alternatives. Half measures never work. You have not promised yourself a career change based on how someone (or something) else develops. You are going to lose weight, and change your life structure so you can keep it off. Period.

You can choose success in your life. You can choose to achieve, to make dead dreams live.

Aren't you tired of the same old job? Living fat, hopeless and helpless.

Change your job. You'll like the new one a lot better.

Before you reach for that extra bite today, ask yourself:
Am I ready to switch my old fat career for a new thin one?
Am I establishing the kind of habit patterns that will help me realize my new career choice?

"I got so excited at the ball game," said one dieter to his doctor, "that when it was all over I found myself with two empty beer cans, a hot dog wrapper and an empty popcorn box."

Is there such a thing as unconscious eating? The answer is yes *and* no. Eating with many overweights has become so automatic (especially in certain situations such as television and ball-game watching) that little thought is given to what is being eaten. Nevertheless, it's very difficult to eat without having some conscious awareness. The excuse, "It wasn't me who really did it, it was my unconscious mind!" is an attempt to take "blame" away from the self.

Dr. Walter Levin, a weight specialist, advises the "unconscious eater":

1. Don't go to ball games.

2. Go to ball games, but buy your tickets in advance and leave the rest of your money at home.

3. Try to get involved in being aware of what your destructive behavior patterns are.

Money is the key link to obtaining extra food at a ball game or in any other public place. If you form the habit of not taking extra money with you, it will be impossible to satisfy any conscious *or* unconscious urge to overeat.

Forming positive habit patterns such as not carrying extra cash will insure success in the living thinner "game" — the game every overweight wants to win. Not only will you lose weight, but you'll notice that your budget will stretch farther than it did before.

Today you are responsible for what and how you eat. You will not try to shift the responsibility to anyone or anything, not even your favorite sport or television program.

That's worth repeating. *Today you are responsible.*

Before you reach for that extra bite today, ask yourself:
Do I overeat, and then attempt to take the blame away from myself? Am I forming positive habits that will insure my success?

Overeaters Anonymous, the international group for overweights patterned after Alcoholics Anonymous, has an interesting saying: *This is a simple program for complicated people.*

If there's one thing our lives are when we are overeating and overweight, that one thing is *complicated.* Ordinary events, events that thin people ("normies" as they are sometimes called) take in stride, we have difficulty handling. Getting an invitation to a party, starting a class, applying for a job — all these simple occurrences can be tremendously complicated by our super-awareness of our bodies.

Some of us have never known simplicity. Would you like to learn what it could mean?

The essence of simplicity, said a great teacher, lies in a direct and uncomplicated approach to both persons and things, so that we see them and meet them *as they are.* We overweights tend to see other people with our eyesight clouded by our own sometimes miserable condition. We complicate unnecessarily.

The great teacher goes on to explain simplicity, saying: *It is only a simple mind which can understand and resolve complexities.*

What does he mean by "simple mind"?

Simplicity is a clean division of necessary from unneccessary; the true from the false. Trying to know ourselves better, for instance, is an effort to simplify ourselves.

Simplicity is not the ability to negate or complicate, it is *the ability to comprehend.* It is mature and wise. It makes sense of the senseless.

Today you have a simple plan. You will eat for health and weight-loss or maintenance. You will reach out for some new knowledge which will further uncomplicate your mind and your life.

Today, you will know the serenity of simplicity.

Before you reach for that extra bite today, ask yourself:
Am I further complicating my life with this act? Have I tried to simplify this day so that I will know true peace of mind?

December 1   Learn to Be a Defensive Guest

December's office parties, club parties, open houses and endless parades of sweet offerings can approach the proportions of a marathon battle for dieters.

For a weight-loser who doesn't want to "fudge" on his eating plan, this month is the time to beware of all those thoughtless folks who frantically shove forbidden food at us in the best holiday tradition.

Where you have good rapport with your hostess, tell her: I won't be able to eat all your fabulous home-baked things. I'm dieting for my health."

On the other hand, if you can't be that direct, you could humorously say: "I'm in a ski tournament this weekend and I don't want to repeat last year's performance where I broke the chair lift at Sun Valley."

If you're still afraid your hostess might feel rejected, then learn to be a defensive guest.

Adding ice cubes to your glass, instead of high-calorie beverages, can make it look full when it really isn't. Or, insist that her salad is the best you've ever eaten, and demand a second portion which leaves you absolutely no room for her 100-year-old-recipe fruitcake.

If you're really self-confident and determined not to regain an ounce during the holidays, you can bring your *own* diet dinner to dinner. Lovable actress-singer Carol Channing always does. If *she* can, *you* can.

All else failing, you can ask a tough question; just how important is this party to you, anyway?

The new image you have, the new approval you have for yourself, these are more precious gifts than any wrapped with tinsel and ribbon. More precious even than the approval of a hostess who doesn't understand your daily struggle to control the need for excess food.

It's not hard to be a defensive guest when you have a new way of life to enjoy every day this month. That's the real holiday spirit.

Before you reach for that extra bite today, ask yourself:
Do I care less about what people might think of me, and more about what I think of myself? Can I escape the holiday food fantasy and get into the real holiday spirit?

About this time during every holiday season the search for just the right present begins. Most of us, carried away with the gift-filled stores, the merry sidewalk Santas, often spend more than we planned or can afford. But there's one gift that requires no shopping at all, and doesn't relieve our pocketbook of one penny.

Did you ever think about giving the gift of forgiveness?

"One December I was suddenly seized with the desire to show my father in some tangible way that I forgave him," said one speaker at an Overeaters Anonymous meeting. "He had been a brutal man who drove his wife and children to hate him, but now he was old and alone.

"I wrote him a short note — my first contact in twenty years — including a photo of his granddaughter whom he had never seen."

The speaker remembered that she felt a new lightness of spirit as she mailed her precious gift. "Almost by return mail my father answered," she told her group, "and in his letter I counted the use of the word 'love' six times. I was amazed and overwhelmed, because I had never believed he knew the meaning of the word, let alone had a human need for it.

"My father died of cancer before another December came, but the memory of that gift given and received has made every holiday season brighter."

Would you like to give the ultimate gift of happiness this holiday season? Give the gift of forgiveness. It will cost you not one penny and bring you a treasure beyond your dreams.

Before you reach for that extra bite today, ask yourself:
Is there someone to whom I can give the gift of forgiveness? Do I believe that as I give, so shall I receive?

The poet and essayist Ralph Waldo Emerson wrote: "Rings and jewels are not gifts, but apologies for gifts. The only gift is a portion of thyself."

Since this is a traditional month for gift giving, it might be a good time to think about the quality of the gifts we give.

In today's world, givers have almost lost their status. People have become demanding consumers, getters, climbers.

Today, let's think about giving a gift that lasts — the only gift that lasts — the gift of "a portion of thyself."

The manufactured gifts you give may be destroyed before another holiday season. Or maybe they won't work at all, and the recipient may become angry at you, the giver, as well as at the manufacturer.

The purchased gifts you give may wear out, or go out of fashion. You may feel that you have to update the same gift every year, which is not giving, but replacement.

There are those who suggest that "secret" gifts are the best ways to exercise the spirit. Do something for someone that he or she does not find out about. If it is discovered, then it will not count.

What secret gift could you give someone today? Something that would bring joy without obligation. Could you give a little portion of yourself? You need not be rich to be generous.

Try giving two gifts. First, give of yourself to others and you may discover that they will spontaneously give a portion of themselves back to you. Second, give of yourself to someone and not be found out. This will be the biggest surprise of all. The paradox is that you will still receive a gift back, except that this time it will be from *yourself*. You will love yourself more for the secret gift than for any other you'll ever give.

How exhilarating!

Before you reach for that extra bite today, ask yourself:
Have I thought of giving the gift of self? Are some of my holiday gifts this year going to be secret ones?

December 4   Eating More and Enjoying It Less

During December a variety of tempting foods always seems to be at hand. Overeating is made easier because holiday foods are most likely to be those which overweights enjoy — or seem to enjoy. But do they?

Researchers at Duke University doubt whether overweights really do enjoy what they overeat. When asked what they like to eat the most, the majority told the scientists that they like crunchy, tactile foods like popcorn and potato chips. Apparently texture and degree of crunch are important to us. But the surprising finding was that overweights as a group, even when they were eating their favorites, were generally *unenthusiastic* about food.

Further research revealed that not only were we overweights not finding pleasure in food, but we didn't enjoy anything else very much, either — from sports to reading. The findings conclude that frustration, boredom, lack of planning and failure to set goals all keep us from enjoying the opportunities for pleasure in life.

Do you feel that overeating is sapping your life of all its pleasures?

Today, you can sidestep the unpleasant pitfalls of overeating. Every overweight knows and talks about the "vicious cycle." What is it? Overeating out of frustration, boredom and lack of planning to reach goals, and then overeating, still more, *because* you are frustrated, bored, and lack well-defined goals.

There's no way to get off that destructive merry-go-round but to *break the cycle of overeating.*

If you've been eating more and enjoying it less — or not at all — today is a new twenty-four hours you can spend to help yourself. One day at a time you can set goals, plan how to get there and then aim straight for your target.

December is a month when too many overweights get off target. The holiday season becomes an excuse to overeat, instead of a month when you can grow stronger and thinner.

Don't get off target today. Get ready. Aim. Fire.

Bullseye!

Before you reach for that extra bite today, ask yourself:
Do I see that overeating causes me not to enjoy food or anything else? Have I broken the vicious cycle of overeating and frustration?

Peace on earth, and good will to men is an ancient prayer of this holiday season. But world peace will never be realized until all of us as individuals make peace with our own selves.

The way to inner peace has been defined as right thought, right feeling and right action. These are the requisites for harmony, which is the absence of conflict.

To have peace of mind means that we must seek a beautiful relationship with our inner selves. All distortions, restlessness and incoherence must be replaced by the positive, creative mind.

It is impossible to feel peace without a sense of positive goodwill toward yourself and your fellow human beings.

You must first feel it for yourself or you will deny it to others.

No one else can give us the sense of unity and cohesion that stills conflict. We must give it to ourselves each day by creating a positive ambience in which to live.

Today, give yourself a beautiful, constructive, secure and unifying inner peace. For overweights, this peace is a matter of getting food out of the way. Overeating blocks peace of mind as surely as the moon blocks the sun in an eclipse, and certainly, we overeaters long for inner peace. In hundreds of diet group meetings every day thousands of us talk about the intolerable conflict overeating brings to our lives. We long for a solution. Secretly, we suspect it would take a miracle to save us from our need for more food than our bodies can use.

But it will not take a miracle. It will simply take right thinking, right feeling and right action to make our desire for peace a reality.

Put the definition of peace of mind into practice in your life today. This is one holiday season that can truly bring peace on earth — to you.

Before you reach for that extra bite today, ask yourself:
Am I ridding myself of confusion and conflict? Have I decided to experience peace of mind for myself?

Some overweights have spent a lifetime proving to others and to themselves that they can't take it. Like a fragile Christmas gift, some of us come wrapped with the words *Handle With Care* stamped all over us.

We're very sensitive people. We've been hurt and some of us let it out a bit too easily. We wear our heart on our sleeve and, just like a chip on the shoulder, it's constantly getting bumped, bruised and knocked off.

Some of us are very good at playing the wounded martyr to our overweight. We see slights that don't exist and we shed many a tear over imaginary insults.

After a while, we stop attracting the attention and concern we're longing for, so we have to escalate the emotional displays. If we go very far, we substitute sympathy and pity — our own and other people's — for love.

Are you all wrapped up in a package labeled *Fragile! Handle With Care?* Do you always have some sad story to tell? Lately, has the sympathy and attention you crave been dwindling?

You don't need to be dependent on your pain. If you are eating right for health and weight loss, you won't need negative attention. You'll be attracting the positive kind.

You will discover that as you grow away from your addiction to excess food, you become strong enough to withstand discomfort. As your confidence builds, a new person will emerge, one that does not need pity — indeed, one that rejects it.

Don't confuse positive help with sympathy. It's a good thing to seek help. It can be a real asset to your master living plan. Who knows? Before long, you may find yourself giving help as good as you get.

Won't that be something? You'll be the one with the strong shoulder — not to cry on — but to put against the wheel.

Before you reach for that extra bite today, ask yourself:
Am I tired of feeling sorry for myself? Have I changed my stamp from *Fragile! Handle With Care* to *First Class?*

Of all the months of the year, this is the month when we compulsive people are most likely to overdo things. By nature we tend toward excesses. We eat too much, worry too much, spend too much and then later we have too many resentments. But whom do we resent most? Ourselves. We think, "Why did I allow myself to get into such a fix?" And what do we do when we resent ourselves? We overeat again, and perpetuate the whole cycle of misery.

Why don't you try to spread some of that good will of the holiday season — within yourself — where it will do a great deal of good? Don't worry so much. Don't overspend and add debt to your other problems. Above all, don't overeat and forge a heavier chain of unhappiness around your life.

But good will is not a matter for bargaining. It has to be given because it is *right*. Sooner or later it will express itself in all your positive thought and action — with yourself and with others.

Easy does it today. Reach for balance. Know that you are entering a happy new era. You are losing weight and growing in self-knowledge with each day. You've stopped thinking of yourself in limiting terms; you no longer call yourself a failure, stupid or undeserving of anything good.

At the very least you deserve your own good will. And from that you can grow to be truly self-loving and self-esteeming. That is the easiest way of all to live.

So — take it easy.

Before you reach for that extra bite today, ask yourself:
Am I doing anything to excess? Have I learned how to take it easy and show myself some of the good will of the holiday season?

Have you ever known anybody who lost a lot of weight — everywhere but in their head? Some overweights never get enough praise for losing weight. (Who was it that gained it to begin with?) They have a tendency to think *too* well of themselves.

Watch out! If your head swells out of proportion to your accomplishment, what will you do when the compliments stop coming? Of course, you could go after them, but this is obvious and alienates many people.

Don't lose your perspective. You certainly have done a marvelous thing. Achieving your natural weight after a period of obesity is like winning the world series of dieting. You have every right to be proud. But try not to rest on your accomplishments. You have more to do.

In order to maintain the weight you've worked so hard to attain, you are going to have to have real growth from within and balance in all things.

Striking the right balance is the key to contented living. Arrogance, or "the big head," will not help you maintain balance. "I discovered that gratitude was a good antidote for my swelled head," says one thinned-down overweight. "Whenever I started to build myself up too much, I remembered to be grateful that I was shown a way out of my problem."

When you reach your natural weight, you will be able to use some of your tremendous fighting energy to start becoming what you want to be. You will no longer be battling *against*, but fighting *for*. This is your positive goal.

But don't go *too* far in your desire to maintain a good balance. Remember, you need to learn to *work with your own mind,* and use your positive mind on *your own side.*

Today, you will strike a proper balance between self-esteem and a desire to continue growing. And you will be content.

Before you reach for that extra bite today, ask yourself:
Am I trying to keep from getting "the big head"? Do I realize that thinking *too* well of myself is a precursor to thinking I can eat anything I want and get away with it?

It's about as important to end your day well as it is to start it off on a positive note. Why not form the habit of reviewing your day each evening with the idea of making any adjustments and improvements in the day that follows? Here are some steps to take. You may think of others just as meaningful to you and your master living plan.

1. *Reality.* Ask yourself if you dealt realistically with situations arising during your day. Did you level with yourself, or did you try to kid yourself or someone else along?

2. *Fairness.* Did you hit "below the belt" today or were you fair in your dealings? Did you put yourself down or lift yourself up?

3. *Involvement.* Ask yourself if you got involved with life today.

4. *Responsibility.* Did you blame anyone or anything for being overweight?

5. *Fun.* Check yourself to see if you found the humor in situations, instead of the tragedy.

6. *Perspective.* Did you practice moderation in the things you ate, said and did?

7. *Flexibility.* Is your mind open to new ways of doing things, or do you get frustrated if the rigid position you maintain is threatened?

Growth is a process that leads to an inevitable emotional transformation. Out of that process comes a new, more whole, and realistic way of experiencing yourself and your relationship with the world.

Such an all-encompassing change doesn't grow out of passive resignation, but out of an *aggressive* search for a way of living that will make life more exciting and fulfilling.

The Welsh poet Dylan Thomas gave us overweights a couplet to live by: "Do not go gentle into that good night. Rage, rage against the dying of the light."

Before you reach for that extra bite today, ask yourself:
Have I formed the habit of reviewing my day for growth? Am I searching *aggressively* for a way to live which will allow me better control of my hunger for excess food?

Curiosity may have killed the cat, as the old tale goes, but it has a special meaning for overeaters trying to get control of their eating. Our perennial problem is two-sided. Either we think we already know everything there is to know or we're too dumb to learn. Neither is the case.

Be curious. The successful person wants to know what makes everything work. He or she collects facts and enjoys learning new skills, gaining new knowledge and meeting new people. Curiosity is an inevitable ingredient of dynamic living. Here's how curiosity can help you mold a new life and body.

STOP. When you feel you're moving through life too fast, take time to watch the sun go down. Recharge your batteries. Just because you are full of curiosity about the way life feels now that you've removed the "drug" of excess food, you don't have to go at an exhausting pace. *Slow down.* You have all the time in the world.

LOOK. Keep your eyes open. Don't limit yourself with tunnel vision that cuts off what's going on to the left and right of you. *Be aware.*

LISTEN. There are many successful people who will share their knowledge and experiences with you. *Everyone has a story to tell.*

There are a few cautions a truly wise person will follow. They have to do with our "old friend," moderation. For example, don't become so enamored of the sunset that you halt all progress toward your weight goal, or begin negative procrastination. Don't become so distracted by all the things around you that you forget your destination. And don't become confused by listening to so many people that you become indecisive. The dynamic life is also the well-balanced life.

Let your natural curiosity flow through your master plan for growth-centered living. It will add a lot of spice to your life.

You can always use more!

Before you reach for that extra bite today, ask yourself:
Have I allowed my natural curiosity to put a little spice in my life? Am I looking for moderation in all things?

When you leave the blur of fatness for the sharp outline of thinness, there is a big payoff in just about every area of your life — especially social. Here are some of the confident new feelings expressed by members of a southern California diet group called The Thin Ones.

"I'm more desirable and I know it."

"Would you believe that I once was afraid to get out of my chair at a party? Now, frankly, I've got a lot of dazzle!"

"A night on the town doesn't mean going to the movies alone anymore."

"I used to be the big sister type, but now that I'm thin, men have to think of me in more sexual terms."

"No more lost weekends at home with bags and bags of goodies to binge on."

"Parties aren't threatening because I know I look like fourteen karats."

"For me, the greatest change between 192 pounds and 125 pounds is the comfort I feel with other people. I know they aren't judging me by my size."

When we were fat during a holiday season, we were lonely, but we felt a special loneliness when we were with people, too. Somehow nothing fit. Not us. Not our clothes.

Today you are on the road to a slimmer, healthier life. You feel more comfortable with your body, It will never inhibit you socially again. You will join *The Thin Ones.*

Have fun at the party!

Before you reach for that extra bite today, ask yourself:
Do I want that "fourteen karat" look? Am I ready to receive the big payoff?

Your brain, roughly speaking, consists of three biological computers, the neural chassis, the limbic system and the neocortex. It has taken hundreds of millions of years to evolve this fantastically complicated brain, and yet it is no larger than a grapefruit. If man attempted to duplicate the functions of even the dullest human brain, the effort would cover acres of ground and still remain beyond the capacity of our space-age technology.

Do you doubt that your brain is powerful? How can you? You have the greatest thinking machine in the world. Don't blame your brain if you haven't achieved as much as you should have. Don't blame your brain if others lose weight, while you seem to mark time.

The difference between people who accomplish their goals and those who don't is a simple matter of programming.

Have you programmed your mind to reflect a healthy self-image, so that you can think better, perform better and feel better?

If you have in-put negative information and got negative results, you can certainly reverse this process and begin to feed in positive information for positive results. When you are thinking positively about yourself, you are happier. Your physical body *knows* when you're thinking happily. Research tests in several countries show that you will see better, even taste and smell and hear better. If positive thinking is this powerful, you can readily accept that your positive, creative brain can help you live the way you want to.

How do you want to live? With pride and dignity and an ability to concentrate on your goal of healthful controlled eating.

Put those trillions of brain cells in your head to work changing your life. You can do it one day at a time.

Your dream lives!

Before you reach for that extra bite today, ask yourself:
Am I in-putting positive image information into my mental computer? Do I believe with all my heart that my powerful brain can help me lose my excess weight?

If you expect little or nothing of yourself, then that is what you'll get — little or nothing. Perhaps you've gone even further. You've told yourself there's no possibility that you can lose weight. You've been telling yourself a lie.

Educators know that children perform in school much as their teachers expect them to. When a teacher gets the word that a child is a good learner then the teacher treats that child as a good learner. Such positive communication helps the child form positive or change negative perceptions of himself.

Do you expect success or failure from yourself? You may say you expect success but if your thinking, tone of voice, facial expressions all tell you you're lying, then your perception of yourself as a failure will not change.

But what if you are truly convinced that you can succeed? You think, feel and act success with every breath you take. You don't let negativity creep in to spoil your image, not for a moment.

The German philosopher Goethe said, "Treat people as if they were what they ought to be and you help them to become what they are capable of being." Apply this truth to yourself.

Don't make the mistake of selling yourself short. You are someone beautiful imprisoned in a dungeon of flesh. Break away. Others have lost weight — *are losing weight.* So can you.

Sometimes we overeaters self-hypnotize ourselves into the most negative and destructive mental habits. Have you done this? One answer is just to expect more from yourself than you ever thought you could do.

Get going!

Before you reach for that extra bite today, ask yourself:
Am I expecting enough of myself? Have I stopped selling myself short?

Learning to live a day at a time is one of the most positive things compulsive people can do for themselves. Whether we're foodaholics, alcoholics or use some other drug, our big problem is never having learned to dwell in the present.

One of the favorite things we overeaters flog ourselves with is a lament over our wasted past. "If only I could have been thin when I was younger," we say. Being unable to change what is already history, we sometimes sink into depression and overeat more. What's the use? We'll soon be forty (fifty or sixty) and youth will be over for good. Of course, it seldom occurs to us that we'll be forty in any event, and that it's up to us to choose whether we'll be forty and fat or forty and thin. We spend even less time concerned for *how we live today.*

When we're not agonizing over our wasted youth, we're worrying about the future. If we allow negativity to rule our minds, the future holds nothing but fear for us. "Next year will just be more of the same," we say resignedly. And with that negative input it probably will.

Both attitudes deny the importance of today. If we spend all our time and emotional energies on the past or future, we have little left to give to the most important time of our lives — today.

This day is the only day you can live. Are you making the most of it? Are you pursuing happiness as part of your positive daily work? William James called the attitude of unhappiness painful, mean and ugly. He said *unhappiness perpetuates the trouble which occasions it.*

Happiness is impossible if you try to live in the past or the future. Failure is almost always the result.

Take this day and do your best with it. When it is done, let it go. Tomorrow you will have another chance.

Listen to Ralph Waldo Emerson. He speaks to you.

"Write it on your heart that every day
is the best day of the year...
Finish every day, and be done with it.
You have done what you could."

Before you reach for that extra bite today, ask yourself:
Am I learning to live one day at a time? Have I been cultivating an attitude of happiness to help make my day as positive as possible?

Today you will come alive with the possibilities in your life. You will make up your mind to act on your dreams.

Do you have weight to lose? How much? You have just stated your goal. Now take some action that will start you moving. Get going, now!

If you have any creeping negative thoughts, get rid of them. Replace them with the thought, "I can." Stuff your mind with positive thoughts. Shatter the barriers that negative thinking has erected.

Do you have trouble getting started? Perhaps it's because you try to take on too much. Take one problem at a time. You may have dozens, but start on your weight problem first. Overeaters kid themselves when they think they can postpone losing weight until last. Overweight is the problem that has them on their knees. After you begin to take off extra pounds, you can tackle your other troubles, one at a time, as you're ready.

Release your natural enthusiasm. You have more than you think you do. You have all you need for the job. Believe it!

Today you will feed yourself on happy, positive goals instead of falling into a sweet-filled fat trap.

Today you will discover that you have a solution to compulsive eating that you can live with easily.

Today, impossible obstacles will just be so many problems to jump over.

During your lifetime you've acquired many habits, some happy, some not so happy. But there is one habit you don't have that you may want very much. Get the happy habit of positive mental attitude. You'll have to work at it. You'll have to cultivate and develop your inner capacity for positive thinking.

Today you are vitally alive, awake and enthusiastic. It will be one of the best days you've ever made.

Before you reach for that extra bite today, ask yourself:
Am I ready to get going on my life? Have I released my natural enthusiasm to help me reach my weight goal?

All your life you have probably been super-critical of yourself. You have spent so much of it just *being* fat. And feeling it. The worst thing about the fat obsession is that you develop great bitterness against yourself. You have no tolerance for a body that has betrayed you.

As you have grown in self-knowledge, you have come to a state of some peace within yourself. Enough, perhaps, to be more honest about your positive self. Give yourself permission to look inside. Begin by asking these questions:

What kind of person am I? Don't just think of yourself as a physical self, but as a personality. If you had to capsule yourself in one phrase (as in an advertisement), what positive statement could you make to sell yourself to the world?

What are six good points to my personality? Make a list of the things you are that make you proud. You may see that you really are not so bad.

What positive things do other people say about me? Write down all the positive things you have been told, overheard or sensed which indicate the way others react positively to you. Do you agree?

The most important lesson we overweights ever have to learn is how to communicate with ourselves. Self-communication makes it possible to triumph over emotions, and, ultimately, our weight problem. It can also mean finding hidden talents which lay unnoticed under all the negativity.

Self-communication, says one psychiatrist, is a form of prayer with yourself. When these communications are positive, the result is positive thinking and that, says the psychiatrist, is another word for *faith.*

You know that you can talk yourself into or out of almost anything. That is not the problem. You're certainly persuasive enough. The problem is allowing yourself to *accept* positive, constructive suggestions. Acceptance will make all the difference.

Give yourself a positive self-appraisal today. Communicate. Get a pencil and paper. Here's a start:

"I have the courage to take this step."

Before you reach for that extra bite today, ask yourself:
Have I made my positive self-appraisal? Do I understand that real self-communication can help me triumph over my weight problems?

Since many overeaters aren't too happy with the lives they lead, long life, with extra years to do all the things they miss while fat, can be an attractive goal. Moreover, as you lose weight and get into a reasonable range, you are apt to become interested in your whole body, not just weight, but total health.

Health researchers in California, after an eight-year study involving over 7,000 people, discovered that there are seven constants if you want to live a healthy, slender, longer life.

How many of these do you follow?

1. Don't smoke cigarettes.
2. Don't drink excessively.
3. Don't skip breakfast.
4. Maintain regular and moderate eating habits.
5. Keep your weight in proportion to your height. Men with the best physical health are less than five percent underweight and no more than twenty percent overweight; among women, those less than ten percent underweight or overweight were healthiest.
6. Sleep at least seven but no more than eight hours per night.
7. Get moderate exercise.

Persons in the study who followed all seven health habits lived an average of eleven and one-half years longer than those who followed none of these habits.

And guess what the scientiests found were the most important indicators of all? "Good eating habits are especially important to good health," said Dr. Ira H. Cisin. "Erratic eaters have poor health generally. Those who ate breakfast almost every day and didn't eat between meals reported significantly better physical health than those who skipped breakfast and ate whenever they wanted."

Did you notice that three out of the seven health constants had to do with eating?

Follow the seven great health habits today and every day. You'll be happier, thinner, healthier and live longer.

Before you reach for that extra bite today, ask yourself:
Am I following health habits that will improve the quality and duration of my life? Do I believe that overeating is the greatest single threat to my life?

Stress in the contemporary world is a good deal like Mark Twain's weather: Everybody talks about it but nobody does anything about it.

We all undergo stress in our everyday lives. A certain amount of it keeps us moving. Stress, in a constructive sense, can even provide challenges for us.

But too much stress and pressure is likely to cause real suffering. We overweights know this. No matter how placid we may appear to be, inside we are churning with conflict.

Good positive attitudes help. We can channel stress into creativity. But if you are getting more than you can handle, here are a few ways you can relieve nervous tension as it develops or even before. Dr. Frank S. Caprio, renowned psychiatrist, has these suggestions:

1. *Take a daily nap.* U.S. presidents take a nap. Even ten minutes will suffice. Why not right after lunch?

2. *Keep telling yourself you are relaxed.* If you tell yourself often enough, you eventually will be.

3. *Learn to forgive.* Hatred and resentment cause more tension than any other emotions.

4. *Pretend you are happy.* Act happy and you will grow into the role.

5. *Learn to laugh more.* When did you start taking yourself so seriously?

6. *Keep in contact with everything that is inspiring to you.* If this means carrying poetry in your wallet or pinning weight-losing slogans to your refrigerator, so be it. Don't be so grim.

The most important thing in your life without exception is learning to live, and live well, without excess food.

In order to realize this goal, you may have to let go of stress, resentments, hatred. You may even have to learn to smile more than you normally would, and pretend to yourself and others that you are happier than you are.

Well, that's not such a big price to pay for the good life, is it?

Before you reach for that extra bite today, ask yourself:
When I feel stress do I do something constructive about it? Have I stopped reaching for my food pacifier whenever I am nervous?

It's not that we overeaters are easier to discourage than so-called normal eaters, but it does seem that sometimes we may have to work at happiness just a little bit harder. For that reason, we need to keep our positive battery fully charged at all times so that we are generating enthusiasm.

If you allow your negative emotions to dominate you, you'll become a frustrated pessimist, and most likely stay fat. You don't want that in a million years.

Allow your personality and developing master plan of living to be guided by positive emotions, and your enthusiasm will help keep you on the path you've chosen for yourself. On the other hand, if you allow negativity to promote disharmony within your thinking you will find yourself constantly out of step with reality.

Don't think for a minute the case for positive thinking is overstated. The philosopher Descartes said: "I think therefore I am." What do you want to be?

Never let negativity take over your life. Counter worry with faith, suspicion with trust, sorrow with joy, resignation with determination, gloom with cheer, anxiety with security, hostility with friendliness, and guilt with forgiveness.

For every negative emotion there is a powerful, opposite positive emotion. You have a choice. You choose your own emotional makeup. Which one — negative or positive — do you chose today?

Before you reach for that extra bite today, ask yourself:
Have I recharged my positive battery today? Have I found an equal and positive emotion for every negative one I encounter in my thinking?

In order to be a winner in the "positive game,"overweights must let it permeate their entire lives. They must select positive stimuli and block negative stimuli. Just like you wouldn't expose your body to the temptations of working in a chocolate donut factory, you shouldn't expose your mind to similarly negative forces.

How can you guard against negative input? Here's how:

1. Check your reading to make certain it stimulates positive emotions.

2. Survey your entertainments — movies, television. Are they positive?

3. Do you have positive-minded friends?

4. Examine your language. Do you verbalize negative or positive emotions? If you verbalize negative ones, you give them added power to control you. There's nothing more destructive. On the other hand if you verbalize positive emotions, you add to their strength.

As you can see, you have to guard your positive self from other people, but most of all from your sabotaging self.

Are you using powerful, positive affirmations in your daily life? Do you say: "Today, I will grow more slender and healthy; I will grow toward the kind of person I truly want to be?" If you have such positive thoughts as these and repeat them aloud, you will have *already started* becoming the slender, healthy, self-knowing person you desire to be.

The nice thing about learning to play the "positive game" is that one day it will become habitual. The concert pianist doesn't think before he strikes each key, he responds automatically, out of habit. And habit is the result of long practice.

Are you *practicing* total positive living each day? What a pleasant day you'll have.

Before you reach for that extra bite today, ask yourself:
Am I blocking negative stimuli from my life? Am I using powerful, positive language when I talk about myself?

All of us are lonely at times. It is a natural part of being an individual human being. But sometimes, holidays can accentuate our inner loneliness, even when we are surrounded by people. Some overeaters feel cut off and alienated from others, especially other people who aren't overweight.

Inner loneliness, when you're fat, is a gnawing emptiness that no amount of food can ever fill. It feels much like being set apart from your *true self*. When you feel this kind of loneliness you are out of touch with the life within you, and you find it more difficult to reach out to others. When you are cut off from yourself *and* other people, you can be as lonely as you are ever likely to be. It is a sad time.

If you feel this kind of deep loneliness, you may want to seek out people who are working toward a common goal. Join a diet group or at least visit one to prove to yourself that loneliness is not a feeling you have to live with if you don't want to.

You'll get a sense of relief at having other overweights around who understand what you're going through, people who have been there. You won't need to pretend for them. You won't have to show them how "right" everything is with you, even while you're crying inside. You can dispense with sham. You just won't need it.

It's good to be alone sometimes, to sort out emotions and thoughts. (Alone is not necessarily lonely.) But the deep "gut ache" of alienating loneliness can be a negative force in your life.

Today, remove the fear of loneliness by reaching out to yourself and others like you with love. Participate in life. Mix. Mingle. Contribute.

Before you reach for that extra bite today, ask yourself:
Am I over-feeding my lonely hunger? Do I recognize that what's going on inside me is as important as what's going on outside?

No matter how hard people try, there are days, especially during this holiday season, when nothing seems to go right. Often nothing at all can be done to change things. What people can do is change the way they react to problems.

It's not what happens to you that creates problems, but how you react.

One of the best ways to train yourself to react in a positive way is to learn self-communication. In other words, talk to yourself.

When you are exasperated, worried or depressed over any emergency — big or small — say to yourself: *I am not responsible for all that happens to me, but I am responsible for how I react emotionally. I will not become disturbed and build up this problem out of all proportion. Excessive concern only causes me to be tired and tense.*

I must remember that I feel better physically and mentally when I choose to be cheerful and self-encouraging.

I will always remember that I have perfect control over my thoughts and emotions. I can make them as positive and helpful as I want.

No one else can upset me or tie me up in emotional knots if I refuse to allow it.

That is the general idea, but practice being specific because it will be an even bigger help. For example, if your husband, boss, neighbor or friend makes you angry, mention them by name in your self-communication. It will help you to focus your positive thought and completely block negative emotional activity.

There will be a great many occasions when you will have to do all your self-communicating in your head. But whenever possible, talk to yourself out loud. You will be engaging another of your senses to help you.

Today is a new beginning. If you learn to self-communicate, you can practically write your own ticket.

Before you reach for that extra bite today, ask yourself:
Am I telling myself that circumstances don't control my life? Have I learned the biggest lesson of all, that I can control my problems by controlling my reaction to them?

For most overweights the biggest crutch of all is overeating. But there are often other crutches we lean on as well. They are negative, sap our creative, positive energy, and eventually, won't support us at all.

Do you use any of these?

1. *What will people think?* This is an all-purpose crutch which can really halt progress. It's fine to be concerned about public opinion, but you may find it necessary to *swim against the tide,* if you want to accomplish your goal.

2. *I don't have the time.* Some overweights console themselves by saying, "It will take too much extra time to do the special shopping and cooking a diet demands. I should give that extra time to my family or job." Who are you kidding? That extra time will be devoted to overeating. Achievers always have enough time in their day to accomplish what's really important to them.

3. *I'll do it next week when things are better.* Somehow things are never better for procrastinators. There's always a "next week" and the diet or needed improvement never gets started.

4. *Those diets don't ever work for me.* This overweight is defeated before he or she starts. There is no enthusiasm in such a life. "Don't," "can't," and "won't" are the operative words and carry this dieter nowhere. This is the weakest crutch of all and generally leaves the user on his knees most of the time.

Using crutches to prop up a negative personality is habit-forming, but they can be replaced by positive attitudes that will help you walk through life with your chest out and head up.

Answer those destructive attitudes with constructive ones:

Of course, you *can* succeed no matter what other people think.

You *do* have the time, no matter how much time it takes. This week is *always* better than next. And you *will* find a diet that works for you because you will make it work.

Unlock the door to your new life today. And throw away your old negative attitudes.

Before you reach for that extra bite today, ask yourself:
Am I using negative crutches which won't support a positive lifestyle? Am I ready to use positive keys to unlock the door to a new life?

We overeaters can't escape it. This time of year causes us to question our lives and make corrections in the directions we are taking.

Have you asked yourself these questions?

1. Have I chosen to eat moderately with such conviction that there is no going back on it?

2. Have I changed from negative to positive thinking?

3. Have I grown in self-esteem so that I can walk proudly and look anyone in the eyes?

4. Have I accepted the fact that overeating will never cause me anything but unhappiness and a sick body?

5. Am I facing life using the principle of one day at a time?

6. Am I willing to reach out for added strength to other overeaters who are winning over their problem?

7. Have I finished with self-hate?

8. Am I helping others who need me?

9. Do I have hope that a better life lies ahead of me?

10. Am I controlling my emotions or letting them control me?

11. Have I fully accepted that I have a lifetime eating problem which can be overcome with a lifetime positive living program?

12. Have I given up all my excuses for overeating?

13. Am I searching for serenity and peace of mind?

14. Do I accept that my inner growth must keep pace with my weight loss?

15. Am I honest with myself?

Asking ourselves questions and deeply probing our minds are healthful exercises to keep us heading in the right direction — and remind us where we came from.

But deep down in your heart, there is one big answer. And you know it. You know that everything is going to be all right, as long as you are eating to live, not living to eat. Food-control is the answer in your life.

Before you reach for that extra bite today, ask yourself:
Am I always unafraid to question my progress, when I do it in a positive manner? Have I learned that the number one answer in my life is food-control?

Like Charles Dicken's timeless character, Scrooge, many an unhappy overeater is haunted by Christmas Past, Christmas Present, and Christmas Future. Psychologists have long warned that the holiday season can be a dangerous one for already depressed people. It certainly seems to be a time when overeaters painfully take stock of their own lives.

For many of us, this holiday season is full of anxiety, especially if we're overeating. Today more than any other single day in the year we are concerned with what other people think about us. And we are even more aware of what we think about ourselves.

Give yourself the most precious gift of all this year — the gift of hope. No matter how heavily your weight problem has weighed you down in the past, have faith that Christmas Future will be a thin one.

You'll be able to go to all the parties, do all the things you feel your fat keeps you from doing today.

The sooner you inject hope and positive energy into your life, the sooner you'll realize the future doesn't have to be a fat one. By putting off positive action, you're not living, you're *waiting*. Don't wait for life to happen to you. Make it happen, starting today.

Enjoy what's going on around you today — the tree, lights, holly, good vibrations. But even more enjoy the gift of hope you have given yourself. There is no past, no future, no present beyond that. There is only the insatiable core of you, longing for peace, freedom from compulsion and health.

You will have them, all of them. Merry Christmas.

Before you reach for that extra bite today, ask yourself:
Have I given myself the gift of hope this Christmas? Am I ready to start living and stop *waiting* to live?

Every day you have twenty-four hours or 1,440 minutes to use, not a minute more or less than the chairman of General Motors or the Queen of England. You've got a lot of time to use, but how do you use it? Lord Chesterfield, who gave lots of good advice to his son in the eighteenth century, left some advice we can use today: "Take care of the minutes," he said, "and the hours will take care of themselves."

When you look at your day to see if you're getting your 1,440 minutes worth, take a good look to determine that you are not "killing" time. There are many ways you can kill time, but one of the most prevalent and destructive of all is the time you spend on self-pity. See if you recognize yourself:

1. *Closed mind.* "It's no use, I can't lose weight," or "I've lost this much, but I'm too old/tired/sick to go any further."

2. *Overreactions to problems.* "I never could do anything right."

3. *Admitting you don't have all the answers.* "I always get blamed when there's trouble around here."

4. *Unable to live with past mistakes.* "It wasn't my fault."

Going on a self-pity trip whenever things don't go the way we want them to is a real waste of time because we fail to profit from experience. If we occasionally lose time, through mistakes we can still make them count by turning them into useful learning situations

How are you going to use your 1,440 minutes today?

Before you reach for that extra bite today, ask yourself:
Am I killing precious time with self-pity? Am I using my time to take control of my life?

Boredom is everybody's enemy, but for us overeaters it can be a two-edged sword. Many a diet has been broken because we allowed ourselves to get into a rut.

Here are some guaranteed boredom reducers. Try them out.

Let your emotions show in a creative way. Your feelings play an important role in your creative life. Don't hesitate to express them. Say "thank you" for a small gift. Share the tears of someone with a disappointment. Don't keep praise to yourself.

Be somebody better. Take on some task today for no other reason than it is the right thing to do. Keep a promise you've made. Pay an apology if you owe one. Be gentle with others (and yourself). Don't talk about anyone, even if you think it is constructive. If it is, tell him or her.

Vary your routine. Do something in a different way than you have always done it. Get up earlier. Go to bed later. Go out with a friend. Telephone someone you never call. Speak up at a meeting. Start reading from the back of the newspaper first.

Do something just for the fun of it. Lie down in the grass. Laugh at a corny joke. Do one completely impractical thing today.

Make a gift. Make something and give it to somebody you care about. Write a check for a cause you have been meaning to support, but haven't got around to until today. Ask a member of your family what you can do for them, and do it.

Doing your own thing is sometimes habit-forming. What started out as a sensible schedule can become a prison of dailyness. When you find yourself sinking into a rut of boredom, shake yourself up. Get out of that rut and out of yourself. If you do, you'll discover that your day will be more complete. You will be able to concentrate the rest of your time on your master plan for controlled eating and contented living.

Do you know something? You've got what it takes.

Before you reach for that extra bite today, ask yourself:
When I get in a rut, am I able to shake myself out of it? Do I believe deep in myself that I have what it takes to lose weight and keep it off?

December 28   Turning Your Liability Into an Asset

One of the best ways to get out in front of life is to convert your liabilities into assets. Even overweight. It can make you stronger, as steel is tempered in a fiery furnace. It can make you more understanding of others and their problems.

The experience of being fat can be valuable too, because if forces you to look squarely at your life and seek solutions.

You readily come to know that your weight problem is not *just* a problem with excess food, but a living problem as well. You could have been thin and miserably unhappy, with no ready way to straighten out your life.

You may find it hard to believe, but being fat can teach you the value of enjoying life, instead of waiting for others or circumstances to do things for you. Many people go through life *pretending* to live. Not you. You know the difference between the real and the phony.

You may find that it is easier to take things on faith than you thought it would be. People care about you. Good things can happen and do, if you put yourself in the way of their happening.

You have found that people who successfully lose weight don't do so by "knocking" themselves or sending negative messages from their brains to their bodies. Instead say: "I'm going to lose weight and keep it off. I'm going to succeed. There's nothing I can't do if I think I can."

No one is trying to tell you that you're lucky to have a weight problem. But you might not have found the person you really are if you hadn't been forced to look under those extra pounds for some answers.

Don't discount what you have done. Aren't you proud of yourself?

Before you reach for that extra bite today, ask yourself:
Am I busy turning my weight liability into an asset? Have I told myself today that I am bound to win?

Whether they're at small workshops or large organized meetings, when overeaters talk about themselves, they have some astounding insights. Often they are surprised (and delighted) with their self-knowledge. One said: "I didn't even know I felt this way, until it just came popping out at a meeting. I really get to know how I feel by listening to *myself*, as well as to others."

Here's what one group of overweights in various stages of recovery from their problem said at a diet group meeting. The group, five women and three men, sat around a table and, each in turn, talked about their feelings.

"For so much of my life I was drifting — drifting and eating. I finally had to *get something going.*"

"I'm going to put myself to better use and less abuse."

"When I slip off my diet, I've learned to be thankful for what I didn't eat, and then to graciously give myself permission to try again."

"I lied to others. I made up a whole different life for myself because I didn't think my real one was important enough."

"I've learned to bear the discomfort of making mistakes. It's not the mistake itself I feared, but the discomfort."

"I don't blame myself anymore."

"I felt so guilty all the time. Now I know I'm not transparent."

"Whatever it is, eating won't fix it."

"I always postponed everything. Then I discovered that NOW spelled backwards is WON."

"Don't be afraid to try again. Trust that you can. And trust means letting go with both hands."

"Following my diet is just food-honesty."

Before you reach for that extra bite today, ask yourself:
Am I being food-honest? Do I *really* listen to myself when I talk about feelings?

The day you join the ranks of the "formerly fat" will be a day as important in your life as your birthday or wedding day. A day to remember.

When you reach your goal weight, you will have become a certain kind of person. Self-motivated is certainly a trait you'll have in abundance. A master's degree in the art of weight-losing would be yours if there were such a degree. You may have actually "learned to eat differently;" you may be on your way to developing a whole new lifestyle.

Your weight-losing experience has definitely taught you to pay attention to *what, when, and how much you eat, your real hunger, and your need for physical activity.*

In some ways, even though your calories increase, you weight-losing lifestyle will need to change little. You should:

1. Continue to keep a close weight check: You may make this daily, certainly weekly; and whenever your scale shows two pounds over your goal weight, you must return to your weight-losing eating plan.

2. Continue eating regular meals. Snacking is never for the "formerly fat."

3. Start from your weight-losing plan and slowly add higher calorie foods to your diet, one food at a time, while watching the scale to see how your body responds.

4. Eat a balanced, nutritional diet.

5. Have some regular form of physical exercise everyday.

Most doctors agree that a careful regimen like this one will keep the "formerly fat" just that — formerly fat.

Dr. Louis B. Crane goes so far as to advise his patients that weight maintenance is the most critical phase of the whole process.

Be determined to keep what you have. You've earned your new body. You've come through it all with flying colors. This is it.

LIVE!

Before you reach for that extra bite today, ask yourself:
Do I realize I can never return to my old ways of eating and thinking? Am I ready to face whatever life holds without a food crutch?

December 31   Celebrations (for the Formerly Fat)

Next year overweights throughout the world will spend 2.8 *billion* dollars to reduce, but you won't spend a penny.

You have a single body. Not one outside and one inside.

You can say, "I can't be stopped," and nobody laughs, least of all, you.

A mirror is no longer your sworn enemy. Somehow it makes you look almost fragile compared to the person you used to be.

You look at your "before" picture and your "after" self remembers the pain, but immediately lets go of it.

There will be times when you won't always win, but it won't be because you were too fat to stay in the running.

By taking away so much from your girth, you have found a new dimension — depth.

You don't know what to expect, but that's all right.

You have never been so close to what you need.

Options have changed for you, or if unchanged, are not limited.

You have a unity within yourself. Perhaps it is called self-confidence.

Maybe all your dreams won't come true, but even disappointment is better than the past realities.

You know more about yourself, enough to know that you want to know more.

Whatever is ahead, you have the strength to accomplish it. And the health to carry it out.

You are ready.

Before you reach for that extra bite today, ask yourself:
Am I guarding my new body and life with all my might? Will I always give myself all the chances I ever need?

About the author

Jeane Eddy Westin is the author of over 250 articles in magazines and newspapers all over the world, as well as six nonfiction books. She now devotes herself primarily to writing novels.

She lives in Granite Bay, California, on "five exhausting oak-studded acres" with her husband and their German Shepherd, Chaser. About her new concern for fitness—which she calls a "complete turnaround" from her former lifestyle, she says: "About two years ago, my husband and I took up weight-lifting, and I've become a strong advocate of (properly coached) workouts. I have a treadmill for aerobic walk-jogging, and I play tennis as often as I can."

Prior to becoming a free-lance author, she was a self-employed communications consultant. She has taught adult education courses and article writing and marketing, and has been a featured speaker for writers' organizations, college and professional groups.

Born in Oklahoma, she attended Fairmont State College in West Virginia, American River College and California State University in Sacramento. From 1951 to 1957 she served in the Women's Army Corp as a cryptographer, with assignments at SHAPE in Paris and in the Pentagon, Washington, D.C.

Other books by Jeane Eddy Westin

NON-FICTION

Making Do

How Women Survived the 30s

Finding Your Roots

The Coming Parent Revolution

The Thin Book 2

Break Out of Your Fat Cell

FICTION

Love and Glory

Swing Sisters

Subject Index

Subject Index

Emotions, feelings
Jan. 15; Feb. 24; Mar. 22;
Apr. 3, 7; June 8, 13, 16,
25; July 2, 22; Aug. 2, 4,
11, 18; Sept. 3, 6, 15, 23;
Oct. 28; Dec. 22, 27.

Energy
Jan. 14; Mar. 19, 28; July
14; Aug. 20; Nov. 24.

Enthusiasm, aliveness
Jan. 16; Mar. 21; Dec. 15.

Exercise
Jan. 3; Mar. 28; Apr. 28;
May 24; May 30; July 14,
16, 31; Aug. 6, 20; Sept.
16; Oct. 2, 31; Nov. 26.

Fear
Jan. 10; Feb. 1, 8; Mar. 9;
Apr. 25, 26, 27; July 7.

Food as love, comfort
Feb. 22; Apr. 8.

Food fantasies
Feb. 4; May 20.

Forgiveness
Dec. 2.

**Freedom to choose,
decisions**
Apr. 1; May 5, 11, 25; June
11; July 30; Aug. 19, 23,
26; Sept. 5, 10;
Nov. 17, 28.

Fun
May 2; June 9; Oct. 28;
Dec. 27.

General health
May 14; Dec. 17.

Giving
Dec. 3.

Goals, priorities
Jan. 5, 26; Mar. 24, 27, 29;
June 18, 28; July 1, 10, 28;
Aug. 14, 21, 22, 28; Sept.
2, 25; Oct. 12, 30.

Guilt
May 19; July 27; Aug. 16;
Sept. 15, 29; Oct. 27;
Nov. 23.

Happiness, joy, pleasure
Jan. 19; Mar. 17, 23; May
21; June 27; July 3, 12;
Aug. 8; Sept. 22; Nov. 1.

Helping others
June 9, 12; Nov. 20.

Hiding
Apr. 29; May 4.

Holidays, vacations
June 6; July 4; Nov. 11, 21;
Dec. 1, 2, 4; Dec. 25, 31.

Honesty
Mar. 25; Apr. 9, 19; June
12; July 19; Aug. 17;
Nov. 9.

Hope
Feb. 26; July 1; Sept. 28;
Dec. 25.

Human needs
July 5; Nov. 7, 8.

Humility
June 12.

Idleness
Oct. 3.

Illness
Nov. 27.

Impatience
Jan. 8; Apr. 4; May 6; June
19; Nov. 25.

Subject Index

Subject Index

Postponement
June 1.

Prejudice
Oct. 18.

Pride
Jan. 25; May 1.

Purpose
Aug. 14.

Rationalizing
Jan. 4; Feb. 15, 25; Mar. 8;
May 27, 28; June 3; July 1;
Sept. 22; Nov. 27.

Reality
Feb. 28; Mar. 27; Apr. 14;
May 4; Sept. 27; Oct. 23;
Nov. 22.

Rejection
Jan. 17; May 11.

Relationships
Jan. 19; Feb. 5; Mar. 3;
May 11; June 27, 28; July
10; Aug. 8, 18; Sept. 19;
Oct. 4; Nov. 2, 5, 7, 20.

Relaxation, sleep
Mar. 20; July 25; Oct. 29;
Apr. 24.

Results, effects
Jan. 11; Feb. 18; June 21,
22; July 8; Aug. 3; Sept. 11,
20; Nov. 6, 10; Dec. 11.

Rewards
Jan. 11; June 22.

Saboteurs
Jan. 27; Feb. 7; June 4, 7;
Sept. 13; Oct. 22.

Self-deception
Feb. 25; Mar. 5; Apr. 9;
May 23, 27; July 19; Aug.
17, 24.

Self-esteem, self-love
Jan. 23; Mar. 6, 13, 31;
Apr. 1, 7; May 13.

Self-image
Jan. 23; Feb. 14, 19, 28;
Mar. 10, 31; Apr. 1, 7;
May 13; June 5; July 5, 24,
26, 30; Aug. 1, 19, 24;
Sept. 8, 11; Oct. 1, 7, 8, 18,
25; Nov. 8, 22; Dec. 12, 13,
16.

Self-improvement
Feb. 19, Aug. 3.

Self-knowledge, growth
Jan. 31; Feb. 21; Apr. 14,
16; May 18, 21; June 24;
Aug. 11, 15, 30; Sept. 11;
Oct. 7, 10, 20; Nov. 8, 23,
30; Dec. 9, 16.

Self-pity
Dec. 6.

Self-punishment
Mar. 10; Apr. 9.

Slips, failures
Feb. 1; Mar. 12; June 7;
July 21; Aug. 16, 26; Oct.
21.

Slow down, easy does it
Mar. 18, 27; June 9, 24;
Dec. 7.

Special diet problems
May 24; Sept. 4, 9, 18.

Special weight-losing
methods
Apr. 11, 17; June 22; Aug.
12, 22; Sept. 1.

Staying power, persistence
Feb. 17; Apr. 10; Dec. 30.

Subject Index

More titles of interest...

Abstinence in Action
Food Planning for Compulsive Eaters
> *by Barbara McFarland, Ed.D. and Anne Marie Erb*

An essential tool for constructing a recovery plan, *Abstinence in Action* provides worksheets, activity records, and inventory checklists to help those in early recovery plan their meals and structure their time. An invaluable resource for assessing food use and tracking progress. 140 pp.
Order No. 5045

Body and Soul
A Guide to Lasting Recovery from Compulsive Eating And Bulimia
> *by Susan Meltsner, M.S.W.*

Body and Soul integrates the physical, emotional, and spiritual aspects of recovery from food addiction. It encourages readers to explore the feelings that have triggered destructive eating behaviors in the past and suggests new coping skills and problem-solving strategies for handling life's challenges. 240 pp.
Order No. 5098

Inner Harvest
Daily Meditations for Recovery from Eating Disorders
> *by Elisabeth L.*

Recovery from eating disorders means more than abstinence and food plans. In this collection of 366 meditations, readers are guided in their personal and spiritual development as they move beyond the early stages of recovery into serenity and self-acceptance. *Inner Harvest* is a bounty for the soul. 400 pp.
Order No. 5071

For price and order information, or a free catalog, please call our Telephone Representatives.

HAZELDEN

1-800-328-0098
(24-Hour Toll-Free.
U.S., Canada, &
the Virgin Islands)

1-612-257-4010
(Outside the U.S.
& Canada)

1-612-257-1331
(24-Hour FAX)

Pleasant Valley Road • P.O. Box 176 • Center City, MN 55012-0176